The Bedside
'GUARDIAN'
36

June 12, 1987

The Bedside
'GUARDIAN'
36

A selection from *The Guardian* 1986–7
Edited by
W. L. WEBB

With an Introduction by
Ken Livingstone

Cartoons by
Gibbard
Bryan McAllister
Steve Bell

COLLINS
8 Grafton Street, London W1
1987

William Collins Sons & Co. Ltd
London · Glasgow · Sydney · Auckland
Toronto · Johannesburg

BRITISH LIBRARY CATALOGUING IN PUBLICATION DATA

The Bedside Guardian. – 36
1. English essays – Periodicals
I. The Guardian
082'.05   PR1361

ISBN 0-00-217982-2

First published 1987
© Guardian Newspapers 1987

Photoset in Linotron Plantin by
Rowland Phototypesetting Ltd
Bury St Edmunds, Suffolk
Printed and bound in Great Britain by
Robert Hartnoll (1985) Ltd, Bodmin, Cornwall

Introduction

The Guardian was the first newspaper that I ever really loathed. Twenty-three years before the *Sun*, the *Mail* and the *Express* went bananas about 'IRA-loving, poof-loving Red Ken', I came to revile not just *The Guardian* itself but also its readers. This loathing had nothing to do with the liberal stance of the old *Manchester Guardian*, although as a 13-year-old working-class boy I had adopted the views of my parents, who read the *Express* and voted Tory. I was therefore in favour of hanging, opposed to pre-marital sex and shared the whole gamut of reactionary views that Lord Beaverbrook was determined to preserve.

It was not the fact that *The Manchester Guardian* stood at the opposite end of the spectrum on all these issues that fuelled my loathing, for in those days I carried my political convictions lightly. My ambition was still to grow up to become David Attenborough II and devote my life to filming wildlife in all those inaccessible places I dreamed of exploring. No, my loathing derived from the fact that at least once a week, copies of *The Guardian* would arrive too late from its Manchester printing works to be included with the Fleet Street papers in the regular delivery rounds at the newsagents where I worked.

Having the misfortune to be the paper boy who lived closest to the shop, I was the one who was invariably lumbered with the task of undertaking an additional late delivery round to the handful of local *Guardian* readers. Morning after morning my heart would sink as I walked into the newsagents to hear the owner announce that *The Guardian* was late again. Little could I have imagined that a quarter of a century later, it would be *The Guardian* alone which would report with reasonable accuracy the whole range of GLC activities. The only other paper to qualify on grounds of accuracy was the *Financial Times*, but the *FT* tended to report only those GLC activities likely to be of interest to the financial community. Because many of its initiatives presented the GLC in a favourable light, the rough trade end of Fleet Street chose to ignore them entirely, and thus ensure that the progression of their editors and owners up the honours list was not interrupted.

A good example of this bias occurred between the summers of 1982 and 1983, when the GLC investigated and exposed a network of fraud involving housing association funds and leading members of the previous Tory GLC administration. As the details of councillors pocketing tens of thousands of pounds of tax-payers' and rate-payers' money emerged, only the readers of *The Guardian* (and listeners to local radio and television programmes) were informed of the scandal. For the rest of Fleet Street, there was no question of such issues being exposed in the run-up to the 1983 General Election. I imagine that it would have been a very different story if it had been Tony Benn, Arthur Scargill or myself who had been caught with our hands in the till.

For this reason alone I am proud to write the introduction to this collection of the best from the past year's *Guardian*. However, there are other reasons as well. The choice of a paper is a matter of style as well as substance. The agonizing and the humour of *The Guardian* are almost as important to its readers as the accuracy of its news columns. I expected *The Guardian* to report the GLC accurately, but I never expected it to give the 1981 administration a blanket endorsement, and I was not disappointed. I still remember and laugh at one of the first and funniest in the *Guardian*'s long series of tortured and highly qualified leader columns, which grew more supportive of the GLC as the years rolled by and familiarity came to moderate the original alarm that had been occasioned by my appearance on the political scene. As press hysteria about 'Red Ken' reached its peak, *The Guardian* of 31 August, 1981 put it all in the proper context:

> If present trends continue, a point may be reached some time next year where it will no longer be possible to switch on Radio Tashkent without finding Mr Livingstone droning amiably away about (say) the British Israelite Movement or the future of handloom weaving in an increasingly faceless technological society. Now some County Hall colleagues are desperately casting about for some way to

stop the ceaseless flow. Too late: the County Hall cater-
pillar is too far embarked on the transformation to media
butterfly . . .

A paper that can laugh at itself and its readers as cuttingly as
Posy has done in her inimitable cartoons, or has the courage to
run Steve Bell's outrageously wicked strip, is worth preserving
and deserves the constant upward progress of its circulation
figures. I have no doubt that my paper-round successors now
have to carry many more *Guardians* than I did all those years
ago.

These last few years have seen the greatest period of change
that British newspapers have experienced this century. The
steady disintegration of newspaper standards finally produced a
reaction which lead to the birth of several newspapers promising
a better quality of journalism, enthusiasm for which was starkly
revealed by the fact that one third of the entire membership of
the NUJ applied to work for the *News on Sunday*. Equally, the
creation of the *Independent* was the signal for an exodus of the
best and the brightest from Fort Murdoch and the *Telegraph*.
We can judge the professionalism of *The Guardian* by the fact
that its journalists stayed.

The hound of the Isle of Dogs

A dog was the last thing I expected to find on the Isle of Dogs. It is anybody's guess why they call it that. Either the royal hunting dogs were kennelled there like the hound of the Baskervilles in the Great Grimpen Mire . . . or a dog stood guard over its murdered master, only leaving the body to swim to Greenwich for food . . . or the river threw up its dead dogs there. Or they didn't. The locals never mention dogs. They call it the Island.

You get the best view, as with the National Theatre, if you turn your back on it and watch the continuous Turner of the Thames. A sailing ship with 'The crew have mutinied' spelled out in flags. Submarines and chaps with binoculars on the conning tower scanning the Thames for torpedoes. The last totter on the river, beaching his little boat on the swathes of mud left at low tide. And a man, hotly pursued, taking a header into the Thames. The police tenderly invite him to come out before he catches a nasty cold; he, treading water, indicates with word and gesture that he's perfectly happy as he is.

And so was I or, like the swimmer, I said so.

It was a dirty night when I saw this dog. You never in your life saw a dog further down the plughole. It was hopping along on three legs. When I touched it, it trembled till its ribs rattled. Then it held out its broken paw. If I had been watching this performance professionally, I would have blasted it as shameless schmaltz. As it was and as I wasn't, I picked him up and took him home.

He was a little brown dog – until I washed him; then he was a little gold dog. As Thomas Hood inquired of a corpse fished out of the river, 'Who was his father? Who was his mother? Had he a sister? Had he a brother?' Had he, for that matter, a name? Shandy . . . Brandy . . . Ben . . . Ken . . . Livingstone . . . Stanley . . . Ginger . . . Biscuit . . . Cracker . . . Jack? He listened intently as if auditioning for His Master's Voice but responded to none of them. I thought I'd call him after the

9

street where I found him. This, I was relieved to see, was Eric. If he'd hopped a little further, it would have been Wentworth and you'd feel such a fool calling 'Wentworth' on the Isle of Dogs.

I feel a fair fool calling 'Eric!' It is surprising how many men appear out of doorways, alleyways, windows and holes in the road when you shout 'Eric!' All, admittedly, fiftyish (it's no longer a fashionable name) but affable and cheerful company except, perhaps, the aerial erector who shinned down from a roof at my imperative cry and had to shin back up again.

The Isle of Dogs, once you start noticing them, is awash with dogs. A tidal wave of dogs all happy as Larry and bending the knee to no man. Dogs of a sporty, larky character. Dogs whose ears and tails don't match. Dogs in combat jackets and trainers out for a jog. Lean, black dogs with cropped ears, walking stiff legged as if they had a sawn-off shotgun down their trousers. Dogs that can get you Janet Reger knickers cheap. Dogs with their ears turned inside out for a laugh. Dogs with a bit of a swing to their walk and plenty to say for themselves. Dogs whose boats would ring no bells at Cruft's.

Apart from elderly, spreading dogs, like snooker tables walking, out on the lead, Island dogs seem to hang about all day in gangs, having a laugh with the lads. Fearing g.b.h. of the ear'ole from 'er indoors, they seem to delay their return almost indefinitely, going home occasionally to wash their socks. They all look exactly like Eric. Mix any three dogs together in a blender, and you get Eric. He's been described as a photofit dog, a frankly random approximation to a dog wanted to help the police with their inquiries. The tail is certainly a mistake. It seems to belong on a squirrel.

Because Eric had been hopping about on a broken leg for some months, the bone had to be forced to fuse with a compression plate, as worn by Barry Sheene. East-Enders do not need an excuse to talk but when offered one they welcome it. Eric's gammy leg drew concerned comment wherever he hopped. It took me two hours to travel from one end of a street market to the other, repeating his pathetic story every yard. Mini-cab drivers – I have never used so many mini-cabs – all turned out to have dogs of their own with colourful histories.

One had to pull into the side to wipe his eyes, remembering an Alsatian. What was.

The plate cost £187 to put in and, now they tell me, will cost another £70 to take out. I staggered a bit at the time but could hardly take him back to Eric Street. In retrospect I consider it the snip of 1986. His eyes never leave me. In shops I see him, paws on the sill, peering desperately through the window. He thinks he's going to wake up and find I've gone. I know I'm going to wake up and find he's gone. He has a tendency to take off without warning and whoop it up with the gang.

I know very well what should be done. ''Ave 'is whotsits off and 'e'll stick to you like 'ot glue,' advised an Eric who answered my plaintive cry in the night. I find it difficult to meet my Eric's eye these days.

24 December, 1986

Nancy Banks-Smith

Calling the shots

'Keep up the fire, sir!' yell a pair of young American infantry-men, as the lieutenant walks up the road where they stand guard. 'Keep up the fire, sir!' they scream, as loud as men can possibly scream, and then perform an elaborate ballet with their M-16s, twirling them round and round and up and down in perfect unison, like cheerleaders' batons. 'Keep up the fire!'

'Rock steady, men,' replies the officer, a giant of a man from Weehauken, New Jersey, who has been assigned to the Republic of Korea for a two-year tour, and is now only 29 days away from reprieve. He passes between the two sentries, through a double barbed wire fence, past a series of death's-head notices that warn 'Mines!', and into the best protected piece of real estate on earth.

The Korean DMZ – 151 miles long and about 2½ miles wide – keeps apart the two most implacably opposed systems of government that mankind so far has devised. On the one side, the North side, are practised the monstrous and doctrinaire barbarisms (as South Koreans and Americans like to put it) of Kim Il Sung and his Democratic People's Republic; on the other is the economically miraculous but, in its own way, no less politically barbarous state of the Republic of South Korea.

No other two countries divided by barbed wire and minefields glower at each other with such venom. The arguments between East and West Germany, Syria and Israel, China and Vietnam have an element of sanity or logic about them that is surely missing from the unending rage that is so evident on and around Korea's old 38th parallel.

Here the bizarre is commonplace. The shouted salutes from the American sentries – formalized and required – set the tone. The exchange between officer and men at the DMZ was just one of a variety heard from the GIs up on the borderline. 'One bullet, sir!' screeches a 'grunt' from another regiment. 'One man, corporal!' returns the officer. 'In front of them all, sir!' shouts a black soldier from the elite unit – all over six feet tall, all experts in martial arts – who police, in the name of the United Nations, an area right under the North Korean noses. 'Keep up the fire, sergeant!' his senior replies.

Loudspeakers, mounted on tall gantries, serenade the southern side with martial tunes. The blue and red North Korean flag on the mighty tower high over Propaganda Village (just over the border, farmed busily by day but said to be deserted at night) is known to weigh a third of a ton. 'President Chun has told us,' said one American marine, 'that if we go and snatch it down and deliver it to him, he'll give us a million bucks. So, I tell you, we's working on a plan . . .'

Balloons drift over the frontier whenever there is a northerly wind, dropping small blizzards of leaflets the size of cigarette cards. Some are dull, mere recitations of Kim's speeches, or expositions of his world-conquering philosophy of Juche, or self-reliance. Others are collectors' pieces. The latest, in bright poster colours, shows a bare-chested and obese American soldier, his chest alive with crawling bugs, labelled 'Aids'. He is leering from cherry-red lips about his passion for Korean women. 'Ladies of Korea!' the card advises. 'The only way to ensure you do not catch this fatal illness is to demand the immediate and total withdrawal of all American personnel from Korea. Yankees go home!'

The North Koreans have been broadcasting this message in a variety of forms ever since the war ended in 1953. The Americans, they insist, are to blame for Korea's tragic problem. The Americans have chosen the Korean peninsula as their Imperial battleground. The Americans, therefore, must go. Now, more than 30 years later, and to general alarm in both Seoul and Washington, there are real signs that their campaign is, perhaps more by accident than design, beginning to bear fruit.

There are 41,000 American military stationed in Korea and their presence is undeniably becoming less and less popular. More than half of them are soldiers, stationed in tactically convenient camps in the north of the country, close to the DMZ. There are in addition six big air bases and naval and intelligence-gathering stations – all of them rigorously protected by guards, dogs, wire, mines and rockets. Dislike of the bases and of their occupants, ever more easy to discern, operates on a number of levels.

The huge fighter base at Kunsan, for instance, sports a three-mile-wide *cordon sanitaire*, within which no American is allowed to live, nor even walk. But immediately outside it is Silver Town, an unlovely muddle of bars and brothels, where the GI can take his ease and forget the nightmare of his assignment far from home. Prices in Silver Town are coming down this month now that the pilots from the annual Team Spirit exercise have gone home: what cost $60 a fortnight ago is back to its regular $15, and the fliers from Kunsan's 'Wolf Pack' profess themselves relieved. 'I'm so horny even the crack of dawn isn't safe,' read one T-shirt on an F-16 pilot. 'It's been a bad month for the wallet,' he said with a grin.

The South Koreans are wearying of this kind of behaviour. One Korean man who has worked for a quarter of a century in a senior job on the base grimaced as he spotted an American pilot with a shoulder patch proclaiming '100 Strike Missions on Silver Town!' 'They should be beginning to realize that we have our pride back now,' he said. 'It's 30 years since the war. We aren't a poor people any more. Our girls can get proper jobs now. We're not a Third World country. These American troops and airmen think they can come in here and treat us like they treated the South Vietnamese. Well, they can't. They're on notice to treat us with respect, or they're in trouble.'

It is not difficult to notice opposition to the American presence in Korea at this most basic, grass-roots level. But recently – probably since the beginnings of the fruitless debate over constitutional reform last year – this antipathy has been joined by opposition on another level. The students and the intellectual community are now questioning the American presence in their country, and apparently see the Pentagon as a more formidable barrier to the possible reunification of Korea than is their own government.

'It is becoming rapidly very clear to me,' said Kim Kyung-soon, a third-year student at Sung Kyun Kwan, the Confucian university near Seoul, 'that America is here for American political interests, not for ours.

'Most Americans don't like Korea, they don't care about the people. They just want to continue to have regional control. They see the Russians at Carn Ranh Bay, and they see the Russians at Vladivostok; they see the Russian navy in Wonsan – they see Russians all over the place. They think the Philippines is going to go Marxist, and they worry about their declining fortunes in the Pacific. So they cling to us.

'They know if they keep up the propaganda about North Korea we'll stay docile, and do as we're told. They know that if they support our generals, the generals will stay in power and support them. There's a lot of mutual back-scratching going on, and none of it has anything to do with reunifying this country, which is what really needs to be done.

'Thirty years have gone by, and there's almost no contact between North and South. Families were divided and have no idea – none at all – what has happened. Mothers don't know if sons are alive; brothers have no idea about their sisters. There's no contact at all. And who stops the contact? Who keeps the two states at virtual war with each other? The Americans, of course. It's in their interest.'

This view, of course, is extreme – though increasingly to be found on the campuses of the Korean universities. But,

14

significantly, it was a view that was essentially shared by one man of towering wisdom and diplomatic knowledge who lives one of the most strangely and delicately balanced lives in this occasionally very strange and delicately balanced land.

Unfortunately it is impossible to identify him, other than to say he is one of those rare diplomats, a European, who has totally free access to both North and South Korea. He lives in one of the countries, and commutes, almost daily, into the other. His status is defined and guaranteed by the terms of the 1953 ceasefire. He is a man who respects confidences, and who expects others to respect his. Everyone seems willing to talk to him. The day I saw him he had had breakfast with a Chinese general in Kaesong in North Korea, took lunch with an American commander near the Imjin River in South Korea, and was planning to attend a small cocktail party given by the North Korean foreign ministry in the Northern capital, Pyongyang, that evening.

He has been in Korea for the past three years, and knows most of the protagonists well. He loves Korea, quite passionately. And he is deeply saddened by what he considers the progressive deterioration of the situation during the past three years.

'The suspicion, of one side by the other, is profound, we all know that. The build-up of military forces goes on, the tension increases, we all know that. But what surprised and truly depressed me is that the obstinacy, the obduracy, the short-sightedness – the real bar to any progress – is nearly all to be found on the Southern side.

'I am not saying the Northerners are angels, far from it. They live in an astonishingly controlled state, as everyone knows. But so do the Southerners. And they, the ones we think might show some tendency to compromise, to reasonableness, show none at all. Every idea that comes down the pipeline and looks reasonable, ultimately it gets rejected by Seoul. The generals in Seoul are utterly intransigent, and that is with the knowledge, connivance and probable support of the Americans. As long as the Americans call the shots in South Korea, there'll be no political movement. Things will simply get worse.'

Officially, all five countries who are militarily involved in the

15

Korean peninsula – China, the USSR, the USA and the two Koreas – are committed to its reunification 'by democratic means'. But there has been almost no progress towards that end in 30 years. And none, to judge from the mood in Seoul, is likely.

And all the while the armies and navies and air forces on both sides are becoming larger, stronger and better equipped. Currently there are 650,000 men under arms in the South, 850,000 in the North and eight million waiting in reserve. Depressing for the diplomat, no doubt, but for the military leaders on both sides an admirable means by which, to use the American phrase, 'to keep up the fire'.

12 May, 1987

Simon Winchester

Plague on the Potomac

The city of Sodom on the Potomac – shaken by a never-ending series of scandals involving alleged homosexual fundraisers for the Contras and sexual liaisons by the 1988 presidential prospect, Mr Gary Hart – was yesterday anxiously awaiting divine retribution.

After biding their time for 17 years buried deep below ground in the luxuriant spring gardens of Washington, a plague of locusts is preparing to descend upon the capital. The curious creatures, which have sent Washingtonians to the hardware stores to block up their windows and doors with defensive screens, have been quietly awaiting their moment to attack.

The first evidence of the invasion has already surfaced. Gardeners across the city, mowing their lawns for the first time last week, noticed thousands of small holes in the surface. It was as if the Lord had taken a giant roller in the dead of night and perforated the gardens, leaving no houses to chance, even those protected by religious symbols.

The locust-like creatures, properly called cicadas, bizarre creatures with five nasty red eyes, have clearly kept them firmly targeted on the newspapers. Revelations that the Contra fund-raiser, Carl 'Spitz' Channel, has pleaded guilty to conspiracy against the federal government and that Mr Hart may have trouble keeping his trousers on, have clearly stirred them.

Many millions of creatures have already tunnelled their way to the surface and are waiting the right moment to take part in one of nature's most unusual dramas. Those people who have lived through it before – in 1902, 1919, 1953 and, most recently, in 1970 – say it is an experience they will never forget. Local garden stores warn there is nothing you can do.

'It's just incredible, the noise they make. There can be thousands of them crawling up in the trees, flying around,' says Mr Douglas Miller, an entomologist at the Agriculture Department's Research Service in Maryland. 'They freak people out because they're big – an inch-and-a-half long – and they'll bump into you. But they can't hurt you.'

In a city where memories are necessarily short because of the large numbers of people who move on with changes of administration, the last locust plague remains as stamped on the institutional memory as the Watergate hearings which followed a few years later.

The city pavements were so thick with the cicadas – colloquially known as locusts – that it was impossible to walk without hearing a nasty crunching sound beneath the feet. But worst of all is the incredible noise. Sufferers told the *Washington Post* of a 'ceaseless cacophony' of thousands of creatures bigger and more noisy than the crickets who chirp their way through hot, muggy Washington nights. The locusts, called Brood X, emerge from their holes when the dogwoods are in bloom and then cling on to the bark of trees to go through their metamorphoses. They use their hypodermic-like mouths to feed on plant juices and stems above the ground, dooming young saplings and some flowering plants to a slow noisy death.

If Mr Reagan's luck holds out, the locusts may drown the noise from the Irangate hearings which open in the Senate today.

5 May, 1987

Alex Brummer

Jollying the Junta

Journalists from around the globe crowded into a small airless room in central London yesterday for a rare glimpse of Field Marshal Thatcher, legendary British strongwoman, who has held this turbulent island nation in her iron grip for as long as most people can remember.

It was the occasion of her quinquennial plebiscite appeal, an event which traditionally occurs every four years. It is one of the most bizarre rituals known to anthropologists, even against the strong competition offered yesterday by the Labour Party.

Every time it is the same. Correspondents from the vast industrial countries as well as the local media are each handed a colourful account of the Field Marshal's heroic achievements in the glorious days since the Revolution, accompanied by threats to do more of the same. As soon as permitted, they ask about the prospects for a return to civilian rule. And every time the Field Marshal replies that she needs another five years to eradicate Bolshevism and other social evils (this time it appears to be state education).

Everyone laughs a lot, but beneath the surface they all know they are witnessing a demonstration of the extraordinary power the Field Marshal has amassed. The foreign media, even holders of yen and other hard currencies, have been ritually humiliated by intense personal searches before being allowed in. They are then forced to wait for hours in conditions resembling a Calcutta January sale, inside the confines of the Blue Hole of Smith Square.

That is bad enough, but as soon as the Field Marshal appears a solid wall of enormous brutes carrying Japanese cameras rises up and she disappears from view for a further five minutes.

But the real cruelty lies in the knowledge of what awaits surviving members of her junta who participate in this ordeal. Legend has it that they used to be brought in in chains. Now that the Field Marshal's grip is so secure the style is relaxed, even jovial, but Junta members know that during the process one of their number is chosen for execution.

Last time, it was a now forgotten figure called Pym, who had publicly called for small majorities. He was taken out and shot before the votes were counted, let alone cast. This time it was rumoured that Mr John Biffen had been tipped the Blue Spot for a similar coded attack about 'violence to leadership'. But he was nowhere to be seen yesterday, and inquiries elicited only vague replies that he was 'busy', on a fact-finding tour of privatization in East Germany or 'gone to the lavatory'.

It could only mean that this Biffen had already become another of the disappeared ones. There would have to be another victim.

There followed an hour in which the pitiful wretches attempted to deflect the Field Marshal's wrath while she toyed with them in a brisk and genial fashion. 'Norman, you should be saying all this,' she would remark. Mr Norman Fowler duly blurted out a few words to the effect that he was sorry and would try harder.

'George, would you like to put it very much better?' she invited the hapless Mr Younger after making a trenchant statement on the importance of the British bomb. Only Lord Whitelaw, who has been on Death Row for many years, seemed impervious to the tension.

Some tried to avoid tension altogether. It did not go unobserved. 'I am sure the Foreign Secretary, who is very quiet, will reply to that,' the PM said at one point, a few minutes after Mr Douglas Hurd had expressed an eagerness to reintroduce the Criminal Justice Bill, 'if the Prime Minister so wishes', and promptly taken a large gulp of water.

The Foreign Secretary, who is very quiet, said a few words and, feeling that perhaps he had not said enough, later made a grovelling plea for continuity so that the Prime Minister could continue her great work for world peace.

His position is serious. It is known that he has been threatened with a torture called 'The Woolsack', which, according to Amnesty International, produces a slow and lingering death.

The trouble with leaderism is that it is contagious. According to the opinion polls, the voters have got used to it. Consequently, those civilian parties permitted to participate in the plebiscite try to get in on the act. Dr David Owen has shown advanced symptoms of leaderism for many years, and yesterday Mr Neil Kinnock came out in something of a rash during the presentation of Labour's manifesto.

Arriving to a fanfare from 'Barry Manilow Remembers Brahms', he walked down the aisle side-by-side with Mr Roy Hattersley. Both men wore red roses in keeping with the party's commitment to florism, the creation of one million new jobs in the flower industry.

Mr Hattersley looked a shade self-conscious, as well he might. It may have been an ad-man's idea of terrific television, but in the flesh it looked like a gay wedding. Not that such notions still appear in Labour manifestos.

On the rostrum at the far end of the Queen Elizabeth II Conference Centre sat members of the Shadow Cabinet, and

"That was wonderful, Mr Brahms – how exquisitely it conjures up a vision of a balding ginger-haired man, accompanied by a tubby man wearing an embarrassed smile, suddenly appearing on a platform full of red roses."

assorted reformed hooligans brought in for the occasion. As gay wedding parties go, they looked rather too uptight to be the bride and groom's families. Rather, they appeared to be trying to pass themselves off as the senior executives of a particularly respectable Yorkshire building society.

20 May, 1987

Michael White

Travels with a Golden Ass

There's a supernova exploding on the cover of *Time*. NASA wants to put a man on Mars (no, don't mention the Challenger shuttle). The President is on TV, apologizing, forgetting, having to correct himself the next day. *Polyps for Reagan*, the graffiti say.

Representative Mario Biaggi of the Bronx and Meade H. Esposito, once leader of Brooklyn's Democrats, are being indicted for bribery, fraud and conspiracy. Bess Myerson, 1945's Miss America and New York's cultural affairs commissioner, resigns after reports of serious misconduct. The CIA has given the Contras ground plans, blueprints and maps of key Nicaraguan installations, to help them with their terrorist programme.

Up in his Prayer Tower in Tulsa, the evangelist Oral Roberts threatens that God will 'recall' him unless his fans cough up $8 million. (The fans come up with the cash.) In New York, it's St Patrick's Day, so the entire city is dressed in green and can be found throwing up all over Fifth Avenue.

California, of course, has its own religions. The Committee for Self-Esteem has just held its first meeting. I thought Garry Trudeau had made it up, but there it actually is, publicly funded and everything, seeking to cure drug addiction, sex-crimes and so forth by making people feel better about themselves.

This is Rome near the end of its power, a famous New York magazine editor tells me. Western civilization hasn't long to go. Islam is coming, the Chinese, the darkness. We may as well celebrate the brightness that we were. Improbable as this sounds to an outsider, for whom the power of the United States is the most glaring aspect of the place, many Americans imagine themselves to be living in their twilight's last gleaming.

It makes them act strange. 'Now that I like you,' I am informed by one Manhattan intellectual, 'I can tell you I thought I wouldn't. I didn't think I could like a Muslim.' And it makes them touchy. 'Salman, as I grow older, I love this country more and more, and I don't like to hear it criticized.'

During my fortnight in the US (Pittsburgh, New York, San Francisco), I pass much time in the excellent company of a Moroccan writer of the second century AD, Lucius Apuleius, a colonial of the old Roman Empire, and I find that his portrait of that Roman world does indeed begin to look rather like contemporary America, but not quite in the way the editor meant.

The narrator of *The Golden Ass*, also named Lucius, is transformed by witchcraft into the tale's eponymous donkey, and his ass's-eye view of his age reveals a world of ubiquitous cynicism, great brutality, fearsome sorcery, religious cultism, banditry, murder.

Friends betray friends; sisters betray sisters; corpses rise up and accuse their wives of poisoning them. There are omens and curses; the items are out of joint.

Eighteen centuries later, with a portentous supernova in the sky, cynicism seeps all the way down from the White House to a Chinese cabbie, who tells me of his hatred for Communism and for poor countries, which adds up to Nicaragua. 'Always the same. Poor countries make trouble for the rest of us.'

Three years out of Hong Kong, he's taken to abusing Manhattan's Puerto Ricans. Doesn't he feel that such bigotry sits uneasily in the mouth of a fellow-immigrant? 'Excuse me, but these people like to steal.' The morning paper carries a story about Chinese involvement in heroin smuggling, but he's unimpressed. 'Have a nice day.'

There have been several race killings of late, blacks murdered by whites, sparking revenge-murders by blacks. Meanwhile, at the UN building, there's a demonstration protesting police violence against blacks in New York City. All this is familiar to the Ass.

22

For sorcery, one need look no further than the mumbo-jumbo of the Star Wars schemes; cultism and Jerry Falwell are everywhere; and as for banditry, Calero and his FDN, let's call them *Contrabandits*, are more dangerous than anything in Apuleius's book.

Now that the so-called 'moderates', Cruz and Robelo, have left the Contra leadership, certain revisionist processes have begun. Conservative columnist William Safire demands that America support Calero; while, on radio, I hear Arturo Cruz described as the 'leftist wing' of the Contras. So we can do without *him*, the pinko.

Pittsburgh reveals a different American malaise. It's pleasant, spacious, 'America's most livable city', a place where the main university building is actually named the Cathedral of Learning. (Inside you find representative classrooms from around the world. The English Classroom boasts desks like church pews and stained glass windows bearing coats of arms: City of Liverpool, Jane Austen, Charles Dickens, City of Bootle. That sort of thing.)

But there's another Pittsburgh, too. Mile upon mile of defunct steelworks bear witness to the collapse of a once-great industry. Unemployment is high. Pittsburgh's super-rich, the Carnegies and Mellons, long ago ceased to depend on steel; their fortunes float, now, on the oceans of pure finance. The poor weren't so lucky, and many, I hear, now earn a crust by servicing the mansions of the rich.

In San Francisco, 20 years after flower power, the feeling of being in a plague city is difficult to avoid. The worst thing about Aids, I'm told, is the speed at which it mutates. The most common symptoms used to be those of pneumonia, but already that's changing. New symptoms, new strains of the plague.

Susan Sontag recently published, in the *New Yorker*, a brilliant, moving short story, 'The Way We Live Now', about living with the illness. Neither the sick man, nor the illness, is named; the story is told by a crowd of voices, the voices of the patient's friends, of his entire world, voices taking on the story from one another, often in mid-sentence, creating an unforgettable vision of the disease as a crisis in all our lives.

I have read nothing about Aids that strikes deeper than Sontag's fiction. Perhaps, then, there is still a place, even in America, for art.

The picture of America emerging from these notes is, of course, in some sense 'unfair'. What you see depends on where you look. But the Apuleian America does exist, and I make no apology for looking at it.

The trouble is, what can a poor ass do? He observes, but cannot act. When donkey-Lucius sees a band of eunuch-priests assaulting a young labourer (and I can't resist drawing a parallel here with the US aggression against Nicaragua) he tries to shout 'Help, help! Rape, rape! Arrest these he-whores!'

'But,' writes Apuleius, 'all that came out was "He-whore, He-whore", in fine ringing tones that would have done credit to any ass alive.'

17 April, 1987

Salman Rushdie

An America we understand less and less

Pause one more time and consider the phenomenon called Ronald Reagan. Six years of power gone, with budget deficits soaring, unemployment biting hard down the Eastern Seaboard and through the Mid-West, with the farm states in parlous poverty, the oldest President in American history is on the stump again, striving to rescue enough Republican candidates to keep the Senate safe. Wherever he goes there is a warm wash of crowds – many of them young voters. What seemed, a couple of weeks ago, the end of his luck and charisma – sudden failure at Reykjavik – is now translated into the most potent campaigning weapon. Reagan's refusal to do a deal with Gorbachev is overwhelmingly endorsed in the opinion polls. More wondrous still, the poor, limp vision that is Star Wars has suddenly become a major plus with American voters. They like SDI; they embrace their President's simple homilies. And abruptly you can find Democrats soft-pedalling on the issue, promising – after all – not to shelve the programme when they take office.

So, we Europeans – this paper, amongst others – got it wrong again. Not wrong about Star Wars itself; wrong, rather, about American public opinion; and wrong – for the umpteenth time – about Mr Reagan's magical ability to spread sunshine, to turn defeat and incomprehension into victory. Will it, though, be enough to turn round the handful of Tuesday Senate races which will keep the Republican majority intact? That still seems too close to call. Until Mr Reagan got his campaign caravan on the road, the Democrats appeared to have just enough going for them. America is a vast continent. Local issues and local disenchantments were chipping away at GOP prospects from California to Maryland. And, of course, that was only to be expected. The mid-term is designed to produce a sizeable swing against whichever party is in government. Today, though, who can tell? It isn't axiomatic that a national President can turn local votes. But Mr Reagan's barnstormings have given the Republicans steam and hope at the end. It will be desperately close on the night; and, even in narrow failure, the President will have shown that his clout goes on and on.

Two reflections follow. One – disheartening, with the Presidential elections only two years away – is the disarray of the Democrats. Still they have no binding philosophy. Still they have no commanding national figures. Still they range from New Deal liberalism to yuppie conservatism. Perhaps that central core can't emerge before some Presidential candidate staggers from the ferocious ordeal of the primary circuit. But there is not even the beginning of coherent identity when you stack the Senate and gubernatorial manifestos end to end across America.

The second reflection returns to Star Wars and Reykjavik. We got it wrong; the BBC and even the sainted ITN got it wrong. Many of America's weightiest East Coast newspapers got it wrong as well. Nobody dreamed that the ashes of Reykjavik could be turned into potential triumph for Mr Reagan. And the lesson of that transformation is clear. Not just that Europe no longer understands what makes America tick; but that many of the Americans closest to the old European values have ceased to understand as well. The United States – in its preoccupations, in its beliefs, in its perception of itself – is not the nation we thought we knew. For good or ill, it is becoming a much more foreign land; and the engines that drive it are new, and surprising, and very strange. When you see Ronald Reagan bathed in glowing cheer you see the embodiment of that strangeness.

3 November, 1986

Leader

The certainties of Two Nations

This is a tale of two certainties. Of the Prime Minister opening her election campaign at a rapturous rally in Scotland, confident that Britain has been revived and restored by her and now bears a proud presence in the world. And of people in the derelict north of England confident, for their part, that if Jesus made his second coming now, Mrs Thatcher would nail him to a cross.

To get into Mrs Thatcher's rally at Perth is in itself an adventure. The murdering IRA have added the piquancy of danger to the event. You are checked by two men with scanning machines, and then frisked by women guards. The friskers are women because women delegates object to being body-searched by men, but men don't object to women.

So there were these girls passing their quick hands around, above, between. When it was my turn, I asked my girl whether no one man had shied at this. 'How can they?' she asked in a candid Scots voice, looking me in the eye and sliding deft fingers into a trouser pocket to verify that a key was just a key.

The Tories make a rally into a state occasion. It is a great political gift. On each seat, including those allotted to the reptile press, was a blue slip of paper giving the first eight lines of 'Land of Hope and Glory', down to 'Make thee mightier yet'. The golden organ in the city hall piped the Prime Minister in to the tune of Scots Porage Oats and she made a triumphal entrance right up the gangway, the length of the hall. 'Thank you for your spirited welcome,' said the text of her speech, distributed to the press an hour before.

She then read a run-of-the mill speech, 45 minutes of it. But she is a personification of the force of Will, and there is no getting away from that. She had some good lines, too. How outdated, she said, socialism now appeared. It had the smell of the late 1940s about it – the atmosphere of shortages, rationing, the black market, and endless restrictions. When she said that, it had the smell of truth.

But she can get away with anything. Talking about the abolition of rates in Scotland, she uttered these three lines, which I here repeat as they appeared in her text:

'They said we couldn't do it.

They said we wouldn't do it.

We did it.'

Here there were irresistible echoes of Doolittle the dustman, waxing eloquent in *My Fair Lady*: 'I'm willing to tell you. I'm wanting to tell you. I'm waiting to tell you.'

A human touch, though not perhaps intended. But had she fixed it so that this election, too, should begin at Perth? The 1983 election did, with much the same speech. And in 1979, though she had already won by the time of the Perth conference that year, she made the first big speech of her administration there. Can it be that she is superstitious? That would be human.

Anyway, on she went, exhorting the faithful to enjoy or endure the election but never (hushed voice) to assume, never to take the British people for granted. Then on to that bit about Britain's proud presence in the world and so on, then a five-minute ovation which she attempted to abbreviate with modest gestures of her hands. She has actressy hands. Then the chairman told us the world expected another Conservative victory, and off the leader went in triumph, pausing to kiss Lady Home in the hall on her way. It was a damn good show.

And he would be a fool, I think, who doubted that she meant every word she said.

I supposed, watching her depart to her necessarily armour-plated Daimler, and glancing at the now-empty platform, that someone had checked that the bottles of mineral water next to the rostrum from which she had spoken were just bottles and did contain just mineral water.

Then I drove to Edinburgh and took a train to Sheffield. This is not Perth. The eastern approach to Sheffield, in the valley of the Don, is through miles of scrapheaps and devastation. I chose Sheffield because, since as far back as 1918, it has been the most loyal of all cities to the Labour Party, and because it is part derelict, and because in the miners' strike I saw such bitterness there as I have never seen in England.

Five of the six Sheffield seats are Labour. Mr Richard Caborn at Sheffield Central has a majority of 16,790. He is the son of a famous communist. He was engineering apprentice, shop steward, and convenor, and then in 1983 took over from Fred Mulley, the former Defence Secretary, who had been deselected. He is anti-apartheid, CND, and bearded. On paper he sounds the type and pattern of Loony Man.

I'll say straight away that he isn't, and that what follows is too brief and selective to be a reasonable account of a long conversation. He says Mrs Thatcher, on her recent visit, walked the streets of Moscow with more ease than she would those of Sheffield. He had heard a man say in a club that she could walk more safely in Moscow, too. Was that also his view? He wasn't saying that: but when she had been in Moscow she had been at ease, buying caviar for the bloody cat and saying Gorbachev was a man she could deal with.

He doesn't see Russia as a menace to peace: Sheffield was twinned with Donietz. Well, I said, what about Hungary 1956, Czechoslovakia 1968, and Poland more recently? 'Not under Gorbachev,' he said. And what, he asked, about Vietnam, El Salvador, Nicaragua?

The Berlin Wall, then? He mentioned fairly free movement between East and West already, different interpretations of human rights, and hopes that the Wall might come down in time.

The talk was more profitable when we came back to his patch. He is worried that a whole generation may have to be written off. So many young people in Sheffield have never had a job. They play pop music till three in the morning, don't get up till ten, and the work ethic isn't there any more.

He agreed he was Utopian, and it didn't put him off that no Utopia has ever been realized. He believes in the human spirit but detests that of Mrs Thatcher and the gutter press, which he says would have pilloried Jesus Christ. I was to hear more about Jesus later.

Mr Caborn drove me to see Hyde Park, an awful city-in-itself of highrise flats on a hill, built when Roy Hattersley was chairman of Sheffield housing committee, but built high, says Mr Caborn, by the edict of central government. He had plans to turn it into dormitories for the World Student Games of 1991, the world's biggest sporting event after the Olympics, and then to sell off part to the university, part to the poly, and part as flats for single people. No more families to live there anyway. He hopes the games may do more for Sheffield than snooker at the Crucible Theatre already does: that brings in £1.5 million a year.

At home, Mr Caborn's wife, Margaret, asked how old Mrs Thatcher was. Sixty or 61, I thought, but at Perth she hardly looked it.

Mrs Caborn: 'No, she doesn't. Say what you like, she doesn't. More's the pity.'

Mr Caborn: 'You're the right-wing conscience of the *Guardian*. They told me not to see you. I said I don't give a bugger. I'll sing the same song.'

It then came out that Mrs Caborn had been born in a pub with sawdust on the floor. I said my father had been, too.

Mr Caborn took me to the Trades and Social Club to meet Mr Ken Curran, a NUPE official, and Mr George Machin, who was for one year, up to February 1974, Labour MP for Dundee East and is now club secretary. We talked about Mrs Thatcher and the miners' strike.

Mr Machin: 'The laws were always made to apply to us, not for the higher-up. I've been saying it's a police state for ten years.'

Mr Curran: 'England is an occupied country. It's under Norman rule.'

What, I said, look at the Thatcher eyes and fair hair, and that English name: her a Norman?

'She's a Quisling.'

A third man, a former county councillor, then said: 'The very word Parliament comes from Norman French.'

Quisling? Norman rule? This was surreal, but Mr Curran turned out, as the evening progressed, to be no joker. He several times spoke about the Highland clearances. It was the same in Sheffield today. The people were no longer of any use and were being disposed of.

Mr Machin: 'The whole history of law has been to repress the people. Look at the Enclosure Acts. They drove people into the factories.' I was then told that if Jesus Christ was born today, Mrs Thatcher wouldn't wait 33 years before nailing him to his cross.

In a lull, I said I had been to the club once before, in the miners' strike, and Mr Machin said: 'I remember. I took you in.' Yes, and there were some miners sitting there and when they were told I was from the *Guardian* they called me a social enemy and pointed to the Exit sign. 'They regarded you as part of the other nation.'

The talk then turned to the police, emphatically part of the other nation, who in that strike had arrested 20 miners outside the club, coming at them in a semicircle of batons and slinging them in vans.

At this point in the conversation a young man in rags appeared near us, got up for a fancy dress party. 'I'm a miner,' he said, 'after the coppers have finished with me.'

Mr Curran: 'I wouldn't say there's any hatred.' Mr Machin: 'Just a guarded wariness.' Well, the nurse I met later that evening at Silverwood miners' club a few miles off was not so forgiving. She refuses to let policemen drink tea in her hospital waiting room.

We got to Silverwood by driving along the Don valley, past places like Salmon Pastures where there once really were salmon, and then steel mills, but now, since Mrs Thatcher came to power, just dereliction and ruins. It has happened in

4–7 May, 1987

31

her time, therefore it is her work.

At the club a young miner, a face worker, told me Mr Scargill was still King Arthur. His executive had asked him to keep quiet but he was still king. Everything he said had been right, except that they had closed more pits than he said. Another man compared Mrs Thatcher to Hitler, in her capacity for devastation. He meant it. They all meant what they said.

The nurse, Mrs Gwen Mellors, works in a geriatric unit. Patients in pain now waited before they asked for help, because they saw there were so few nurses. But surely more was now being spent on the health service, in any terms, than in 1979? She repeated what she saw herself every day.

She also said she was lucky. She had 'little luxuries' like a telephone, but had never been able to afford a holiday abroad, except when the NUM, thanks to Russian donations, had taken her to Russia and Bulgaria during the strike. She belongs to a women's action group which still meets every Monday in Rotherham.

Many miners laid off or sacked have never worked since. Their children run round in plastic shoes. As Mr Curran said, if it wasn't that people got a drink, there'd be a great deal of despondency.

Suppose Mrs Thatcher did get in again? A miner said: 'If she does, I really do think that Broadwater Farm is going to look like a tea party, up north anyway.'

The certainties of Sheffield and Silverwood were as deeply held as those of Perth. I do not question the good faith of anyone I listened to or spoke with all weekend. Mrs Thatcher on the smell of the Forties was eloquent.

Certainties, certainties. There was only this glimmer. As we were saying goodnight at the club, Mrs Mellors said: 'When she first came in I thought it might do the country some good. A woman. To bring up a family. But she's never ever had to want. To be honest, say she gets elected again, and she puts my sons in employment, then I tell you what, the next time she came up I'd vote for her. But she won't. Things have really gone from bad to worse.'

18 May, 1987   **Terry Coleman**

Why it will be all my fault

Sir, – First they came for Liverpool City Council, but I did not speak out: I thought they were all Militant Tendency.

Then they came for the miners' leaders, but I did not speak out: they seemed a bit ultra-left for me.

Then they came for the constituency parties, but I did not speak out: I didn't realize so many were disbanded.

Then they came for the 'loony Left', but I did not speak out: I thought they were all gays and lesbians.

Then they came for black sections and they took away Sharon Atkin, but I did not speak out: what she said was over the top.

Finally, they came for me and everyone told me: 'You must have brought the party into disrepute or they wouldn't have come for you.'

One morning I woke up and we had lost another election and everyone said it was my fault. There was no one to speak for me.

I still don't know what I said, but it must have been awful. I feel there should be a trial so that I can confess.

Yours sincerely,

6 May, 1987

Richard Chessum
Leamington Spa

War on the streets

Without a driving licence, I would not be able to fetch a loaf of bread in Los Angeles. The nearest bus is three miles away and goes once every two hours. Having survived happily in Bournemouth, London and New York as a non-driver, it was clear that my time was up.

To judge from the average taxi driver, any cowboy can

get a licence in New York. There may be more dangerously daredevil drivers: the French, one is told; the Saudis, perhaps. There cannot be anywhere else the same lethal combination of ineptitude.

Hit the gas pedal, hit the brake, swing the wheel: the three rules of New York driving. No matter that traffic lights along main avenues are linked at 25 mph – just screech from stop light to stop light, 0–60 and jam on the brakes. Radios at top volume muffle the reality of other cars. To yield is to lose face; 'Stop' is a relative term. All of this excludes the pothole as a New York institution: a great lump gouged out of the city's main artery. Taxi drivers hurtle across, over and through them, swerving, speeding, changing lanes without signal. Most drivers can neither speak English nor understand much of it and few can hear anyway behind the thick, bullet-proof screen.

A yellow cab medallion changes hands for $50,000 to $100,000, so someone is making huge profits – not the drivers, certainly. Gypsy cabs, known euphemistically as livery cars, are in even worse condition, running without set tariff or, frequently, even rudimentary insurance. What they all have in common is this sense that *anyone* can drive. It is as if a licence is a constitutional right.

Imagine my surprise, then, to discover that it is actually difficult to get a driving licence. It requires enormous amounts of free time, nerves of steel and quite large sums of money. On the whole island of Manhattan, there is only one office for the New York State Department of Motor Vehicles. This is way down-town, opens at 7.30 a.m. and by that time has a three-hour queue in place, every morning, every day that it operates. It is the only democratic meeting place. No one can skip the line. In a city in which money buys anything, no one can do this for you.

There are ways around it. Of course. They involve not so much money as cunning. Out in Yonkers, for instance, in that far-off haven of shopping malls, there is a tiny Motor Vehicles' office which is full of sunlight and uncharacteristically helpful clerks. (Bureaucracy elsewhere is as thick and ungiving as the city at its worst.) Taggart's Driving School even operates a mini-bus that sets off for Yonkers three times a week, holding

34

the hands of its soon-to-be-pupils as they apply for a learning permit.

The application for a permit is tricky. It is a lot harder than you think to prove you exist. Cancelled cheques may or may not be proof of residence. Baptism certificates do not count as anything, passports might, depending where from and in what name. If one piece of paper has a middle initial that is missing on another – go back to the beginning. Electricity bills might do, rent books are unlikely. It is quite common to set aside the morning for Yonkers, only to find that a veritable sheaf of papers will still not satisfy as proof of birth, name and address.

Then comes the written test. Taggart's no longer bother to hand out highway code books. Each putative driver is given a white booklet with the questions and correct answers filled in. 'Don't try and think,' says Jolly Joe at the free introductory lesson. 'Just learn it, folks.'

Lessons cost $39.95 an hour; a package of six gives one free. Each pupil is given one instructor. These instructors are all-powerful, full of swagger and jaunty confidence. They are the bull-fighters, the sports stars, the stunt men. Nothing like dual control to make a tiger of a mouse. Only the Mets' pitchers have the braggadocio of Taggart's instructors milling in too-tight trousers on Lexington Avenue outside the Manhattan office. The Cubans come into their own – smart, full of charm and a hard edge. The Haitians, Puerto Ricans and cool strutters from Harlem walk here as kings. If the car is a metaphor for American life and sex, it goes without saying that its practitioners are stars of the street.

Only the very young book a driving test on Manhattan. It is like war. Moderate to heavy traffic, the test laws say. Heavy traffic down there on Delancy Street is murder. Taggart's likes to recommend the gentle backstreets of the forgotten Bronx. Unfortunately, to get to these byways in order to practise in peace, you have to drive along some of the most vicious highways out of the city. Lesson after double lesson, I quivered, sweated and almost fainted through underpasses, tunnels, junctions and four-lane death traps. After that, the test itself was nothing. Five minutes, two turns, a bit of parking and a U-turn.

The stoic woman examiner had failed the driver before me

whose instructor exploded in rage and threats. (Perfectly normal response from a rejected star.) New York is full of white middle-class women who have never driven and never will; they fail the test five, ten times before giving up. The atmosphere on that Bronx corner where testers and testees gather is enough to defeat any namby-pamby West Side liberal type – it is earthy, tough, cowboy country.

I passed first time. My face fitted. I danced downtown to queue all morning to have my photograph taken, my final application stamped. The licence should arrive any time now through the mail. Dreadful news, however, has just reached me. To insure a car in Los Angeles, I have to get a Californian driving licence. New applications, new queues, new tests. I should have known; last year, we had to file twelve separate income tax returns across America. Sometimes, the founding fathers and the federal system of independent states is enough to make you sick.

23 June, 1987   **Linda Blandford**

Dinkie Docklands

There is no school, no shop, no social life and no transport, but the yuppies are paying up to £1 million to live here. This is Docklands in the East End of London, where speculators have retired on their profits and the local housing estates blend effortlessly with their up-market counterparts – Cascades, Clippers, Gun Wharf and Tobacco Dock.

'It used to be called Wapping-on-Thames,' says 73-year-old Jim Smith sharing a lunchtime pint at the White Swan and Cuckoo. 'That's what it says on my driving licence – Green Bank, Wapping-on-Thames. Green Bank? Huh – not a blade of glass in sight.'

Jim, born and bred within sight and sound of the docks, is saving up to go across the road from the pub to the newly built Java Brasserie, where they serve up nouvelle Indonesian cuisine – tiny portions but beautifully arranged on the plate.

36

'It costs about £20 a head. If I like it, I'm going to save up to go back next year,' he says. Jim is a rounded man, wearing a flat corduroy cap and sporting a shirt and tie under his mustard pullover and belted trousers.

He finds one of the advantages of the new intake is that the original Wapping residents can now get cabs home from the West End. 'They'd never come here in the old days. They was frightened of being eaten. We used to ask for Wapping police station 'cause that way they didn't know who you was and they had to take you.'

His nephew Alan Smith has been in Docklands for 17 years. 'We were offered a flat and my wife looked it up on the map and said: "Oh, look! There's a big high street so it must be all right." We got there and found one shop.

'We spent two years trying to get out again, but no one was interested. If we advertised today we'd have to put the phone off the hook after half an hour.'

Cue, estate agents: Hugo Kidston is 21 and sounds like Prince Andrew. He's transferred from the Chelsea office of Savills, the international property company – Berkeley Square, Hong Kong, New York, Amsterdam and now . . . Wapping.

Hugo and his colleagues come from and sell to the kind of people who think 'my old china' is a reference to the family Wedgwood and a 'nice boat race' is the correct thing to say about Henley. It has fostered a resentment locally that occasionally rears its ugly head through the activities of an organization called Class War.

The dog and bone is ringing relentlessly in the background with new inquiries as, elegantly crossing brogued and pin-striped legs, he explains: 'A lot of people came here after Big Bang in the City because it's near to their work and a lot have come in from Essex and Chelmsford on the east side of London. It appeals to everyone.'

Everyone, that is, who can afford around £80,000 for a tiny one-bedroom unit, or about £250,000 for an average converted warehouse space.

Fresh-faced and full of life, Docklands veteran Paul Austin, of Carleton Smith, has moved there himself. 'We've been here since 1970. We were the first estate agents in the area,' he says, from an office that could be described as light and spacious with superb river views.

'It all started when some of our clients, who had empty warehouses after the closure of the docks, came and asked us what they should do with them. We turned them into homes. They only cost £50,000 in those days and were mainly bought by artists and creative people. Now the Dinkies (double income no kids) are moving in. 'In the future, this will be an international market. We'll have some of the best recreational activities and shopping areas in London.'

In the meantime, there is of course the Asda supermarket on the nearby Isle of Dogs. This is the new London enterprise zone where commercial properties, including the new *Guardian* print works, will not have to pay rates until 1992.

It is here that one unearths some genuine East Enders selling conversions to the converted. David Galman and the crew from Collins and Co. used to sell in neighbouring Newham, but they got into Docklands when they merged with the West End agents Druce.

'We've got East End knowledge and West End clout,' he explains, providing a verbal sketch of the area that transforms the barren wasteland, with its lack of beauty and amenities, into the most exciting property prospect in the capital.

David, aged 24 and looking like a stockbroker in his shirt, tie, red-rimmed glasses and the essential brogues, is a believer.

He has already bought a home on the island and says that once the infrastructure has been created, which should be around his thirtieth birthday, the island is going to be the greatest place around. His property has increased in value by 50 per cent over the last two years.

'The only thing we haven't got is a school, but that means that the place is full of young and single people, which makes it great fun,' he says.

His colleague, Andrew Thomas, fielding phone calls while his tuft of blond hair leans in all directions with a life of its own, agrees. Young and lippy with the rough, tough ways of a local, he is constantly pursued by clients and associates.

As we talk, a girl from the nearby office of Parris and Quirke calls to ask him to meet her about a property. He listens, incredulous. 'You want to meet at ten tonight? Well, I can't. Honestly, I'm having my hair cut. Does your boss know you make these calls? Whaddya mean, I'm naive?'

Sighing, Andrew confides: 'This only happens in Docklands. One of the blokes here, Graham, took a girl to see a property and ended up seeing her. He even took her to meet his mum and dad. But then she went to see another property with another agent and he found out she was seeing him as well.'

So much for loyalty. But then, you can't expect to find old East End virtues amongst those whose only experience of cockney life was being taken to see Tommy Steele in *Half a Sixpence*. Not that you'd get much for that in Dockland these days.

25 May, 1987

Shyama Perera

Lambeth's walk on the wild side

'I'll f...... cross their f...... picket lines. I don't give a f... for their trade union! I'll f...... kill them! I'll get private security guards to f...... pay the money!' Linda Bellos, leader of Lambeth Council, had just stamped out of yet another meeting with striking members of the Civil and Public Servants' union and her own NALGO officers. The unions were refusing to allow her to pay out a pittance of £14 a week to welfare clients who risk starvation when their giros are stopped by the CPSA strike.

There was chaos in the town hall that day and in the leader's office in particular. She gave one of her rare wry smiles and said airily, 'But it's always like this. Something's always happening.' She is in charge of a borough the size of Luxembourg, with a £209m budget, about the same as that of some African countries.

Her meteoric rise to power, public prominence and notoriety came as a result of a remarkable conjunction of events: she was the right person in the right place at the right time. She only joined the Labour Party in 1984, approached by a black organization to join the struggle for black sections within the party. She was only elected to Lambeth Council in 1985.

She arrived at an opportune moment. Ted Knight, the previous leader, and 30 left-wing councillors were just being disqualified for refusing to set a rate, causing financial loss and chaos to the borough. She arrived too late to vote with them and be disqualified herself. When the others were finally disqualified, it left her and two other councillors as the only remaining Labour members.

There was an inevitable power struggle between the three and all the other councillors who were elected last May in place of those disqualified. She was not Ted Knight's choice, though it was still thought that he would expect to rule from exile through her. She rapidly made it clear she was her own woman. The hard Left did a deal with the soft Left, whereby she got the leadership, the mayor's post and all the main committee posts, except Housing, which went to the soft Left.

There she was, the perfect choice – hard Left, a woman, black, a lesbian, and Jewish. The one social disadvantage she lacked was a physical disability. But to show her credentials in that field, she carried through a policy of recruiting only disabled people from May to September last year, until the 3 per cent quota of disabled people on Lambeth's staff was reached.

It led to a huge number of posts, including many directors of key departments, going unfilled. A leaked draft of a letter to her from her own chief executive in January this year warned that the council was heading for dire trouble and might have to start closing services down, because of its inability to attract, recruit or retain enough middle and senior level officers.

In February, the Federated Union of Managerial and Professional Officers representing the senior officers in Lambeth threatened to strike over pay and the number of evening meetings they were obliged to attend. (There are now 90 committees and working parties – at least 12 more this year.) The chief officer also complained of the excessive power the trade unions held in the council, confusing the role between councillors and officers.

However, the day I visited her, she was clearly not in the least confused about the frontier between her own left-wing self and her trade unions. She jabbed her finger and sliced her hand in the air. 'I don't care what any of them say. I'll f...... cross their picket lines!' she shouted. 'I'll do it, make no mistake.' If she hadn't been wearing a Chairman Mao blue jacket with a black fist lapel badge reading 'Support Black Sections', she could have been any infuriated Tory leader or plutocratic company boss.

Her opponents smirk with a certain glee. It is she and the Left who have fuelled the volcano they now sit on, they who have allowed the unions to get out of hand and prevent the carrying out of some of the policies left-wing councillors now wish to impose.

Certainly her experience in trying to deal with the unions has not altered her ideology one iota. Reality, even the harsh realities she deals with day by day, seems not to dent the fervour of her purist Marxist ideals. Shortly after I had observed her rage at the unions, she dictated to me this careful statement, waiting as I wrote it down verbatim: 'The trade unions are the legitimate representatives of the workforce and it is not for me to determine their view. My duties are to take into account the views of the trade unions and balance that with the overriding duty to deliver services.'

She was born in Lambeth. Her mother was a Jew of Polish extraction, her father a Nigerian. Her father worked in the Osram Lamp Company, and at Battersea Power Station, her mother at a Sunpat Peanut Butter factory. They were both Labour Party members. 'They were both *manual workers*,' she says emphatically. 'I will not accept the slur that I might be middle class.'

She went to a Brixton comprehensive, which she left at 19 with one A-level in music. She played the clarinet. She was married immediately to a cellist. 'He was *very* middle class.' She had two children and a very hard life indeed. She is deeply reticent about her marriage, for fear of jeopardizing her children. The worst time appears to have been after the birth of her second child, living in a town outside London. She was still breast-feeding when she went back to work in a tax office, with no car, dragging them off each morning on the bus to a child-minder, going to work, returning to fetch the children, shop, cook, wash and iron. 'I was a beast of burden.'

Lesbianism and divorce followed. Because she had become a lesbian she lost her children – as lesbians often do. The trauma of that loss, she says, still affects her deeply, though she does have access. In all the nonsense and absurdity churned out by lesbians and gay rights committees, this one brutal issue – the treatment of lesbians in the divorce courts – gives her militant feminism a real and bitter edge.

After divorce, she took a driving test and went to Sussex University to read politics, where she graduated in 1981. She came back to live in Lambeth and was involved in Revolutionary Feminist groups, Black Women's groups, and Women against Violence Against Women, but never, she says, in any other political party.

Her public persona is harsh, hatchet-faced, grim and relentless. Of all the Labour Party black sections activists adorning the TV screens of recent weeks, she looks the most alarming. Her private face is only a little more relaxed and easy-going. Smiles are rare. She speaks in long, perfectly formed sentences. She is extremely clever, astute and direct, not warm but not unfriendly either.

Racism is everywhere, in everything, in every person and institution, she says. Who is to gainsay her? For she is surely right. And with that single, simple truth she has the power to exploit white middle-class guilt in her own party. It's the ace she puts on the table, which is why the whole black sections issue causes such angst and rage to the Labour leadership. Her own impeccable catalogue of disadvantages gives her a lever to help shake the foundations of her party.

She sharply refutes the suggestion that race can be used to trump all opposition. 'I say, "Don't come bleating to me with your white liberal guilt. Could you spare us the guilt till after the meeting? I am the one suffering discrimination, and that's worse than guilt."' She talks of the racist hate mail she receives every day bearing messages like: 'I hope you die of Aids.'

Arriving as Lambeth's leader, with less than a year as councillor, she was undaunted by her inexperience. First she decided to carry through the policy on employing the disabled. Then she had to tackle the mounting bureaucratic bungling in dealing

42

with Housing Benefit. The computer department has been swallowing ever increasing sums trying to operate it. Then she set up an inquiry into the inefficiency of the housing repairs department. The results of that inquiry, though, sound like a foregone conclusion. She says she has promised the unions that, whatever the outcome of the investigation, she will increase the direct labour force and reduce the numbers of private contractors.

She has also been managing the creative accounting of the budget. Lambeth has borrowed £13m from an Irish bank, on the newly discovered wheeze of selling them buildings and assets and leasing them back again, piling up interest payments for the next 25 years. 'There's still plenty more we can sell and lease back to cover future years,' she says. Presumably she doesn't expect to be there on the day of reckoning.

But Lambeth's problems are so manifold and so complex they defy solution from within that benighted borough itself. Half the households in the borough live on less than £4,400 a year. Five hundred families at any one time are living in bed-and-breakfast squalor at a cost of £4m a year. A third of families are one parent families. Loony or feckless policies, putting ideology before needs, putting the council workforce issues before the needs of the borough, don't help. There is a certain ramshackle charm about the life in the leader's office, as meetings come and go, crisis follows crisis and her attention is tugged from one issue to another in rapid succession. She says it's always like that. She is certainly decisive and emphatic but her centre of operations hardly has the air of a powerful hub of authority.

She is good with words – if not politic. She has a gift for providing a short sharp pithy quote that gets splashed across the hostile tabloids. She called the local police 'bent on war' one tense weekend. 'I am a lesbian and proud of it,' she announced, and of course she repeatedly calls the Labour Party a 'racist institution'. She even says her own council is racist, despite having raised the number of blacks employed from 16 per cent to 30 per cent. She made the point neatly by throwing open the door to a meeting off a corridor. There was a large table around which sat a score of white middle-aged men in ties. 'There, you see!' she said. 'There's still a lot to be done.'

That day she came out of one meeting smiling and waving a eulogy of herself, a poem written by Lambeth poet Michael Archangel. The chorus read:

> Sister Linda's phone is
> always ringin',
> Sister Linda's on de line,
> Ring Big Sister Linda
> An get some peace ah mind,
> Phone Sister Linda
> An liberate yuh mind.

11 May, 1987

Polly Toynbee

Two more nations

Sir, – The belief that Britain is now two nations is obliquely supported by the details of a recent 'Guardian Offer' for a waxed cotton jacket, 'at home, in town and country'. An almost identical article, obtainable from the same address, is advertised in *The Times* as 'invaluable for a whole range of country pursuits, from fishing to shooting to horseriding and point-to-point'. Such activities are not for *Guardian* readers, of course, but the consolation is that their jacket is ten pounds cheaper.

The descriptions differ in only one detail: the *Times* jacket features 'a waterproof gamekeeper's pocket', the *Guardian* one 'a waterproof poacher's pocket'. The actual jackets are identical, except that the *Guardian* version has a detachable hood – presumably to help the wearer avoid being recognized by gamekeepers.

Yours faithfully,

2 February, 1987

Tony Lurcock
Oxford

Cold comfort statistics

The politics of atrocious weather is rooted in the fact that the misery is actual for everyone. On balmy days and even dank ones, it is extremely easy to forget the privation in which many people live. When, merely by venturing outside, it is possible to experience the insensible limbs and frozen bloodstream from which luckless citizens are suffering, and sometimes dying, in their homes, governments live, for a salutary moment, under the baleful eye of heightened public awareness.

This government has responded adroitly. It saw the political danger and acted, by making nonsense of its own tortuous scheme for giving extra heating assistance. Bureaucratic objections were cut through, in best Thatcherite style. Those who qualify would get the money now, not after the statutory days of suffering had been endured. John Major, the Social Services Minister, confirmed his reputation as a capable performer.

It can be a great advantage to be in government, not opposition, in these circumstances. Governments can act, oppositions only bleat. On Tuesday, Labour thought it was coming to bury a bunch of stony, inflexible ministers. To its chagrin, it discovered that the government is not quite so stupid as it assumed.

It was also reminded how long it is since it was in power. Nothing now inhibits the Thatcher people from proclaiming the immensity of their contribution to public spending. And since inflation alone would mean that virtually every figure has gone up over eight years, there will be scarcely a category of public spending where Labour's promises cannot be capped by the Tory claim that they have spent far more than Labour ever did when it had the chance.

Since the Tories can now show they are spending £400m on regular heating assistance as against Labour's £90m they take the trick – as long as one overlooks the loss in pensions produced by changing the basis of indexation.

Behind this well-constructed forensic barricade, Tory backbenchers chortled with relief. They continued to feel good

45

yesterday, during Labour's all-day emissions of outrage. They felt saved from a booby-trap. Were they not now the caring party? How they had stolen one of the few remaining shreds of Labour's clothing? It was all a reassuring piece of politics.

Yet those heightened perceptions cannot be banished so easily. Bitter cold as a universal experience gives fresh life to questions which this great society of ours has got used to treating with evasion, excuses and a kind of impossibilist shrug of the shoulders.

On heating itself, is it seriously contended that the enormous resources of this country cannot be organized in such a way as to ensure that no citizen dies of hypothermia by accident of poverty? Is the best regime the Government can devise one which requires 63 weather stations to send in their seven-day records, requires hundreds of DHSS offices to establish proof of need, and places at its apex a Met Office that now declines to answer questions about the temperature on the grounds that this has become a political issue?

Is this not government stringency gone mad, departmental line-drawing taken into realms of the higher lunacy? Is no minister prepared to concede that the cash limits and the PSBR he now invokes as restraints on his freedom of action are, compared with the need to keep all the people warm, gods worshipped only by those whose well-upholstered seats insulate them from contact with the real world?

And doesn't this life-and-death quibble over whether £5 should be handed over to the neediest people in society, on the minister's weekly say-so after consulting the Met Office secret statistics, sit oddly beside other current events? For example, on the day Mr Major was making his little concession, it emerged that the deposed chairman of Guinness was to retain his salary of £375,000 a year, even though his colleagues had apparently decided he was unfit to continue in his job.

This is mystifying enough as a fact on its own. When set beside the pittance of a heating subsidy with which ministers have a good chance of stilling public outrage, does it not suggest some dislocation of the ground-rules by which society is organized?

Similarly with homelessness, also brought to life by the

46

shared experience of this brief ice age. In 1985, 93,980 households were accepted as homeless within the meaning of the Act. The figure is now running at over 100,000. And it takes no account of single people, childless couples and others outside the meaning of the Act.

The number without even a bed-and-breakfast roof over their heads is not known, but in London alone amounts to many thousands. What has Government to offer them? While defending her generosity on heating, Mrs Thatcher washed her hands of the homeless, saying they were a problem for the local authorities.

This was administratively correct, no doubt. And designed to place the blame on Labour as much as anyone. But when the snow and ice oblige you to contemplate the cardboard boxes that pass for home underneath the arches, it becomes a horrific confession, not of the limits, but of the abdication of government.

These are sour thoughts from a comfortable life. I fear I shall forget them in the spring.

15 January, 1987

Hugo Young

In the steps of Comrade Penis

I do not mind being called Banks-Smith. Admittedly Ernie Wise said it reminded him of someone falling off a horse at Badminton but people get used to falling off horses at Badminton. I rarely feel that shooting Mrs Thatcher would solve matters except, of course, that I could then marry Mr Thatcher.

'What is your name?' Lady Penelope Fitzwarren, a clerk in a DHSS office, asked a particularly dilapidated claimant, who sat dripping before her in *Keeping Score* (Channel 4). The extent life had it in for the lad can be gauged from the fact that, of all that down-trodden throng, the rain seemed to have rained on him alone. And with some vim at that.

He said, damply, that his name was Banks Smith. Pressed

47

(at which more rain ran out of him), he admitted his full name was Banks Chalmers Cheeseborough Norman McLintock King Appleton Riley Walsh McIlmoyle Keyworth Smith, the Leicester City side in the 1961 Cup Final. The losing side, of course, which you could have deduced from looking at him. Lady Penelope showed the incredulous delight of a woman who had been called after the Tottenham Hotspur team. The winning side, as you could have guessed from looking at her.

There had been, as P. G. Wodehouse put it, raw work at the font. He himself had been called Pelham Greville, a fact, you notice which he did not publicize. No doubt he comforted himself with the thought that his brother was called Armine. There is always, thank God, someone worse off than yourself.

Personally I think Banks Smith could count himself fortunate he was not called Nancy. Look how violently John Wayne reacted against being christened Marion and Big Daddy against Shirley.

There is absolutely no limit to the labels parents slap on innocent children. Consider Tarquin Olivier, so called because his father thought it would look nice over a theatre. Absolutely nothing further was heard of Tarquin, who retired violently into healing obscurity. Or Fifi Trixibelle Geldof who, one prays, will look like her mother.

I commend to you in your prayers Ub Iwerks (an animator of Popeye), A. Toxen Worm (a critic), Le Bum Suk (who was assassinated and probably found it a relief), Loxton Juliant (a dairy cow who once wrote to the *Daily Telegraph*), Hans Utterfucker (who was rejected by Coward for *Bitter Sweet* and couldn't think why), Comrade Penis (whom Fenner Brockway met in Poland; Brockway sent him a postcard hoping he was still strong and erect), Bent Olsen (who produced Liberace), and Pasta (a prima donna).

Banks Smith and Lady Penelope proceed to get even by playing a series of rather tedious practical jokes on authority. The first – setting a policeman he disliked to arrest a nun she disliked – resulted in a headline: 'Halo, Halo, Halo.' The newspaper *Today* is currently running a poster with the face of James Anderton and this very same phrase, which only goes to show what a hard time the comic writer has trying to improve on life, itself a farceur of a high order.

There are not many laughs in black comedy – the very word often seems an offence against the Trade Descriptions Act – but those who stuck it out to the end were rewarded with a dazzling impression of Mrs Thatcher by Gaye Brown.

The producer was, surprisingly enough, William G. Stewart, who produces *The Price is Right*, a show to rot your socks. One wonders in passing what that G stands for.

5 March, 1987

Nancy Banks-Smith

A piece of America

A new American doll, described by its owners as a piece of art, is skirting the boundaries of bad taste even by the quick buck standards of many entrepreneurs. 'It is utterly offensive and bizarre,' the National Coalition for the Homeless charged yesterday.

The object of scorn is the 'bag lady' doll, which made its debut in a Boston department store and is now going on sale across the country for between $49 and $500 a time. The doll is a replica of that adorable American character, the starving street person, depicted by its designers as a cabbage-patch-like figure adorned with trinkets, mismatched socks and the rag-tag clothes of a street person. All that is missing is the supermarket trolley in which street people traditionally carry around their worldly goods.

The bag lady made her first appearance in the window of a department store in Boston's elegant Copley Place Mall, home to Tiffany's and not the sort of place which normally welcomes any of the country's swelling ranks of homeless, which had reached an estimated 3 million at the last count.

Despite some intense picketing by the city's homeless, the doll's manufacturer, Mr Donald Gourley of California, has decided to press ahead with national distribution through 2,500 shops.

49

In the face of the protests, Mr Gourley remains unrepentant. 'We're sensitive to the fact that these people are sincere, but the artist has a right,' he argued. 'When we developed the bag lady there was no intention of it being a homeless person. Bag ladies are part of America. We make joggers, ballerinas, baseball players, golfers. It's a piece of America,' he said. The doll was designed by Mr Gourley's son Ryan, who says he created the original after he met a street lady some three years ago.

Even though the bag lady has generated some unexpected publicity for the homeless cause, the doll is being loudly condemned by the National Coalition for the Homeless. Its Washington director, Mrs Maria Foscarinis, said yesterday that sale of the doll, at prices which only the richest could afford, was an appalling contradiction. 'It is puzzling that the public is paying more attention to a homeless doll than the homeless themselves.'

Over the last seven years, broadly covering the period since President Reagan took the oath of office, the number of homeless people in the United States has soared. 'This is largely due to a lack of affordable housing,' Mrs Foscarinis said. She noted that the problem had become so acute that Congress, despite current budget constraints, has just passed a bill which would provide up to $400–500m of emergency aid to the homeless. The measure is soon to go to President Reagan for signature.

The bag lady doll comes in several sizes. The smaller 20-inch model sells for $49, while a larger 3ft version sells for $110. The most luxurious in the series sells for $500. 'The doll is clean, the doll is cute,' say the marketing team at Mr Gourley's company, Sher-Stuff.

It was noted that under the most efficient conditions it is now possible to feed and house a homeless person for $15 a night. Thus the price of one bag lady doll would give a homeless American at least three nights of comfort away from the ravages of life on the streets, where whole families now have to survive.

17 April, 1987

Alex Brummer

It's a Fax

Proof, at last, that yuffies (young, upwardly-mobile filo-folk) take their personal organizers to bed. Hang about. I mean, they tuck up with their little ring-binder pocket filing systems. A new version, called Safe-Fax, is now on sale. The distinctive thing about it is that it's fitted out with four condoms.

13 May, 1987

Andrew Moncur

Some people: 1

Millionaire Robert Maxwell has been economizing on his Christmas presents. Three thousand of his employees have again been given copies of a book which was produced by one of his companies, Pergamon Press, but is still lying around in large numbers. Last year it was the history of Maxwell's team, Oxford United, and this year it is a volume which commemorates both the royal wedding and the Commonwealth Games. On the packaging it is firmly declared that you will find inside a medal showing the heads of Andrew and Fergie and a £2 coin as a games souvenir. Imagine the feelings of the employees on opening their gift and finding the £2 coin is simply not there – only a piece of card with a tape hanging off it. Some were speculating yesterday that the cash has gone to help with the debts incurred by the games, which the big man saved from financial disaster. 'Mr Maxwell never ceases to amaze us,' said one publishing worker.

When Sir Frederick Lawton retired as a Lord Justice of Appeal at the weekend, the most fulsome tribute came from Lord Lane, the Lord Chief Justice. 'If Fred has ever made a mistake,' he declared, 'I have yet to come across it.' Well, there was just a tweeny-weeny lapse back in 1936, when the same Frederick Lawton was selected as parliamentary candidate for Hammersmith North by Sir Oswald Mosley's British Union of Fascists. *Action*, the BUF newspaper, welcomed the young lawyer as 'a fine fighting Fascist candidate'. Sir Frederick told *Tribune* newspaper not long ago that he withdrew as candidate very quickly, and left the party not long afterwards. He later joined the Conservatives.

23 December, 1986

Stephen Cook

Spectre in the palace

There was speculation in Vienna yesterday that Dr Kurt Waldheim, who has been transformed from triumphant Cheshire cat into a pale, spectral figure, would be psychologically incapable of carrying on for more than a few months. Sources in the conservative People's Party, his campaign backers, describe the Austrian president as a broken man.

As he broods amid Hapsburg treasures in the presidential palace – 'a living corpse in a mausoleum' by some accounts – America's rebuff will seem the cruellest he has suffered since his election. While the snubs multiplied from Japan, Ireland, Belgium and the Israeli ambassador, he resisted pleas by the People's Party that he resign on health grounds. But America is different.

Waldheim was fond of popping over to the United States, where as UN Secretary-General he kept a Manhattan house adorned with works of art. A small consolation is that no one has yet suggested stopping his imports of American toilet paper (ordinary mortals in Austria silently endure particularly tough varieties).

Nor has there yet been any serious concern over his habit of carrying a gun. This was confirmed during the election campaign by his son Gerhardt, who said: 'When I asked about the pistol he told me it was from Greece. He said: "My God, those were the days," but he would never expand on it.'

In an attempt to brush up his image abroad Waldheim appointed a special adviser for 'international questions' who has been conspicuously silent. This is not surprising, since he is none other than the Austrian ambassador to Japan, who prematurely cabled that Waldheim would be welcome in Japan, only to have the invitation repudiated.

Waldheim has been sustained by his wife, a dynamic Lady Macbeth figure who was briefly a member of the Nazi Party and who reportedly would never countenance his resignation. But as he goes about his ceremonial duties of opening fêtes, factories and nurseries he seems visibly shaken. 'He resembles one of those Thunderbirds puppets, with a bizarre habit of extending his arms like a wraith,' reports an observer.

A theory now gaining currency is that, while Waldheim has consistently lied, he suffers not so much from Reagamnesia as from an advanced form of Austrian syndrome which genuinely scrambles unpalatable wartime memories.

No one can write him off: he has a remarkable capacity for absorbing traumas. As the writer William Safire recalled: 'It was impossible to talk to him before his impending Nobel Peace Prize, and equally impossible to talk to him after, when he found he hadn't got it.'

29 April, 1987

Stuart Wavell

How war saved the British Right

Writing here the other day, Hugo Young drew attention to our current Leader's breath-taking arrogance in contending for exclusive rights to patriotism, and for the general desirability of wiping the Labour Party 'off the board as a foreign excrescence'. Now, such contentions are nothing new from Tory squires, members of MI5 and 6 transferred to Tory benches, and variously interested scribes. But they are something new from a Prime Minister whose office has traditionally supposed a care for the whole body politic.

Whether or not this prime ministerial ploy will be payable politics has yet to be seen. Everything is possible, even if the electors may have learned a thing or two since the 'Zinoviev Letter'. But Hugo Young's central point provokes thought in another way. Nowhere else in Europe, he reminds us, is a challenge made 'to the very right of a "socialist" party to exist. Nowhere else are questions asked about its patriotic reliability.' Why this strange uniqueness?

Other right-wing parties in Europe would no doubt like to join Mrs Thatcher in portraying their opponents as actual or prospective traitors to the national cause. They do not do it because, without dragging the rug from under their own feet, they cannot do it. The reason lies in the history which still shapes our ends; the history of the 1930s and the Second World War.

The historic fact, as solid as that the Normans came in 1066, is that the British Right were unique in all of Europe in having escaped total discredit from the Nazi–fascist triumphs of the 1930s and the early war years. Throughout continental Europe, with rare personal exceptions, the Right welcomed the rise of fascism and its partner in Germany, refused all serious challenge to either, and duly paid the price.

Worse, the European Right held to the same attitudes, after Nazi–fascist conquest, with responses ranging from anxious quiescence to eager collaboration. All patriotic resistance, save in some individual cases, was the work of the people of the Left and Centre, but above all of the Left. By the end of the war, accordingly, the continental Right were in traitors' jails, in flight across the Atlantic, or silent and incapable of entering the smallest patriotic claim.

Something drastic had to be done about that, and something was. Brutally assisted by Stalin, Churchill and Truman launched the Cold War. With the Truman Doctrine of early 1947, and the subsequent destruction of Left–Centre coalition governments in France and Italy, the continental Right could

54

at last look forward to times less bleak and profitless. I happened then to be the Paris correspondent of what has since become Mr Murdoch's principal paper, and recall interviewing a French tycoon who was waiting to recover his fortunes. 'Ah, my boy,' he confided with the large grin of a crocodile in sight of prey, 'at last it's done. The mortgage imposed by the Resistance is off our backs.' The rise of the Right had become possible again; and this is just what came about.

All this makes a complex story, involving the political suicide of the French communists in their obedience to Moscow, the wriggling of French socialists with some shame of their own to leave behind, and the ambition of new-cooked Christian Democrats for whom the star of Washington now shone more brightly even than the planet in Rome. But essentially the story is simple. Only with the Cold War and its consequences could the years of appeasement and collaboration be thrust aside.

But not therefore forgotten. Even today the communists of Italy may still be banned from government by Washington's decree, but no sober Italian democrat is going to raise the spectre of the past by accusing them of betrayal of the national cause. Who fought through the years of enemy occupation, and who died?

As similarly major parties, the socialists of France and West Germany may hold to their beliefs, but nobody there will think it payable politics to call them candidates for betrayal. The skeletons would tumble out in landslides if they did.

The record in Britain is the same but also different. Our 'Men of Munich' sailed in the same sinking boat as their colleagues on the continent, and shared the same guilt for shipwreck. But in their case the war gave them the chance to reach dry land, and go to fight against Hitler and Mussolini with the rest of us. And when the war in alliance with Russia duly arrived, instead of the war against Russia they had happily expected, well, they again went along with that as if it were, for them, the most natural thing in the world.

The ironies are tremendous, however lost on Mrs T. If any man saved the British Right from paying for its political betrayals, it was the Churchill whom they had abominated all through the 1930s, just as it was the same Churchill, victorious in 1945, who lent all his oratory to reversing the tide of the Left which came out of the victory.

It was again the war that saved Churchill's own credit. He might be warning of the Nazi danger late in the 1930s, but in 1935 he could still describe Mussolini as 'a really great man', and refer to Hitler, in another article in 1935, as someone who might possibly become, no matter through what horrors, one of the 'great figures whose lives have enriched the story of mankind'. Some enrichment.

As it was, the Tory Party were glad to be able to entitle their 1945 manifesto as no more than 'Mr Churchill's Declaration to the Electors'. And the electors proceeded to confirm that a lot of time was going to be required before traditional Tory arrogance could again become an asset.

Churchill did in fact present Labour as a balefully intended tyranny, even suggesting that Labour in power would bring in some kind of Gestapo (now, presumably, it would be some kind of KGB?). Beaverbrook's *Evening Standard* thought it useful to print photos of Labour's NEC with a caption warning that 'These People Want To Be Dictators'. But it didn't pay: the Tories were soundly beaten, and history tells that people danced in the streets.

Time has duly passed. The British Right are now heard to speak as though their 1930s record was reliably forgotten. Still, one senses an inner faltering. If Labour is to be boxed into the political traitors' corner, some solid alibi against past attitudes which sent Tory enthusiasts scurrying to Berlin and Rome may still be advisable.

I suppose this need to transfer guilt is what lurks behind our current spy extravaganzas, lately playing to packed audiences not supposed to overhear. That senior MI5 operatives could be loony enough to embark on lies and slander, so as to depict Labour as the true home of traitors, and do it off their own bat, is of course conceivable. But that the thing should not have become known in Tory high places, then or later, is something else, and very hard to believe. And if it did become so known, and has received no public censure since 1979, what conclusions follow?

There is another sombre echo. Nothing reminds one of

Neville Chamberlain's bland self-congratulation, when giving Hitler the green light at Munich, as much as Margaret Thatcher's when relying on Reagan for salvation. The cases are hugely different, but the resultant Tory attitudes are not. For Mrs Thatcher now, as for Chamberlain then, British patriotism must be the servant of a blindly unabashed Right. It is indeed a strange provincialism.

12 January, 1987

Basil Davidson

How the King met his deadline

The final hours of the life of King George V, always associated with the rival versions of his last words (official: 'How stands the Empire?'; unofficial: 'Bugger Bognor'), has provided fuel for another controversy. Previously unpublished evidence has revealed that the celebrated medical bulletin, 'The King's life is moving peacefully towards its close', was the prelude to death by euthanasia – with the timing arranged in part to catch the morning newspapers.

The details are recorded in a private notebook kept by Lord Dawson of Penn, the royal doctor, who is alleged to have prompted the unofficial last words by telling the King that he would soon be convalescing at Bognor Regis. His entry for 20 January 1936 describes how the King was given a lethal combination of morphia and cocaine at Sandringham as he lay in a coma, terminally ill with bronchial and cardiac disease.

The decision was not made to relieve pain, which the British Medical Association today considers the only ethical grounds for intervention which may also hasten death in the terminally ill. Lord Dawson, whose notes are quoted for the first time in the December issue of *History Today*, wrote candidly that he had other motives.

'At about 11 o'clock it was evident that the last stage might

57

endure for many hours, unknown to the Patient but little comporting with that dignity and serenity which he so richly merited and which demanded a brief final scene,' he recorded. 'Hours of waiting just for the mechanical end when all that is really life has departed only exhausts the onlookers and keeps them so strained that they cannot avail themselves of the solace of thought, communion or prayer.'

The notebook, which is quoted by Lord Dawson's biographer Mr Francis Watson in an article on the death of the King, goes on to the third reason – 'the importance of the death receiving its first announcement in the morning papers rather than the less appropriate evening journals'.

The royal doctor phoned his wife in London to tip off *The Times* – whose editor, Geoffrey Dawson, was no relation – to delay publication because the death of the 70-year-old monarch was about to be announced.

Lord Dawson, who had saved the King's life eight years earlier when an abscess complicated an attack of pleurisy, continued: 'I therefore decided to determine the end and injected (myself) morphia gr.3/4 and shortly afterwards cocaine gr.1 into the distended jugular vein.'

Mr Watson said yesterday that he had not included the details in his biography of Lord Dawson, first published in 1950, because Lady Dawson had thought that they might be too controversial at that time. The notebook was among Lord Dawson's papers which were later given to the royal archive at Windsor by the doctor's son-in-law, Lord Eccles.

The BMA said that Lord Dawson's actions, if repeated today, would be ethically and legally wrong, but in the 1930s the public attitude had been more one of 'leave it to the doctor'.

Lord Dawson put the same argument in helping to defeat a voluntary euthanasia bill in the House of Lords in December, 1936. 'This is something which belongs to the wisdom and conscience of the medical profession,' he said, adding that any law might 'deter those who are, as I think, carrying out their mission of mercy'.

27 November, 1986

Martin Wainwright

The monarch of masochism

On 2 May the QE2 was sailing towards New York barnacled
with complaints about juddering turbines, unfinished interiors,
empty swimming pools and vibrating rooms. The British
nation, enjoying one of its regular bouts of self-denigration,
wondered why the country which had invented the steam
turbine and once commanded the lion's share of all shipbuilding
orders couldn't even get the turbines on a luxury liner ready
in time for the agreed delivery date. All that, of course, happened in May, 1969, when the QE2 finally embarked on her
maiden transatlantic voyage, delayed for months by faulty
turbines and half-finished interiors. Cunard's public relations
were not helped by the fact that the operations director was
called Cocup.

Since then the QE2 has rarely failed to stir up the industrial
hypochondria which we love so much to wallow in. There was
political controversy in 1983 when a £2.5 million contract for
refitting went to Germany. It was described by a Labour
spokesman as 'an insult to British yards'. But this was nothing
to the insult when Cunard announced at the end of 1985 that
the £100 million reconstruction of the liner was also to be
undertaken in Germany. Not a single yard in the country that
once ruled the waves had felt able even to tender for it with
any confidence of delivering on the required date.

What is, perhaps, surprising is that even when a German
yard does the rebuilding and things go wrong, we still grasp
the opportunity for yet more maritime masochism. Whether
this is really justified or not hangs on whether the current
problems (water leaks, overheating, empty pools and a 15
degree list) were down to the builders in Bremerhaven or – as
they claim – Cunard's plumbers.

But that's not the point, because we would surely have found
something else to grumble about. Think of the national disgrace
if the German yard had rebuilt the QE2 faultlessly . . . and on
time. Just why the QE2 emerges so regularly as a barometer of

the popular conception of national decline is more difficult to fathom. After all, there are plenty of industries which have declined almost as fast as shipbuilding. Some have disappeared altogether. Others have never got off the ground. The avalanche of imported cars and Japanese consumer electronics which has hit this country never seems to qualify for national self-flagellation in the same way that a £2.5 million refit for an ageing liner in a foreign yard does. It is all the more baffling because – unlike imported cars – the QE2 is earning foreign exchange for Britain by plying her lucrative trade around the world. Ensuring that the refit is done more or less on schedule, albeit in an overseas yard, means the ship is ready to resume her duties earlier than otherwise, thereby earning more profits and providing more employment.

Maybe the symbolic importance of the QE2 lies somewhere there. Born of Britain's declining manufacturing base, she is now part of the 'leisure industry', a floating signpost of the way (if Mr Lawson is right) manufacturing is yielding to the service industries in economic importance. Cunard gave the passengers a 40 per cent refund, which seemed to satisfy most of them. The company could have done without the publicity. But whether the rest of Britain could is a moot point. Suppose, horror of horrors, that the QE2, complete with nine new German diesel engines, sails into a new era of reliability and, in terms of bad news, oblivion? Goodness knows what we will find to complain about instead. We can't rely on the weather all the time.

21 May, 1987   **Leader**

Getting used to violent change

Some things never change. 'Is it not a disgrace . . .' Martin Flannery (Lab, Hillsborough) prefaced his first question of the new Parliament yesterday, just as he always seemed to do in the old one. 'No, it's not,' the Tories roared, not even waiting to hear what had upset him this time.

'Is it not a shameful indictment of this Government . . . ?' Michael Meacher complained in another time-honoured formula. It usually is, with Michael.

But elsewhere there are new dispositions, violent changes in fortune, which will take some getting used to. Norman Tebbit, assured a few weeks ago of a seat at Mrs Thatcher's right hand, stood wistfully at the bar throughout Prime Minister's questions yesterday: the front bench below the gangway, his usual perch since he left the Cabinet, was too crammed with knights of the shires and other distinguished duffers to spare him even an inch.

With the PM absent in Brussels, there appeared instead John Wakeham, famed in his years as Chief Whip for authoritative silence, now reduced to halting evasions, answering even the friendly questions by reading from his brief.

As for John Biffen, Mrs Thatcher's regular stand-in last session, he lay slumped in an anonymous spot three rows back below the gangway, where a neighbouring MP thoughtfully fanned them both with his order paper.

The Home Secretary, Douglas Hurd, who opened for the Government in yesterday's Queen's Speech debate, exudes a reassuring air of continuity in these times of dizzying change. Running his hands caressingly up and down the Despatch Box (no doubt some Home Office psychologist is preparing a monograph), he soothed and smoothed his way through his Home Office text as if it were *A Book at Bedtime* and his mission in life was to put the whole nation to sleep.

Little conclaves formed, whiling away the time as Douglas chuntered along. John Biffen and Julian Critchley met no doubt to deplore, as stylists, the Home Secretary's abject resort to terms like 'civilianization'. More interestingly still, David Owen and the veteran Tory backbencher Julian Amery – the author, one recalled, of a life of Joseph Chamberlain, a man who broke with two political parties and left them bleeding.

Gerald Kaufman, for Labour, reminded the House that recently Mr Hurd had been trying to lure Doctor Owen and friends into the Tory fold. It was significant, he suggested, that

61

the offer had not been repeated today. Douglas had no doubt realized that the doctor's arrival would threaten his chance of the leadership: he would be outflanked from the right.

But mostly his speech was serious and solid, with the added merit, which Mr Hurd's conspicuously lacked, of addressing the meat of the matter: the inequality and deprivation which, according to the order paper, were the subject of this debate.

His comprehensive indictment stretched from perinatal mortality to the riots in Chapeltown, Leeds, where Gerald lived in his youth.

John Biffen, who followed, was greeted with cheers, the loudest coming from Labour. He started with Scotland. Left with just ten of that nation's 72 parliamentary seats, the Government could not simply try to sail on with the slogan 'Business As Usual'.

Then the Baker reforms: authentic Tory thinking in the Butler and Balfour tradition – but only if firmly set in the context of collective educational provision, and not designed to achieve some form of oblique privatization.

And they certainly would not work if the Government grudged the resources to support them. The weekend speech by the new Chief Secretary to the Treasury, John Major, trailing an era of unparalleled public spending rigour, seemed to him very unwise. The economic strategy, which he gladly saluted, would need to be balanced by an equal commitment to a positive social policy.

The Queen's Speech, he declared in conclusion, was a magnificent radical document which he was happy to support. The Opposition benches rocked with mirth. Ministers present looked decidedly thoughtful.

1 July, 1987   **David McKie**

How the Tories rule the roost

The Conservative strategy for the inner city can be seen most clearly at the back entrance of Clapham Junction station in south London. There, straight ahead of you, is The Falcons, a luxury housing development with a swimming pool, sauna and jacuzzi, a security fence around the estate and a video entry screen in every flat – a perfect pied-à-terre for the City gent.

Only four years ago this was a hard-to-let, down-at-heel council estate. The tenants were moved out when asbestos was found, but they were never moved back. Instead the Conservative-controlled Wandsworth Council sold the entire estate to a property company which rehabilitated and renamed it. Two-bedroom flats on the eighteenth floor of Osprey Heights, one of the buildings, are now on the market for £106,250.

The same has hapened to other council estates in the area. Archer House, named after a black mayor of Battersea in the Twenties, was decanted for a council modernization programme, but the tenants never moved back. It was sold to a property company who put geraniums on the window-sills, parasols in the courtyard and renamed it Battersea Village. Jay Court, named after Douglas Jay, Battersea's Labour MP for 37 years, was emptied because of asbestos and then sold to a private developer and renamed. The flats sell for up to £120,000.

This does more than anything else to explain why the Conservatives won Battersea in the election last week. Sales of council blocks and council estates have removed more than two thousand tenants from the electoral register and replaced them with very high earners. The Labour Party regards it as a deliberate attempt to use housing policy for political ends, a kind of demographic gerrymandering, and Conservative councillors make little attempt to deny the charge.

'I don't think any of us has ever tried to hide the fact', says Peter Bingle, chairman of the property sales committee, 'that we have sought not just to run Wandsworth more efficiently but to change Wandsworth into a Conservative borough . . .

a borough that will stay Conservative regardless of national swings.'

Some of his party colleagues might regard his remarks as a little too extreme, or at least too explicit, but Councillor Bingle has no time for such faint-hearts. 'There have been too many Tory councils just trying to "manage the service". We have done that, but we have always remembered that we are primarily Conservative politicians and that the aim has been to make Wandsworth a Conservative borough. We are one of the few Tory councils that has actually realized the political potential of running a town hall.'

No one can deny the rapid progress the Conservatives have made towards their aim. In the Seventies, Wandsworth had a Labour council and three Labour MPs. In 1978 the Conservatives won control of Wandsworth Council and laid the foundations for their subsequent victories. In 1979 they took Putney from Labour and have increased their majority in 1983 and 1987. In this election they took Battersea, one of the earliest socialist strongholds in London, which has had at least one Labour MP almost continuously since 1892. In the next election they hope to take Tooting (where the Labour majority is now down to 1414) and to realize their ambition of a Tory council and three Tory MPs.

Bingle believes that their success is due not so much to the Yuppie invasion, which has been overplayed as a factor in Battersea, as to the council's housing policies. Alf Dubs, the defeated Labour MP, agrees with him at least on this. 'Councillor Bingle said his aim was to use his housing policies to convert Battersea into a Tory seat and he succeeded,' he says drily.

But Bingle ascribes only half the change to the sale of council estates or council houses on the open market. The other 50 per cent he puts down to the sale of council homes to existing council tenants or their families. This has been pushed very hard in Wandsworth by a high-pressure housing sales team and by huge discounts on houses that can be sold again in three years.

The first policy results in a change in population from council tenants, who are perhaps 75 per cent Labour, to high earners, who may be up to 90 per cent Tory. The second policy can

64

result in a change in attitudes. Bingle claims that many staunch Labour voters have become staunch Conservatives after buying their houses. 'Particularly in Battersea, where socialism has been part of the culture, when they do make the break they adopt their new political allegiance with the same fervour as somebody who changes religion,' he says.

There is little evidence that house purchase has been a decisive factor in changing people's views, but equally there is no doubt that there has been a rise in the working-class Tory vote in Battersea and Putney. There are still huge council estates in both seats (39 per cent in Battersea, 44 per cent in Putney) and Bingle accepts that 'in social terms it should still really be a Labour borough'. But he believes that Wandsworth's unique brand of 'Thatcher populism' has been able to 'break through the class divide and establish a Conservative stronghold in previously strong Labour areas'.

Conservative Central Office has been paying close attention to what is happening in Wandsworth. After all, if the Tories can win a seat like Battersea they can win many others like it. And if they can break down Labour's power base on the council estates, they can equally break Labour's power base in the inner cities.

If Wandsworth is a jump ahead of national politics, it would not for be the first time. In May 1979 it elected a Conservative council that earned a reputation for being 'Thatcherite before Thatcher'. In June 1979 the country followed suit.

By May 1982 the council had stirred up so much bitter opposition to its cuts that it seemed to be heading for defeat, but in a Falklands-dominated election it survived by 33 seats to 27. In June 1983 Mrs Thatcher did the same, but by a larger margin. By May 1986 it again seemed to be doomed to defeat. But in the last days of the campaign it used a Labour rates scare to squeeze votes from the Alliance, and survived by 31 seats to 30. In June 1987 Mrs Thatcher did the same, but by a larger margin.

This makes Wandsworth the ideal testing-ground for the next stage in the Thatcherite project, which is likely to involve the two key policy areas in the inner city: housing and education. Wandsworth has already volunteered to be the first borough to opt out of the Inner London Education Authority and apply its ruthless brand of Thatcherism to schools.

At the same time Peter Bingle has not been shy in putting forward his own ideas for the next stage in housing. After breaking up Labour's electoral base on the council estates, his new challenge is to break up local authority housing departments and ideally to remove council housing from housing departments entirely.

If local authorities won't play ball, he believes the Government should take housing away from local authorities and give it to urban development corporations, 'impose the Wandsworth factor', and sell it off block by block.

Bingle argues that the only way to finance the repairs needed in older council housing is from receipts from council house sales. Wandsworth can boast a fairly high level of capital spending on housing – £800 per dwelling – and that feeds off a high level of sales. Labour councils, less keen to sell, are short of capital and end up defending their own bureaucracies against angry tenants.

The lessons of Wandsworth are not lost on Peter Hain, the defeated Labour candidate in Putney, who analyses Labour's failure in much the same way that Bingle analyses Conservative success. 'The Yuppies are a delusion,' he says. 'It's an attack on Labour's electoral base on the council estates and we need to warn the Labour Party in the north and in Scotland of what has happened in London because Wandsworth is a forerunner of what will happen up there. It's a dress rehearsal.

'The Tories are about wiping us out in the inner cities. They're trying to do a Putney and Battersea on the rest of Britain.'

19 June, 1987   **Martin Linton**

Going West

Every Tuesday morning, the real-estate brokers of Beverly Hills set off in a procession of Mercedes to inspect the goods.

It is called 'the caravan'. All the newly listed houses are thrown open to be swarmed over and assessed. It is a beady and narrow-eyed moment and the air is filled with the sound of orange and dandelion-yellow hair breaking in the urgency to get there first. A thousand painted casting directors in pursuit of younger, fresher talent.

The houses themselves, for the most part, are just so much raw material. The odd Basque farmhouse has been over-restored already by an award-winning (1958) television producer with its living-room stained-glass window hand-crafted in Santa Fe *après* the transept at Chartres. But delicate pink half-million-dollar cottages with wisteria growing beneath the shade of Wilshire Boulevard are sold only to be bulldozed. They call them 'tear downs'.

Sallow-faced owners, waiting to move to adult retirement colonies in Arizona, sit in authentic Spanish-styled (i.e. part Moorish, part Hendon Central) living rooms beneath 16-foot cornices, grimly outstaring those who come in search of glamour. An inappropriate owner on the premises reduces the cost, it is said, by $100,000. At least.

Pity poor David Puttnam, that Isaiah Berlin of the film industry (no, Solly, not Irving). He laments in the press that he simply could not find a house without a pool. His search is usually introduced by the writer in order to illustrate (a) how thoughtful and serious and (b) how free-thinking is Mr Puttnam. Never mind that the hills of Los Angeles are full of houses without pools, spas, jacuzzis, 5½ baths or neo-Italiante fountains after Bernini. It is the tyranny of The Concept.

The Concept is what rules the movie business – and therefore the earth – in place of natural laws. The Los Angeles Concept goes this way: there are only houses with pools by which everyone is either writing or wishing he was writing the big one: the soon-to-be-optioned major mini-series.

Few people here work in the movie business. Fewer still earn any kind of living from it. The place is full of perfectly nice history professors, teeth bonders and holistic allergists. It is also full of homes being put up for sale by banks after repossession. Divorce fights, bankruptcies, spending binges: just the stuff of life. Since the ideal is that of the set design, all is but a painted flat to be shoulder-tossed lightly and moved on.

The world is calm, full of oil (California uses 3 per cent of the world's annual consumption) and there are no such things as earthquakes, floods, fires or other disasters, which may explain why, on the day a mortgage closes, earthquake, flood and fire insurance must be immediately and expensively put in place.

The make-believe was almost punctured by the new law that holds estate agents responsible for Whatever Happens if they have failed to make full disclosure. The gushing, pushy, rapturous prose of the sales agent in full flight now has to encompass such tit-bits as the news that the place is falling down ('Where can it fall, let's face it?'). Then there is geological disaster to communicate: that the whole hill is falling down. ('It's been here so long, where's it going to go?'). Or just that it's in the dangerous brush area and might burn down ('. . . all you need is to paint the number on your roof so the helicopter can find you').

Property divisions are strangely fuzzy; few buyers have their new homes surveyed. Full disclosure means passing lightly over the news that your neighbour's pool is in your garden or simply that your garage and kitchen are standing in his. The picturesque underground spring running past the gate may cause a mud slide; the pretty river outside the living-room window is a flood control channel; the crack in the dining-room floor was the 1971 earthquake; the gorgeous view over the canyon was achieved without the help of a building permit and the whole upstairs is illegal. None of which stopped us buying the house into which we are shortly moving. Going West is to embrace adventure.

Our house is, or rather was, what is usually described as 'a rustic redwood sleeper', i.e. an extremely ugly wooden shack that no one wanted to buy. Dark outside, dark inside, but huge and warm. 'I can see it now,' exclaimed the first architect. 'All white. A French provincial chateau. No, a *petit* chateau. I've got it: a *chateaulet*.' The second architect said glumly: 'I'd worry about the roof if I were you. It leaks.' 'What a find,' said our friends. 'What integrity.' 'You can't afford him,' said our cream-soft, moisture-replenished lawyer. 'He's too cheap.'

Just a coat of paint, we said, and new roof please. Walls came down, floors came up, the flood channel was dredged, the windows went, the back door became the front door, the pool was dug. Last week, the insurance company's inaptly named 'silent alarm system' was installed. It goes off at the sight of a dancing moonbeam whereupon Westec Armed Response – men, guns, dogs, sirens – scream up the hill at our expense. Doubtless the fire helicopter will find us easily now that our address is written on the roof in day-glo.

Our tiny and gentle neighbour popped in last time we were there. 'When you get here, give me a call if anything goes bump,' she said sweetly. 'I'm an exorcist.'

16 June, 1987   **Linda Blandford**

Some liked it hot

IN MEMORIAM

Type is cast in alloy of lead, tin, and antimony by moulds or matrices. It is assembled in three ways:
Hand setting: characters for headlines are selected from a case or tray and set into a stick.
Automated setting letter by letter: Copy is typed on a Monotype keyboard which sets type from matrices, producing galleys of type.
Automated setting line by line: Matrices of letters are selected by keyboard strokes on a Linotype.
Pages are made up from galleys, sticks of type and picture blocks in a metal frame or chase resting on the bench or stone. When complete the frame is locked up and flattened with a mallet and leather-backed block of wood, a planer. It is now called a forme.

Last Wednesday's paper was the first edition of the *Guardian* to be printed without hot metal playing a part since the foundation year of 1821. Last Monday was the last use of type cast from molten metal on the paper. It was a glorious and rueful night, the momentous 'end of 400 years of history', as one printer said, thinking of Gutenberg and Caxton.

It was a night of wet-eyed sentiment as, after most of the *Guardian* had been computer- and photo-set and the pages pasted up by gum, scalpel and Sellotape, the front page was locked up in its forme, every line and rule and space hand-fitted and precise.

Conducted to the stereo by the compositor-pallbearers Peter Postance, Danny O'Shea, Terry Littlechild and Geoff Claydon, accompanied by Mike Thompson on the saxophone, it was banged-out by hundreds of printers, journalists, and their folk beating out the traditional music of retirement in the print – every piece of heavy metal that could be lifted rhythmically beaten against the metal benches known as the stone.

Thus hot metal had a decent burial, leaving behind a barrel of laughs about the frustrations of transforming the *Guardian*'s production from Manchester in 1821 to the direct input of computer technology and printing in the Isle of Dogs later this year.

Working on the stone with comps had its frustrations, too, but many mourn the passing of the Linotype machines, the smell of the casters, the sticks of type, the galleys of lead spacers, the mounted blocks, and the humour and skill of those who filled the chases with a myriad bits of metal.

Last Monday was the last chance to get ink literally on your fingers, and strong men declared they would never wash their hands again and admitted that they had never, ever laundered their aprons. For sub-editors who nightly read upside-down and back-to-front type and argued, joked, and sparred with these princes of craft, the passing is a mixed blessing, too. To experience a composing room at full stretch was a nightly miracle and wonder of skill. Speed and flexibility were of the essence.

In Farringdon Road the composing room became known as the engine room on good days or the underworld – or even the de-composing room – on bad. There was sometimes aggro between comps and subs, stemming partly from the jealously guarded craft divisions among print workers and partly from parallel chains of command.

Theirs is a symbiotic relationship in which the sub is answerable to editorial decisions, the comp to the printer, but both are responsible for the page. Thus both could call upon authority yet neither could necessarily command it.

Some journalists were fortunate to sub-edit in the *Guardian*'s old Cross Street office in Manchester. Unlike the converted Farringdon Road warehouse with carpet tiles which now houses it, this was a real block-floored, mahogany-lined newspaper building which smelt of ink and paper, each night running like a majestic liner leaving port, the lights twinkling in the canteen on the top floor, the whine of the basement presses starting up and tuning to a distant rumble, and the yellow vans flitting about the loading bays like tenders.

I once saw Ben Eastwood spring a page there five minutes before the first edition. Mr Eastwood was the imposing skipper of the composing room, every sinew of him a Master Printer. The trolley he was pushing caught its wheel on a wooden floorguard and the metal cascaded onto the floor.

He summoned Cliff Forth from Page 1 and they worked with the speed of light, one at each end of the chase with myself and a proof reader called Dodd (no relation) calling out the first words of lines from galley proofs. Cliff arranged stories along his arm and shuffled lines like cards. The page was complete again in five minutes and we found only three minor transpositions.

Second-in-command at that time was Ted Cooper, a little barrel of a man who spoke Lancashire Anglo-Saxon incessantly and incomprehensibly. He had an ear-to-ear smile which he only displayed after closing time; he wore bottle-glass specs and clumped about in army boots, frequently foot-butting Lino machines like the original bovver boy. But he also read the paper thoroughly from Cardus on cricket to Cardus on Mahler, and there was nothing he didn't know.

He was truly explosive. Ian Breach, a precise and neat-handed sub, once drew in a missing line on a page proof and asked Ted to put it in for the next edition. 'The blank's already blankly-well there,' said Ted, peering at it through his bottle-glasses, and after Breach explained that he was looking at a Biro mark, Ted went apoplectic. But he did it.

Cross Street's composing room was only quiet on nights when United were playing. This was partly because of the workload brought about by absenteeism and partly because every man had his ear tuned to the banned tranny under the stone describing another virtuoso Best performance.

Then there was Pegleg Lou, a Lino operator whose mischief was as long as the night. He would set corrections on lines which were wider than the standard column and try to persuade comps to fit them in by cutting column spacers, or subs to change the layout.

At the *Guardian*'s old London office in Gray's Inn Road, Mr Borrett was in charge when I got there. Don Borrett was every bit the Guv'nor, blustering and old-boying his way through the evening, and capitalizing on editorial mistakes by allowing five minutes flat to cut 45 inches of excess type from a features page. (Quite right too – Ed.)

When the editor sent him a clever-clever leading article to be set in Latin one evening Borrett appeared, waving it in a dither. 'I can't set this, Mr Hetherington,' he said. 'We haven't got the fount.'

Borrett prided himself in composing during the 'cut' when the rest were at supper. The trouble was that unlike all his craftsmen underlings he would start by inserting the column rules and run the metal in from the bottom of the page, which defied all the logic of newspaper writing and the flexibility of hot type. Often the comp would have to start again surreptitiously while the sub retired hurt to curse Caxton and all his works in the Blue Lion.

Composing rooms were a man's world, and the introduction of women sub-editors caused some discomfort. Like all newcomers their mettle was tested. In the heady sixties Carol Dix was the first to venture bra-less there, and she was presented with a handsome pair of cups when she left, in a strangely bashful ceremony.

One who didn't see the joke is now a nearly-famous thriller

writer whose handbag was filled with metal – which subs were not allowed to handle – so that she was nearly armless when she set off for a dignified exit. The culprit, Postance, will no doubt come to a sticky end in a whodunnit.

In the new world of small-screen and paste-up the terminology is still of Caxton, while the tools and the skills and the smells and the frustrations are different. I thought of Ted Cooper when I saw someone thump a computer the other day. I once came upon him hacking his boots at the legs of a Lino and asked him cheerily what was up. In broad Lancs he snapped, 'The phooking-phooker's phooking-phooked.' RIP hot metal.

18 May, 1987

Christopher Dodd

Fascinating Editorial Cuts of Our Time:

The Times *carried an important letter yesterday about 'frightening' levels of unemployment in Europe in general, and Britain in particular, signed by five internationally distinguished academics. But whatever happened to the original opening sentence of their missive? They had wanted to say: 'Hands Across Britain rightly dramatizes the need for policies against unemployment . . .'*

Professor Rudiger Dornsbusch, at the Massachusetts Institute of Technology, one of the signatories, received in a phone call from London the explanation that this would be cut 'for editorial reasons'. The unmentionable Hands Across Britain is expected to involve 350,000 people, in a long line from Liverpool to London, on Sunday coming. Don't tell a soul.

29 April, 1987

Andrew Moncur

Fleet Street pack and the KGB

It was hardly the most helpful media example to set before a Soviet press grappling with the limits and implications of their own forays into *glasnost*.

The Fleet Street pack can make strong men weep at the best of times. Unleashed upon a prime ministerial walkabout in the depths of the Soviet Union, they have shattered even the arrogant aplomb of the KGB.

The sight of a free press determined not to miss a single image of a publicity-conscious Prime Minister with elections on her mind must have made even the most reformist Russian ponder the wisdom of all this new talk of freedom. The Foreign Secretary, Sir Geoffrey Howe, was locked out of churches as the pack bayed in. Mr Bernard Ingham, Mrs Thatcher's spokesman, and his aides were locked out of a museum as the Soviet security men battled to regain control of what they had expected would be a stately and dignified progress by Mrs Thatcher.

Their collapsible step-ladders swinging like the fearsome weapons of medieval peasants, the TV and press cameramen sprinted around and ahead of Mrs Thatcher, outflanking and ambushing the bewildered KGB.

'Are they always like that?' asked the man from *Komsomolskaya Pravda* of a colleague who had once served in London. 'They can be worse,' came the reply. 'You should see the press cover the wife of their Prince Charles.'

Indeed, it got worse later. In the monastic precincts of Zagorsk, there was at least a touch of restraint. But when Mrs Thatcher went walkabout in the Moscow suburb of Krylatskoye, something went wrong in the programming. A cry went up from the press bus 'we're missing something', and Fleet Street's finest, accompanied by US and Japanese television crews, 500,000lb worth of video equipment on the hoof, stampeded after the story. The melting snows and unmade paths made it a kind of urban Passchendaele, and Russian grannies and children went sprawling as the herd thundered into the newly stocked supermarket and spruced-up sports centre.

The KGB had no idea how to handle this anarchic crowd with the licence that comes from decades of confidence in the rights of the press, and from the presence of a visiting Prime Minister whom the Kremlin does not want to see offended.

The Russians who crowded into the fringes of the media circus to stare at the Iron Lady had never seen anything like it. Russian television rarely mounts more than one camera crew at a time. Suddenly, there were lenses and boom microphones and miniature tape recorders coming at them from all sides. Over 100 British television and press journalists came out to swell the 15 permanently stationed here. But almost every foreign news organization based in London has taken advantage of the Thatcher trip to send in representatives to cover what one of them called 'the sexiest Soviet story since Chernobyl'. Another 100 of the foreign correspondents based in Moscow joined the throng. It was chaos at Zagorsk monastery as hacks missed the press buses, and the highly respectable vice-president of the Academy of Medical Sciences found his private car commandeered as the free world's eyes and ears tore back to watch Maggie look politely at the sad shelves of a Soviet supermarket.

By contrast, yesterday was a period of calm. Talks in the Kremlin, and the standard laying of the wreath at the Tomb of the Unknown Soldier, are familiar events that the Russians know how to handle.

31 March, 1987

Martin Walker

Another job for Sir Robert

The news from Whitehall is that Sir Robert Armstrong, the Cabinet Secretary, is trying to make his escape. Not many people know this. Even the Prime Minister may only have known after the event. But a few weeks ago, Sir Robert quietly put in for another job that would have taken him away from his post at the nerve-centre a year earlier than he is contracted to leave it.

Whether this should be ascribed to the 'Australia effect' – the unbearable afterglow of two weeks' public embarrassment in a Sydney courtroom – or merely to the belief that his special services will not, after all, be needed until September 1988, Armstrong's attempt to depart the scene has a number of sharp resonances with present discontents; especially as they relate to the matter which has made him famous – his connections with MI5.

The job Sir Robert applied for was President of Trinity College, Oxford. It is actually rather a pathetic story, which does not reflect well on the college. The job falls vacant in September, at the start of the academic year, and Armstrong was invited to put his name forward, which he duly did after what must have been long deliberation.

There were 13 candidates for the post, each of whom was asked to write down why he wanted it and what he would do if he got it. In the event, however, the most distinguished civil servant in the country, having been urged to apply, was then abruptly disinvited and did not make it to the final shortlist of six. This week it was announced that the new President would be Sir John Burgh, former civil servant and presently head of the British Council.

So Sir Robert may be imprisoned in Whitehall for the duration, after all. The other Oxford colleges likely to be available are rather less classy than Trinity. But before asking why he would really want to go, and more especially what he would leave behind if he did, one should recall why he is still there.

In normal circumstances Sir Robert, who is 60 in ten days' time, would now be about to leave Whitehall anyway. That is the statutory retirement age for civil servants. But some months ago it was announced that an exception would be made for him, and he would stay on for another 18 months. This was by mutual agreement between him and the Prime Minister, and was explained by the novel constitutional pronouncement that it would be desirable for the new Cabinet Secretary to be chosen by the new Prime Minister.

The old ideal that civil servants provided the continuity while governments came and went was, in other words, significantly mutilated. A Cabinet Secretary, we were now to understand, was henceforth to be regarded rather like a minister, or perhaps a prime ministerial press secretary: co-terminous with the government of one party, and held to be so committed to it that a successor government should have the right to pick a new one.

Additionally, and rather more respectably, it was thought that an old hand like Sir Robert would be better equipped than a new man to handle the transitional complexities thrown up by a hung parliament.

Armstrong's readiness to disturb this special arrangement, by getting out early, may simply reflect a new judgment about the outcome of the election. Perhaps we have here the loftiest evidence yet available that Whitehall is getting ready for an inevitable third term of Thatcher government, in which case Sir Robert's familiar ministrations would not be required; and that, after an early election or before a later one, Mrs Thatcher will be able to slide Sir Clive Whitmore, or another of her protégés, into the Armstrong chair.

His departure, however, would have left unfinished business of a more ominous kind. Just as his non-departure now threatens to engulf him in it. His absence might have been quite convenient for the Government, as things have turned out. His continued presence exposes them, and him, to further embarrassment that would be far better avoided. For Sir Robert, better than anyone else in Whitehall, knows where certain bodies are buried.

Pressure is now mounting to exhume these: pressure the Prime Minister is resisting but probably cannot go on resisting for ever. I refer to the most important substantive outgrowth of the Peter Wright trial in Australia: the contention Wright makes in his notorious unpublished book that he was involved with other MI5 officers in attempts to destabilize, by means of numerous dirty tricks, the Wilson Government of 1974.

These are serious allegations – confessions, more like – and they are being amplified by other dodgy figures from the nether world of security in North Ireland. They made a *prima facie*

2 February, 1987

case for believing that certain people in the lower reaches of MI5, in conformity with Muscovite conspiracy theories then raging in security circles and also, as I've reported here before, in senior Conservative circles, operated outside the control of their directors to undermine ministers to whom they were supposed to be responsible.

When these allegations were first made, by Harold Wilson himself in 1977, an internal inquiry was set up by the then Prime Minister, Jim Callaghan, and produced a report which was meant to assuage the more lurid fears. There was no evidence, apparently, that MI5 people had acted in any such way.

In rejecting a new inquiry now, as a result of Wright's and other evidence, Mrs Thatcher falls back repeatedly on a hallowed, but sometimes perversely unsatisfactory, doctrine. Because the 1977 inquiry was held under the previous Administration, she has not seen the relevant papers. Governments are never allowed to see the papers of their predecessors, and the civil service takes seriously its duty to see that, in the name of supposed good government, they don't.

This can have some strange results. After Argentina invaded

the Falklands, for example, Foreign Office officials agonized for a long time before permitting themselves to notify Lord Carrington, the Foreign Secretary, that the Callaghan government had secretly sent a small naval force of its own to peer over the horizon of the South Atlantic. In the case of MI5, one cannot help concluding that Mrs Thatcher is using the doctrine as a way of trying to wash her hands of the 1977 problem. Sometimes it is very convenient to be able to make a virtue of ignorance.

However, just as the Foreign Office's punctiliousness about revealing what the Callaghan Government had done did not deter its successor from mobilizing for war, so there are no serious grounds for saying that because there was an inquiry in 1977 it would somehow be improper, still less impossible, for her present government to hold another in 1987 in the light of the new evidence. This is shallow stuff, as Mrs Thatcher must surely know every time she trots it out at Question Time.

One person who certainly knows is Sir Robert Armstrong. But then he occupies a rather special place in this whole affair. For although one set of ministers are not supposed to know what another set were doing, the civil servant, of course, is privy to both. He is the repository of secrets they are not allowed to know.

At the time when Peter Wright and his friends say they were up to their dirty tricks, Armstrong was Deputy Under-Secretary in the Home Office, in which post one of his tasks was to be the highest-level link-man between the Home Office and the security services. He was still in that position when Wilson, having retired, published his allegations. And he was either in that post, or had just been promoted to Permanent Secretary, when the short 1977 inquiry was conducted.

We thus have a situation, somewhat bizarre even in the annals of Whitehall and its protocols, in which the Prime Minister piously says she does not and cannot know about an episode in which her principal civil servant, who is also her main personal adviser on security matters, was a prime actor at the time and must know almost everything that can be known. In his position, Sir Robert knew all the allegations and at least some of the facts, and has done so for the last ten years.

Wheel on, however, Sir Robert in his role as Cabinet Secretary and prescient counsellor against future political trouble. One can see, with more than the usual clarity, his natural human interest in supporting the Prime Minister's insistent stand on the narrow ground she is taking, and averting an inquiry into distant events, of which he was obliged to be a ringside spectator, however blameless.

Not the smallest of the consequences of Sir Robert's fortnight in the box in Australia is the precedent it has set. If he was able to appear, the first Cabinet Secretary to do so, as a prime witness in a court case about security, he could scarcely plead that it would be wrong for him to testify at an inquiry into events of the mid-1970s on which he is uniquely qualified to throw some light – even if the most he could reveal was that the topmost official in the Home Office was kept in the dark.

A complex ball of wool might then begin to unravel. One can certainly begin to understand why, were the process to be set in motion, Sir Robert would find it less endurable to be in the witness box, yet again, as the serving Cabinet Secretary than as a man retired from office, now ensnared only by the perquisites and dignities of the President of Trinity College, Oxford.

19 March, 1987

Hugo Young

A Country Diary: Oxfordshire

Many of our larger birds – particularly predators, gulls, herons and rooks – eject pellets or castings of indigestible matter orally instead of through the usual alimentary tract; and, of course, since these are proportionately large, they may regularly be found. Less well-known practitioners of this technique are members of the thrush family, such as the blackbirds which are strewing my garden with small cylindrical pellets consisting of the tough skins and seeds of rose-hips. Another member of the same family, the robin, uses the same method, but its minute castings are most rarely found. Now the second example I have ever come across has provided an interesting link with the MI5 court proceedings in Australia. Many years ago, on the old BBC Third Programme, I served on a panel which included a naturalist who shared my interest in birds' pellets, and needed an example of one from a robin for his collection. A few days later my very tame household robin, which knew its way about the house, deposited a pill-like black pellet on the sheets of my turned-back bed, and this was duly sent to fill the missing gap. Now a robin has deposited a similar pellet – consisting mainly of the legs and wing-cases of small beetles – on my bird-table. Of course, my mind went back to the former occasion, and soon afterwards when reading of the complicated proceedings in Sydney, I was amazed to discover that my pellet-collecting acquaintance was mentioned: not as a naturalist, but as once head of the counter-subversion department of MI5.

3 December, 1986

W. D. Campbell

Yes and No, Minister

Ah, Humphrey. The list of Gongs for the Great, the Good and the Useful. Remember what I said last year? No more tedium. No more boring buns for your clapped-out Whitehall chums. This must be a life-enhancing, dynamic and frankly controversial roll of honour from a government unafraid to bat for Britain.

Quite so, Prime Minister. I think you'll be very satisfied with my headline catchers this year. Lord Maxwell of Mayhem, for services to the Commonwealth Games. Lord Murdoch of Wapping, for services to Central Office and police overtime. Sir Ian Botham, for services to medicine and freelance journalism. And, of course, a Companion of Honour for your great friend the President of the United States. I can see the *Express* front page now. Premier toasts Bob, Rupe, Ronnie and Boths in New Year Shocker. The ghost of Lord Kagan will simply put on his Gannex and shuffle into the shades.

Well, er, Humphrey, when I said 'bold and controversial' of course I meant judicious, courageous, but careful to foster essential unity within society . . .

Quite, Prime Minister. Perhaps, after all, CBEs for the Director of Spent Fuel Services at Sellafield and Rupert Murdoch's haulage contractor would be sufficient to set your special stamp on the list . . . ?

Isn't that still a bit stark, Humphrey?

Well, Prime Minister, I'm sure we can always find ways of sugaring the pill. Knighthoods for the Chairman of the Export Guarantees Advisory Council; the Chief Executive of the Property Services Agency; the Regional Procurator Fiscal for Strathkelvin . . . that sort of thing.

And Welsh Water, Humphrey?

Indeed, Prime Minister; never forgetting the Chief Commissioner for Northern Ireland boy scouts; or for that matter the director of Huntingdon Poultry Research Station.

No one can say I'm chicken, Humphrey.

Alas not, Prime Minister.

How do you think it'll play in the media, Humphrey? Fair, honest, unflinching, that sort of thing?

The press, as ever, have little to complain about, Prime Minister. An OBE for the lobby correspondent of the *Sunday Express*; an MBE for the editor of the *Concrete News*.

Solid thinking, Humphrey. And those little in-jokes you love so much in Whitehall? Apart from making the Governor of the Bank a Privy Counsellor for services to sterling.

I think perhaps the CBE for the Archbishop of Canterbury's appointments secretary is the one I relish most.

For services to keeping Runcie out of my way, Humphrey. But, you know, I do think you've got a little puddingy. Orders of the Warm Bath for all your mates at Defence and the FO and Agriculture. Where's the raisin in the cake, Humphrey, the *joie de vivre*, the Politician as a Cultured Polymath?

Dame Iris Murdoch, Prime Minister. A big gong for Maxwell

Davies. A little gong for Simon Rattle; another for Graham Collier; Alan Ayckbourn; racing drivers; badminton girls; old Irish goalkeepers. They're all here. It is a most catholic collection, if I may say so.

But I still don't see the headline, Humphrey. Something that shows the acceptable, light-hearted face of international statesmen, something that reveals the smiling warmth behind the mask of resolution, if you see what I mean.

Something that makes you seem a human being, Prime Minister?

Exactly so.

That, Prime Minister, is a task carrying many intrinsic difficulties, but if I might suggest . . .

Yes, Sir Humphrey?

One for you; and one for me, Prime Minister.

31 December, 1986

Leader

In diplomatic circles

'For a person involved in the British diplomatic service in Athens,' the judge said in a recent divorce case, 'it could hardly have been more embarrassing.'

What happened was that the British Consul in Athens had gone to the cinema with Maria, his mistress, in the normal way, when his estranged wife turned up, having taken the trouble to come out all the way from Maidstone in Kent for the purpose. 'I think she went out there to stir things up,' the judge said.

He described just what happened. 'She attacked Maria, tried to pull her hair, and made a lot of allegations. There was a lot of shouting and a scene. There may have been some scratching of Maria's face by her.'

While the incident can't have been much fun for Maria, for Our Man in Athens it was even worse. It was embarrassing.

Positively blush-making. Almost as bad as that time in Istanbul when Mrs Consul (as she was then) told the wife of the Consul-General that if something wasn't done about the sewage she would fill a pail with the stuff and throw it over the Consul-General's dining room table.

She also had a tendency to scream and shout at her husband in public. This 'caused problems'. Our Man eventually went off to Athens on his own, where he found the absence of his wife 'something of a relief'. He shacked up with Maria, and the rest is history.

Of the incident involving the Istanbul sewage (or Turkish delight) the judge said: 'That sort of behaviour is extremely damaging to a husband in the sensitive area of the Foreign Office and the wife knew it well.'

But did she? I only ask this question because there has come into my hands a document published by the Diplomatic Administration Office in 1965. Since the document is RESTRICTED, I would certainly be prosecuted under the Official Secrets Act if I were even to quote its title, which is (it's a very long one): 'Guidance to Diplomatic Service and other Officers, and Wives, posted to Diplomatic Service Missions Overseas, or some "do's" and "don'ts" of Diplomatic Etiquette and other relevant matters.'

Here's a sample from the document: 'In many countries, a senior lady guest will expect to occupy the right-hand end of the sofa and ladies and senior persons should always be placed on your right when you are walking with them.'

Funny people, foreigners. Or are they? The next section of the document, and this is probably really Top Secret or even For Your Eyes Only, is on the subject of HUMOUR. At the risk of being sent to the Tower and beheaded, I will quote this state secret in full: 'Until you know people well, beware the temptation of wit and the dangers of humour. It is exceedingly hard for a foreigner to understand the sort of humour which comes naturally to us, and almost equally hard for us to indulge naturally in the humour which appeals to foreigners. Failures in this line can lead to sad misunderstandings.'

At any rate ex-Mrs Consul wouldn't have been helped much by perusing 'Guidance to Diplomatic Service and other Officers, and Wives . . . etcetera' because in the entire work there is not a single mention of the correct behaviour when dealing with sewage problems in Istanbul, or when meeting your husband's mistress in a cinema in Athens.

31 March, 1987

Richard Boston

A Country Diary: Keswick 1

All the months this year seem to have got out of joint. They have been late in their timing and November has simply emphasized the effect with yellow-tipped orange trumpets on the desfontania (only suitable for mild climates) and snow on the fell tops. A strong, sleety gale is tearing the leaves roughly from the oak trees. There are only a few leaves, yellow and fragile, on the lowest birch twigs sheltered by the green tips of the tree heath and the blue-green branches of a juniper, but, in contrast, the last leaf-stems of a tree peony are an astonishing carmine. There is, however, damage in the garden, but not connected with the storms. I went this morning to look at the nerines which should have been in flower now – only one flower was left, all the rest were eaten almost to ground level. The early cherry-red pulmonaria has had its flower heads neatly nipped out too, surely by mice or voles, but it was the sort of situation which really does make you 'lift your eyes up to the hills'.

November is a silver month between the gold of autumn and the green of spring. The lateness of the seasons has had other odd effects. The redpolls arrived on the birch cones in October, they left and were followed by black-headed siskins but now those have gone and a second wave of redpolls are here. The cloud-masses over the fells have each an outline of pure silver and when the sun gets through it touches everything else with silver, too. The redpolls hang up-ended, feeding, their always pale underparts turned to the purest of silver.

1 December, 1981

Enid J. Wilson

85

Richards lets fly with 87

Vivian Richards, cricket's best batsman, who was so unceremoniously sacked by Somerset last summer, helicoptered down to his new home in a Lancashire village yesterday, put on his pads to score 87 runs with a sleepy, jet-lagged venom, then put his feet up and said: 'Well, I've never scored runs in a hail-storm before, but it's good to be back.'

The West Indies captain had left Antigua basking in over 100 degrees. Rishton managed about 35. His flight to London had been delayed but, appropriately for once, the *Star* newspaper chipped in with a chopper, so he arrived just in time for the toss.

He was greeted by a couple of thousand and an excited mob

'. . . and God said, "on the seventh day thou shalt rest from playing all this one-day cricket".'

12 February, 1987

86

of urchins, as well as a cruel wind which lanced in off the moors bringing with it a whole season of weather in one afternoon – sleet and hail, stair-rod-rained showers, rainbows and pockets of sharp sunlight.

It's a new world for him. His first innings in England – a half century for Lansdowne Second XI Bath, on 26 April 1973 – was for a sedate English country house club. This is the Lancashire League. Different culture. Viv is probably the nattiest dresser in cricket, but here he emerged from his helicopter, brown trilby rimmed in Rishton garish green and gold and a tracksuit bearing the legend 'Hollands' Pies – makers of quality puddings since 1851'. Within an hour of touchdown, he had Michelin-manned himself into a thermal vest and two thick sweaters to take bleary guard as first-wicket down against Haslingden.

First ball, a raucous lbw appeal turned down – 'who d'you think they've come to watch, lad, him bat or me umpire?' He played a couple of groping maidens from a post office clerk then eased the sleep from his eyes with a hook which was dropped at long-leg by young David Jackson, a factory worker.

Then the giant stirred. Homer was not going to nod off, and nine fours and six sixes followed in a voluptuous flurry as if a man was on a stroll topping dandelion heads with a walking stick. He put on 66 with Phil Sykes, a 22-year-old management trainee, and 50 with Dave Wilson, a computer programmer. He was caught after 72 balls trying to repeat his most handsome hit. When he bowled he took two for 26 in 12 overs as Rishton won easily, restricting Aslingdean to 131 for seven.

His £15,000-plus perks – full board in the plushest local hotel and the BMW is delivered this morning – is as much as he earned at Somerset. The feeling has persisted for the last couple of summers that the phenomenon they call 'the master blaster' was mightily in need of a decent rest from the county treadmill.

Mind you, heroes have to work for worship in the gritty Lancashire League. 'He's a good'un, they tell me,' said one muffled ancient, in the statutory know-alls' huddle near the pavilion yesterday, 'but no flashy batter has ever got us much up here. Unless he's the very best, like.'

This one most assuredly is, I told him. 'Let's see come September,' said Mr Grouser, munching his gums and huddling challengingly back into his overcoat.

4 May, 1987

Frank Keating

Reporting a nightmare

What kinds of life should we call 'ordinary', here in the late twentieth century? What is 'normal' in these abnormal days? For many of us, any definition of the quotidian would still include notions of peace and stability. We would still, perhaps, wish to picture everyday life as rhythmic, based on certain settled and repeating social patterns. Ryszard Kapuscinski's work seems to be based on his knowledge that such conventional descriptions of actuality are now so limited in application that they have become, in a way, fictions.

There's this 'spry old dame' whom Kapuscinski meets in the emptiness of Luanda, Angola, during the civil war of 1975. She's worried that the white race is about to enter 'the vestigial phase. Barely 2 per cent [of the inhabitants of earth] will have naturally blond hair. Blonds: . . . a rarity of rarities.' You could say that humdrum, predictable lives are getting to be as abnormal as those blonds.

Kapuscinski's own life hasn't been dull. He's been to 27 revolutions in 55 years, which could be a record. The statistic reveals more than just his line of work. It suggests that the revolution, that thing of rumours and broken rhythms, amorphous, bloody, fitful, is now one of the normative processes of human affairs.

When peace becomes abnormal, combat fatigues, automatic rifles, missiles, hostages, hunger, fear become the building blocks of a new, uncomfortable definition of the real.

In such a brave new world, it's not surprising that the foreign correspondent has become a myth-figure. He goes out there, doesn't he, and sends us the bad news. And when we've had

88

too much reality, we turn the pages, we switch channels, enough is enough.

Alas, our intrepid correspondents tend to run into brick walls. The situation is too confused, they can't find anything out, it's time to file a story. In these stories Ryszard Kapuscinski is able to admire 'the opulence of human fantasy'. 100,000 Cubans were in Angola, according to the world's press, whereas in truth the total fighting strength of the leftist MPLA was about 30,000 soldiers, 'of whom about two-thirds were Angolans'. The MPLA's Cuban allies had brought over lots of extra uniforms, because a Cuban uniform scared the pants off the right-wing FNLA and UNITA troops.

If war reportage is so often make-believe, from whom are we to hear reliable accounts of the horrific, metamorphosed reality of our age? To answer this question is to understand the profound importance of Kapuscinski's writing. There is a difference between invention and imagination, and Kapuscinski possesses in abundance the gifts of the true imaginative writer.

In his books on Haile Selassie and the Shah, and now in *Another Day of Life*, his description – no, his *responses* – do what only art can manage; that is, they fire our own imaginations. One Kapuscinski is worth a thousand grizzled journofantasists; and through his astonishing blend of reportage and artistry we get as close to what he calls the incommunicable image of war as we're ever likely to by reading.

Another Day of Life is about the birth-crisis of independent Angola. It is also a superlative, vivid piece of writing, containing many of the resonant surreal visions that have become Kapuscinski's trademarks.

In the opening section, the capital, Luanda, is emptying rapidly, its inhabitants convinced that Holden Roberto's FNLA forces, backed by Zaire and the West, are about to devastate the city. 'Everybody,' Kapuscinski notes, 'was busy building crates.' From this prosaic beginning he launches into a rhapsodic account of the emptying of the city's stone buildings into the wooden crates: 'Gradually . . . the stone city lost its value in favour of the wooden city . . . Nowhere else in the world had I seen such a city . . . But afterward, [it] sailed away on the ocean . . . I don't know if there had ever been an instance of a whole city sailing across the ocean, but that is exactly what happened. The city sailed out into the world, in search of its inhabitants.'

The seagoing crate-city belonged to the Portuguese who had fled Angola. Kapuscinski finally traced the crates to their destinations: Rio, Capetown, Lisbon. His ode to the wooden Luanda is perhaps a shade too long, but it's still a little bit of genius. Of all those who wrote about Luanda, only Kapuscinski *saw* the wooden city. It was there under everybody's noses, but it still needed eyes to see.

After a journey down one of Angola's many dangerous roads, past the Russian roulette of roadblocks and the constant probability of ambush, Kapuscinski's companion Nelson murmurs, 'Another day of life.' He is celebrating their survival, good, so we live until tomorrow at least. But Kapuscinski appreciates that the phrase has a secondary meaning: this is how life is now, this is just the way of it, it is what living has become; a daily escape from death, until you don't.

Kapuscinski counterpoints his portrait of this shifting, uncertain, terrified world with his telexes home to Warsaw, setting up a tension between the rich, ambiguous truth of life in war-crazed Angola, and the need of newspapers for facts.

This concluding, albeit temporary, victory of facts over uncertainty shows us that Kapuscinski is not the kind of purely 'literary' writer who might have been content with an open-ended, unresolved portrait of life as chaos, studded with his many brilliant metaphors of unknowing. The truth may be hard to establish, but it still needs establishing.

'Overseas, they don't know,' Kapuscinski writes, but he often does. He knows that the whole war has depended on two men: the pilot Ruiz, who flies ammunition to besieged border cities, and the engineer Alberto Ribeiro, who manages to keep Luanda's water supply going. Without these two, the cities would have had to surrender to the South Africa-backed enemy forces.

Such details are, like the wooden crate-city, proof that Kapuscinski's is a very piercing eye indeed. He hears well, too. Of an MPLA commissar, he says: 'Ju-Ju's communiqués are brief and calm when things are going well . . . But when something turns rotten, [they] become prolix and crabbed, adjectives proliferate, and self-praise and epithets scorning the enemy multiply.' Ours is the most cryptic of centuries, its true nature a dark secret. Ryszard Kapuscinski is the kind of codebreaker we need.

13 February, 1987

Salman Rushdie

The end of the word is nigh

'It darkles (tinct, tinct) all this our funnanimal world. We are circumveiloped by obscuritads . . .'

Finnegan's Wake, Joyce's odyssey through the night mind of the human race, his vespers for a fallen world, might be the Urtext of literary Postmodernism (which has a classier pedigree than the same phenomenon in, say, architecture). In that great babbledebook, that boadeconstructor of narrative tradition and decorum, we surely sense the approaching End of the Word. Or as Joyce himself more Postmodernly put it, 'I know it is only a game, but children might as well play as not. The ogre will come in any case.'

Alternatively – since half the debate is about whether Postmodernism is a continuation from 'classical' modernism (Baudelaire to the death of Eliot) or an alteration, a real mutation – you might place James Joyce just that side of the divide and Samuel Beckett on this. For Joyce's legitimate son and heir shows even more of the stigmata of the new consciousness: radical irony and the blackest of comedy or 'self-consuming play', dire attenuation of the human, and a minimalism so tight that a late piece called *Breath* squeezes out a life in just fifteen seconds, with a birth cry that turns into a death rattle.

Much of the rest you can find in the books of his lovely bastard Flann O'Brien: the multi-layered, many-voiced narrative, the pastiching and juggling with genres and the myths of pop and high culture.

There are other arguments about this juncture in literary culture and the culture in general that seem more political. Is Postmodernism, as it has developed, progressive or reactionary, essentially subversive or incorporated by capitalism, deeply liberating or really rather infantile? Well, yeah, right on: it's *anti* all that old Modernist elitism, all those myths, all that *foreign* stuff, but it's also, wow! *for* being one of the boys, and all the easy reading and looking and listening, no sweat – except of course the sweat of keeping in with the new elitism of pure, blank fashion, of *keeping up*, like any teeny bopper or colour supplement editor, to recall a few tropes from a receding, already charming, perhaps due-for-a-revival, past.

I simplify a little. Some of the most characteristic Postmodern texts – John Barth's *Lost In The Funhouse*, say – are by learned profs, likely to be discussed in impenetrable post-structuralese by buttoned-down Yaleo deconstructionists. Italo Calvino's marvellous reader-teaser, *If On A Winter's Night A Traveller*, with its false starts and sudden button-holings, will keep you on your toes quite as elegantly and compellingly as Nabokov. And generally, the better sort of this writing makes an authentic response to the surrealism of everyday life in the flood tide of our times.

Still, the question about continuity or a break is the crucial one, as Frank Kermode betrayed 20 years ago in a parenthesis in *The Sense Of An Ending*, his argument about what had been happening to the novel in an apocalyptic age.

How you view it depends largely on what you think has been happening to the rest of the human enterprise. If you look at Daniel Bell's *The Coming Of Post-Industrial Society*, you can see in three or four pages an extraordinary thing unfolding: a whole generation of intellectuals, anxious to register the great changes they see, and able to do it only in terms of what had gone, what was no longer. Throughout the Sixties, these historians, philosophers, sociologists and critics could tell us only that we were living in a post-traditional, post-Christian, post-bourgeois, post-capitalist, post-Marxist, post-liberal, post-civilized, post-literate, post-*Modern* age – in all, Bell lines up 20 of these posts.

It is a curious phenomenon, this period which seems to think of itself only as an after-life, a half-life, a social and spiritual demonstration of entropy. 'If it sounds strange . . . ,' wrote Ralf Dahrendorf, elaborating his account of managerialist post-capitalism, 'this strangeness is due to the strangeness of reality' – thereby echoing Norman Mailer on the problems of the novelist in an age when 'the trouble with reality is that it isn't realistic any more'.

What's at the back of these estrangements seems clear enough. It is that our imaginations still cannot digest the historical facts of the Holocaust and Hiroshima, or the 'balance' of nuclear terror that won't let us forget them. They do not merely haunt our dreams, but our other fictions too. Look at the more radical thinking and writing of the last few decades: what the work which is most clearly of this time seems to be saying is that these man-made apocalypses have exploded our culture and history, disrupting our deepest sense of what we are and making us doubt our sanity, even our creatureliness.

Certainly they are what made Brecht conclude that the grand house of culture was built on bullshit, and Adorno feel that to write lyric poetry after Auschwitz was itself 'barbaric'. But more than that, these black facts carry, as increasingly our fictions do, 'the sense of an ending'. This does not mean merely that our future is threatened by even bigger bangs. What it sometimes feels like is that, to adapt Virginia Woolf's famous sentence, 'in or about' August 1945 something in human character actually died. At some deep level, we seem to believe that the Bomb and the death factories were in fact the End to which our civilization had been tending, the coming event of which the assembly line, the Somme, Guernica and the apocalyptics of the old modernism were but shadows.

So: we live in a Postmodern culture in a post-historical world and feel strange, and a prized part of our literature (Beckett, Burroughs, Ballard) occupies purgatorial landscapes peopled with autistic or schizoid characters, or is lost in the funhouse of pastiche and near-pornography, equally affectless and soul-damaged. At the very least, we know that Humpty Dumpty, that greedy Prometheus with the monkey morals, has suffered a second Fall, and it may be that his murderous hubris is part of the reason for the insistence of structuralism's anti-humanist thrust.

Perhaps now is the moment to remember Vladimir's bracing exchange with Estragon near the end of *Waiting For Godot*:

'I can't go on like this.'

'That's what you think.'

We must go on, we can't go on . . . we go on. There is the glow of apocalypse at our backs, yes, and the shadow of Something ahead, yes, but meanwhile we must attend also to this ever more speedy getting and spending which is the lot of the saving majority still of Thatcher's Brits and Reagan's Middle Americans.

Postmodernism is what has grown where the tension in this split consciousness is greatest. Which means, of course, that it has flourished more and madder among the abounding contradictions of postwar American society. (The British, leafing through another nice book on country houses while supping their real ale and munching their ploughman's lunch between the twittering Space Invaders, should reflect, however, on how much of their self-satisfied cultural conservatism has desiccated into thoroughly postmodern pastiche and self-parody.)

Could anyone be surprised that writers mix genres, confuse fact and fiction, fantasy and reality, in the land of Watergate and Star Wars? In retrospect, it is the Nixon years that seem the prime time. How could Philip Roth hope to compete, in his Watergate satire, *Our Gang*, with the *real* absurdism of the Nixon tapes, which often sound quite remarkably like Beckett or Pinter, or the Czech absurdist Vaclav Havel – for instance in this powerful scene between Nixon and Attorney-General Mitchell:

Nixon: He won't talk on the phone with anybody, according to Kleindienst. He thinks his phone is tapped.

Mitchell: He does?

Nixon: Who's tapping his phone?

Mitchell: I don't know.

Nixon: Who would he think, who would he think would tap his phone? I guess maybe that we would.

Mitchell: I don't doubt that.

Some American writers – rather a lot – committed suicide in

these years. Some were moved to play with a more or less amiably psychotic view of the world: see Kurt Vonnegut, recurrently, and Donald Barthelme; see the quietly crazy pastoral of Richard Brautigan's *Trout Fishing In America*, especially the visit to the Cleveland Wrecking Yard to buy a used trout stream (stacked in lengths out back there; waterfalls upstairs in plumbing).

I suppose Vonnegut and our own J. G. Ballard in their different ways are the paradigmatic postmodernists. Vonnegut as an adolescent prisoner of war survives the Dresden firestorm, and spends his writing life in the strictly mad task of trying to reconcile his childhood in the old German–American mid-West and today's gobbling consumerism with the sights that met his eyes 40 years ago when he emerged from a butcher's cold-store into the charnel-house our bombers had made of 'the first fancy city I'd ever seen'. Ballard, born in Shanghai and growing up in a Japanese prison camp, plants his Max Ernst landscapes in the gardens of bricky Shepperton and the exotica of his boyhood dreams of science in the interstices of motorways and abandoned runways; only in his fifties does he write a novel registering something almost like ordinary human contact between the characters.

Mostly with such people the writerly talent and authenticity of vision is unmistakable. Where it isn't, there's often a kind of infantilism involved in postmodernist capers that makes one think of Empson's 'smack' at the young Auden's stagey apocalyptics fifty years ago:

> Waiting for the end, boys,
>   waiting for the end,
> What is there to be or do?
> What's become of me or you? . . .

And

> Shall we all go wild, boys,
> Waste and make them lend,
> Playing at the child, boys,
>   waiting for the end?

It's possible to be more optimistic, less nervous about the

95

import of all this. An American critic, Marshall Berman (a continuity man like Kermode, though I think for different reasons), takes Marx's marvellous line about a time when 'All that is solid melts into air' as the title of his account of the experience of modernism. 'To be modern,' he writes, 'is to experience personal and social life as a maelstrom, to find one's world in perpetual disintegration and renewal . . . To be a modern*ist* is to make oneself somehow at home in this maelstrom . . . to grasp and confront the world that modernization makes, and to strive to make it our own.'

It is noticeable, though, that he doesn't produce many positive postmodernist heroes, and that when Fredric Jameson, another American Marxist critic interested in this debate, seeks to, what he has to concentrate on are E. L. Doctorow's fictional 'archaeologies' of the broken history of the American Left, in *Ragtime, Loon Lake* and *The Book Of Daniel*. Then there are the young 'dirty realists' Bill Buford has been publishing in *Granta* – Jayne Ann Phillips, Richard Ford and the rest. They're hardly the Baudelairean heroes and heroines of modern life that Berman might wish them to be, though they do seem to accept, rather glumly, that the strange present is where they live, that this is after all their historical address, like it or lump it.

But if you are looking for a more convincing optimism of the will in contemporary literature, you will have to turn away from the stoned comedy and twitching revels of the old world and look to the new. By that I mean of course not a North America, which is no longer Hegel's 'land of the future' (unless in an altogether grimmer sense than he meant), but to the writers of Latin America and the Indian subcontinent, where 'to grasp and confront the world that modernization makes' is still a new and welcome task. Note that both Garcia Marquez and Salman Rushdie resist the 'magic realist' label and think of themselves rather as realists of a kind appropriate to their cultures at this stretching moment in history when, as Carlos Fuentes says, 'you have the Iron Age in the mountains and the 20th century in our cities'.

Where magic comes into the equation is perhaps best described in the words of the Russian formalist Victor Shklovsky

96

– for once a figure from the history of structuralism has something to say for our comfort. 'Habitualism,' he wrote over 60 years ago, 'devours objects, clothes, furniture, one's wife and the fear of war . . . Art exists to help us recover the sensation of life, it exists to make us feel things, to make the stone *stony*.'

2 December, 1986

W. L. Webb

To All and Sundry

The Spanish Prime Minister.
Dear Mr Gonzalez,

You will doubtless be aware that the Cat and Fiddle Inn on the road between Buxton and Macclesfield is a corruption of Catherina Fidelis, in reference to Catherine of Aragon. Derivations purporting to trace it to Caton le Fidele in remembrance of a former governor of Calais should be disregarded.

You will further be aware that Elephant and Castle is a corruption of the Infanta of Castile. These testimonies to the longevity of relations between our two countries, notwithstanding the frequent conflicts of interest which have arisen and the naval engagements in which you are still one down, will excuse what might otherwise appear an interference in your internal affairs.

I understand that you had a million people on strike last week. I also understand that you have not appeared in parliament for eight months. My advice to you would be, in the Spanish idiom, to take the bull by the horns and face the Opposition.

Traditions evolve, and it is true that Prime Minister's twice-weekly Question Time in the Mother of Parliaments has developed into a cacophony. Nevertheless it serves the necessary purpose of allowing members to shout and jeer within the chamber, which they might otherwise do outside, to the detriment of us all.

If you would care to be present at one of these occasions, where you will find close similarities to your own national sport,

I will drop a word in the right quarter and engage you a seat in the distinguished Strangers' Gallery.

I write as a true friend of Spain. Not having been there or followed its fortunes professionally, I can, I hope, claim that degree of detachment which is essential to the well-intentioned counsellor.

With kind regards to your fellow-members of the Cortes,
Yours sincerely,

The Wykeham Professor of Logic, Oxford.
Dear Professor,

It was shown here last week that we have no knowledge of the present but only an historical knowledge of what happened some time, however brief, ago. On the other hand, we do have knowledge about the future, assuming the regularity of the world. For example, on Wednesday of this week those so inclined will join festivities to mark the 30th anniversary of the Treaty of Rome.

It is matter for regret that your department has given insufficient attention to this anomaly. I am sure you will recognize that to have greater certainty about what will happen in future than about what is happening now is not a satisfactory state of affairs.

If I were to venture a criticism, it would be that so many persons occupying your illustrious chair should have allowed the anomaly to continue. I trust that the matter will receive closer attention in future than it has in the past.

Hoping this finds you as it leaves me, as it were, at present.
Yours sincerely,

The Cabinet Secretary.
Dear Sir Robert,

I trust you will not allow the current controversies to distract you from your work.

I do not have to remind you that you are the Prime Minister's principal adviser. Where should we be if every senior civil servant, let alone the Cabinet Secretary, were appearing in court and writing letters to the press? The tradition of reticence

98

in these matters should not lightly be abandoned for, after all, the record will be made plain for posterity in a mere 30 years' time.

I urge you to keep your head below the proverbial parapet and, if another vacancy should arise at Oxford, you may rest assured that your candidature will have the unremitting support of this column.

Yours sincerely,

The Controller, Radio Three.

Dear Mr McIntyre,

At the time I thought it was a good idea to put the BBC World Service news on Radio Three twice a day. Having listened to it, I am not sure.

The World Service depends for its authenticity on being hard to receive. Even with repeated fine tuning on short wave, it is impossible to escape the crackle, whistles and sudden changes of volume which persuade the listener, wherever he may be, that he has made a genuine effort to keep in touch with Bush House.

I would ask you to remember that the service is not intended for suburban intellectuals in the comfort of their drawing rooms, but for geologists in the Amazonian jungle and hard-pressed diplomats in such difficult postings as Bangui and Ras al Khaimah. Even they should need to give it their utmost concentration.

To hear it on stereo VHF is almost a descent into decadence of which, goodness knows, the evidence abounds on every side.

Yours sincerely,

The Chairman, Red Deer Commission, Inverness.

Dear Mr Mackenzie,

I note that you are slap in the middle of the close season, which for stags does not end until 1 July. You have all my sympathy in what you must find an extremely frustrating time of year.

In the light of the restrictions imposed on you, I thought it worth mentioning – and you may, of course, already know –

that the close season for stags in England and Wales does not begin until 1 May, so that there may be some decent stalking to be had down here as the weather warms up. If you wish me to make a few inquiries on your behalf, my facilities are willingly placed at your disposal. On the other hand, you may have contacts of your own.

In either case, I wish you all the best when the long silence in your part of the world comes to its inevitable end, and in the meantime I would commend to you the wise advice of Milton, and on occasions forelock watchful wait.

Yours sincerely,

The Astronomer Royal.
Dear brother-scientist,

I noted your strictures on the box the other night about the Government spending cuts and, for what it is worth, I heartily concur with them.

It so happens that I have a disused outbuilding which I am thinking of turning into an observatory. I should be grateful for any advice you can give on how best to proceed. It won't, I fear, be another Mount Palomar, but I always say that every little helps. Please telephone when you are free to come, and bring a 20-inch telescope with you. I have a friend who is a joiner and would help us to rig it up.

I see that on 2 April Mars will be in conjunction with the moon, which you may feel would be an appropriate time to make the first observation, weather permitting of course. We do get a fair amount of cloud cover, but I expect you are used to that.

Don't hesitate to bring a colleague. It will be open house.

Yours sincerely,

● Correspondence with the Archbishop of York, the Liberian ambassador, and the general manager of Cork Airport is unavoidably held over.

23 March, 1987

Geoffrey Taylor

Hartless

Sir, – Goodbye Gary Hart:

How sad about the tender trap,
  We know just how you feel;
Too bad your greatest handicap
  Was having broad appeal.

11 May, 1987

Roger Woddis
London N 13

Affair of the Hart

Donna Rice, served up as the sizzling doner kebab who has skewered Gary Hart's prospects as Democratic presidential candidate, was 'never anything but nice', according to her school principal. What's more, 'she didn't dabble in politics at all while at high school, to my knowledge.'

The 29-year-old model, aspiring actress and part-time pharmaceutical saleswoman, is emerging in much the same wholesome mould as Fawn Hall during the last celebrated case of smoking trousers in high places, the Olly North affair. This time, however, there is speculation that Ms Rice, who appeared topless in a poster, might not spurn *Playboy*'s blandishments.

Described as stunningly attractive, with an outrageous figure, she has had small parts in *Miami Vice* and *Dallas*, between modelling swimsuits in Miami. The latter work was summed up by a former employer as ranging from 'your average mom-type thing to your more fashion-orientated, good-looking-lady-type thing'. Recent pictures depict her in a slashed-to-the-waist-type thing.

Brought up in South Carolina, where her mother works for the Forestry Commission, she graduated from Irmo High

School in the capital, Columbia, to read biology at the state university. A former Miss South Carolina, she is a registered 'emergency medical technician', an indispensable asset on the campaign trail.

At least two of her other interests (acrobatics, skiing and sea sports) have been mentioned in connection with Gary Hart. By her account it was in Aspen, the Colorado skiing centre, that she first met him as hostess of a New Year's Eve party.

In March she met Hart again at a yacht party. 'I was very embarrassed,' she recalled. 'But of course everybody was ready to strike up a doo-dah, or whatever.' She has admitted to striking up a duologue with Hart, offering to help his campaign as a fund-raiser, whereupon he asked for her telephone number. A few days later he called to invite her on a yacht trip to Bimini in the Bahamas with his companion, William Broadhurst, and a woman friend.

'It was all very innocent,' she said, explaining that closure of the island's Customs post had forced them to stay the night, the men and women sleeping on separate boats. Asked if Hart had made any advances, she replied: 'Oh no, not at all.' Although Hart was 'very relaxed with me' and had phoned her a few times since their outing, 'I'm more attracted to younger men,' she insisted. Hart is 50.

Ms Rice, who denies spending Friday night with Hart, commented on the propriety of their relationship in Washington: 'I figured, hey, if he doesn't have a problem with it, then I don't have a problem with it.'

And why not?

The ideology of enmity

The contrast is striking. While controversies like Contragate, insider trading and Gary Hart's love life burst with volcanic ferocity and speed upon the American public, spewing lava and ash in all directions, the process which shapes US foreign policy moves with glacial speed and temperature to acknowledge what even Mrs Thatcher seems to think may be the most significant development in the long history of the Cold War: Gorbachev.

Why are American attitudes so deep-frozen? It is 40 years this summer since the scholar–diplomat George Kennan first inserted the fateful word 'containment' into an article he published in *Foreign Affairs*, flagship, then as now, of the internationalist elite, under the pseudonym 'X'.

'X' did not advocate the sweeping and military version which the Truman Doctrine was already implementing in Greece by the time the piece actually appeared. He did challenge America to stop appeasing Uncle Joe Stalin and embark on a policy of 'long-term, patient but firm vigilant containment of Russian expansive tendencies' – for as long as it took for something better to emerge, perhaps in 10–15 years.

Whether that something may finally have arrived nobody knows for certain. But Europeans, with the characteristic exception of the French, are hopeful. Americans, by and large, are not. The Reagan administration is willing, nay eager, to cut a deal on Euro-missiles to clinch a Washington summit in September, but that has all to do with Reagan's domestic plight and not with changed basic assumptions about the East–West conflict.

And those hawks who do acclaim the prospective deal see it as a triumph for hanging tough against an enemy who needs a respite from the arms race more than Washington does, rather than a reflection of fundamental rethinking. Or as one participant at a recent seminar said of Gorbachev's patience with Reaganite provocations: 'Why is Misha a wimp?'

It is not that there is no intense debate on the Gorbachev phenomenon in the interlocking worlds of scholars, diplomats and spooks, just that it has barely affected the tone and assumptions of public debate. True, the White House no longer contents itself with reflex jibes that Gorbachev is only a slick PR man – a severe case of pot slandering kettle. Now that so many opinion-formers have met the man (and George Shultz privately concedes his brilliance) it is respectable to admit that something seriously different may be being *attempted* economi-

13 April, 1987

cally – even politically. But, we are usually assured in the next breath, it can't work given the constraints of a system which Misha says he is committed to modernize rather than dismantle.

Hence the quip 'Reagan will outlast Gorbachev', an extreme case of *chutzpah* when we consider the Prez's age, health and political circumstances. But it is advanced on editorial pages and in small magazines by hard-line conservatives like Marshall Goldman and Richard Pipes up at Harvard and by many officials. Al Haig has helpfully predicted that the General Secretary may be assassinated.

As the INF debate underlines, the 'zero-sum' mentality persists: what is good for Moscow must be bad for us. Nixinger, as the wits call the revived Nixon–Kissinger axis, warns that the West cannot, should not, try and help Gorbachev achieve his domestic goals. The West must judge its interests only in the light of his conduct of foreign policy – as it unfolds more clearly.

The arms control community is impressed, but lacks influence. Some liberal Sovietologists, like Professor Jerry Hough, are deeply impressed by Gorbachev's domestic aspirations ('an implicit deal with the middle class') and his survival prospects (Gorbachev isn't Khrushchev) but even Hough joins conservatives in suggesting he may adopt a tough foreign policy to sustain it. Workers already suffering domestic Thatcherism will accept it if they think Mother Russia is in danger, the argument runs.

In any event, the dominant tone remains apprehensive. To the question: 'Is it in the interests of the United States that Gorbachev succeed in his reforms?' comes a boisterous 'yes' only from the political Left, some Liberals, and (let us not forget them) those Armand Hammer types eyeing markets for their agriculture, mineral extracting and high-tech exports. To the Right such pragmatic capitalist calculation remains anathema: it will only help create a more efficient tyranny.

The triumph of ideology over export markets contrasts sharply with the benefit of the doubt constantly given here to China's faltering economic experiments, of which Shultz – also privately – despairs. Pardonable caution is one thing and some analysts point out, 'we've been burned before', most recently by Yuri Andropov's brief, false dawn, but why is US anti-Sovietism so ingrained, so rooted in its distinctly shaky ideological threat as much as the military one?

The answers are not all negative. Because Americans take their civil liberties, their free press, the accountability of their government (Contragate) more seriously than world-weary Europeans and *dirigiste* Japanese, far greater offence is caused here not merely by the past horrors of Stalinism, but by human rights practices which Gorbachev has only now begun to modify. 'That's why Sakharov's release made such an impact here,' says one US official. 'Its importance was exaggerated,' snaps a liberal academic.

Of course, the Reagan Administration has sustained a high level of ideological fervour against the still-evil empire. But what Harvard psychologist John Mack has called 'the ideology of enmity' is a recurring theme of American society – innocently looking out on a wicked world for the source of its own disappointments. George Kennan's cerebral musings in 1947 thus touched a sensitive public nerve. Forty years' hard pounding have not deadened its responsiveness. With even many US radicals defining themselves in terms of being anti-Soviet it is not surprising that the American peace movement has usually chosen to attack the symptoms of 'Soviet-phobia' weapons – rather than tackle its underlying causes head on.

If a reluctance to rethink is rooted in public prejudice, it is reinforced by the vested interests. Indeed, arguments about the resistance to change that Gorbachev faces from the party, the bureaucracy, the military and the security apparatus, could well be invoked here if there was any serious indication that the Howard Baker 'regency' was contemplating more than a holding operation.

Military Keynsianism alone, with jobs and bases in every state of the Union, gives all but the doughtiest politicians little incentive to look at the warfare state and say, 'Hey, let's call it off.'

At elite levels neither institutions nor bureaucratic and academic disciplines have decisively divergent interests which could significantly open up the debate. CIA analysts may be less gung-ho than their counterparts at the Pentagon. Shultz may be smarter than Weinberger. Columbia University's Russian Institute may have more liberal credentials than Harvard's Russian Research Centre. But centrist think-tanks like the Brookings Institution, let alone leftist exiles at the Institute for Policy Studies, lack effective leverage this side of a new presidency.

What is at work here is the unhealthy fact that campuses and think-tanks are locked into government patronage and research contracts, or into private money with commercial strings. The result is an intense but narrow debate among historians, economists and political scientists. Natural scientists actually have a better record of vocal opposition to nuclear folly – even at the risk of losing Star Wars dollars for their labs. But reinforcing caution and conservatism among the scholars in the humanities is the inhibiting lure of office which few physicists share. When asked if there would be new thinking on the campuses Henry Kissinger contemptuously replied: 'Why should there be when every professor thinks he can become an assistant secretary of state?'

It goes without saying that the media reinforces conformity in a society which has riotously anarchic edges but a surprisingly solid centre. The *New York Times* is judged a little more susceptible to Gorby now that the neo-conservative A. M. Rosenthal has departed the editor's chair to write a neo-conservative column. The opinion pages of the admirable *Wall Street Journal* are run by ayatollahs who regard Nigel Lawson as a fiscal socialist. The liberal *Washington Post* is surprisingly severe on Misha. American TV is . . . well, American TV.

If there is consolation in this portrait of a deep-frozen Cold War glacier it is that the imminence of the post-Reagan era may soon force the ice to crack. Even sooner, the threat of economic rather than military catastrophe may rub home the inter-dependent nature of the modern world in which wealth and power is far more diffused than in 1947. Someone calls it 'a soft landing' from the Cold War. In the current edition of *Foreign Affairs*, alongside the reprint of his original 'X' article, George Kennan, ironically transformed in old age from a cold warrior into a paid-up dove, urges his countrymen towards the crucial change in perception: from the dangers of Soviet aggression to the dangers of unintended war.

As for 'containment', he tactfully notes that 'a large pro-portion of the sources of our troubles and dangers lies outside the Soviet challenge, such as it is, and some of it even within ourselves'. It may be a way of hinting that, instead of writing off Gorbachev, Washington should be asking itself how it is going to elect a President of similar mettle.

20 May, 1987

Michael White

Lenin and company

The image of a theatre filled with 600 Soviet actors impersona-ting Lenin was conjured up on the 117th anniversary of the birth of the founder of the Soviet state.

'Fifty years ago, only five actors had the necessary authorization to play this role,' the celebrated Lenin actor Kirill Lavrov said in *Kommunist*, the party's main theoretical journal. 'But by the second half of the 1970s, their numbers exceeded 600. And in Moscow, organized actors' seminars for them would be held. The participants would sit in a hall, all looking like Lenin, and would swop experiences and insights.'

The bizarre sight of massed Lenins might be calculated to strike fear into the heart of any politically aware capitalist, but *Kommunist* also found it unwholesome, arguing that the image of Lenin should be more precious.

'An alarming tendency appeared. One of our great actors, Maxim Strukh, told me once how he got a phone call from the party youth organization in one region,' Mr Lavrov said.

'Please get yourself dressed and made up like Lenin and come along to our meeting,' they asked him. 'We want you to come up on stage and we report to you on our work as young Communists.

'And then?' asked the actor.

'In the role of Lenin, you praise us for our work,' came the reply.

'These young people had not thought of the monstrous profanity they were committing,' *Kommunist* said. 'The great image of Lenin was being turned, whether we wanted it or not, into a stereotype.'

Lenin's birthday, 22 April, is a national holiday in the Soviet Union. The streets are festooned with flags, and *Pravda*'s normally staid black and white pages explode into red headlines proclaiming: 'The cause of Lenin will live for centuries'.

Pravda devoted almost half its six pages to Lenin's anniversary, but the *Kommunist* article is remarkable for the thespian perspective it throws upon Lenin's role and presentation in the modern Soviet Union.

In the past, Mr Lavrov claims, whenever an actor strode towards the stage dressed as Lenin, the entire company would stand up. 'I cannot say the same happens these days. But still it seems to me that at no other performance is there such tension behind the wings, such iron discipline.'

A new challenge is emerging for Soviet actors – learning how to play the roles of people who have been shunned by Soviet history for 50 years. A spate of plays is being written about 1917 which include the roles of Trotsky, Kamenev and Zinoviev – heroes of the revolution who became victims of Stalin.

Brest Peace, a new play by Mikhail Shatrov about the decision to end the war with the Germans in 1918, will be premièred on the Bolshoi stage this year. Fyodor Burlatsky, one of Mr Gorbachev's speechwriters, is completing a play called 1927 about the events after Lenin's death, which includes a role for the old dictator, Stalin, himself.

23 April, 1987

Martin Walker

A civilizing mission to Greenham

Amidst all their troubles with traditional enemies like Russia and Congress, Pentagon planners have not forgotten the beleaguered US service families of Greenham Common. Buried among the million-million dollars worth of small print in the new 1988 budget is a modest $2.1m plan to build a youth club for the base along with a repair centre for amateur car mechanics and even an arts and craft shop.

First indications from the Pentagon last night suggested that the scheme is not part of a belated hearts and minds gesture to win over the Greenham peace women, which would have ranked as the worst policy misjudgment since arms for Iran. The arts and craft shop would be solely for the 5,000 US military personnel and their dependants who service the 96 missiles and protect them from the peace women.

As such, it is part of a $776m package of schemes to improve American military facilities worldwide – including $70m in Britain – and appears to suggest that the Defence Department is banking on a long stay in rural Berkshire, whatever deal Reagan and Gorbachev may have contemplated in Reykjavik to remove all cruise missiles and their Soviet counterparts from European soil.

With congressional Democrats and budget-cutters sharpening their razors to get to work on the 1988 budget, the arts and craft shop may never bloom with New England quilts or New Mexico pottery. 'We have nothing more specific on it at this stage,' said Lieutenant-Commander Chris Baumann, one of the many middle-ranking officers confined to less exciting Washington duties than Colonel Oliver North, as instruments of the Reagan Administration's overt action strategy press relations.

'It is something we are working for and until it is approved not even the specifics will be laid down. We have a lot of other things to be funded and we're not going to start spinning our wheels for something which may not happen,' said Lt-Cdr Baumann with the caution of a man whose own department is seeking 16 new ships this year, including $660m as down payment on an aircraft carrier.

Congress is supposed to be impressed by the defence planners' concern for the welfare of its voters-in-uniform, which is an integral feature of this year's budget sales pitch, along with investment in Star Wars technology and some hi-tech weaponry.

The planners may be onto a better thing with their assumption that no interim agreement between the superpowers is imminent on zero-zero Euro-missiles. At a briefing here this week, the Greenham women's *bête noire*, Assistant Defence Secretary Mr Richard Perle, was optimistic about arms control progress now that Moscow has given up its efforts to derail Star Wars. 'Far from mobilizing pressure from our allies, our allies have been having second thoughts about how fast and how far they wish to go with respect to nuclear disarmament,' he noted with satisfaction.

9 January, 1987

Michael White

Live babies

'This sense of critical fragility (myself, my wife, my daughter, even the poor planet baby-blue in its shawls), it drove me from my study in the end,' says the fraught young writer who narrates the best story in this little bomb, I mean book.* What it drove Martin Amis to do was produce a set of variations and dark fugues on the theme: Nuclear weapons – will they get us (and our children and our children's unborn children for ever) before we get rid of them?

It's a touching comeuppance for the brilliantly gifted fiction-brat who called his first novel *Dead Babies* that the arrival of a baby of his own should have made him come out so fiercely and vulnerably. In fact, Amis tells us in an urgent polemical preface, half the stories were written before he realized what they were on about; and then, he says, he saw that in a sense this had been his theme all along.

It's easy to see that the first story, 'Bujak and The Strong Force', is a strong one and the last – an immortal's jaded reflections on the whole peculiar human enterprise – rather weak. But the insight at the heart of them all and Amis's response to it produce an effect that seems more than the sum of these varyingly successful parts.

The most curious story provides a clue to this effect. In 'The Little Puppy That Could', the earth itself is retching and fevered in the aftermath of some nuclear extravaganza. A sickly community of survivors partly-living on the rim of a reeking crater is terrorized by a vast and monstrously misbegotten man-eating dog, the incarnation and end-product of all that has gone wrong with a corrupted nature: a dire and dirty dog, 'boiling and bursting with whole ecologies of trapped viruses, germs and microbes: anthrax, foul brood, rinderpest, staggers, scours, glanders . . .' And into this dark shambles hopefully gambols the title's parody of innocence and tender amiability, a *puppy* . . .

* *Einstein's Monsters* by Martin Amis (Cape).

'Deliver my darling from the power of the dog': even before one has tuned in exactly to the ironic tone (a mixture of Nabokov, Kafka and Sendak) one picks up suddenly another powerful signal, a memory of that strange cry in the psalm. The effect of the parable and of the book as a whole comes from the tension between that primal protective terror for the young and the realization that love's vulnerability generates its own 'strong force' to oppose to the stock-piled monsters of the nuclear sleep of reason.

'Failing to get the point about nuclear weapons is like failing to get the point about human life,' writes Amis in his introduction, and who better than the little people to remind you what the point is? Who better to make ineluctably clear what it is, by contrast, that nuclear weapons stand for, in all their fear-corrupted, life-denying, future-devouring, suicidal fatuity? ('They make me feel,' says Amis, 'as if a child of mine has been out too long, much too long, and already it is getting dark.')

In 'Bujak and The Strong Force', the insight is mediated differently. It is about a huge, heroic emigré Pole, 'all his life in the resistance', a man who 'had lived the twentieth century. And then, one day, the twentieth century came calling on him.' His cherished family of improbable survivors is wiped out in a night of moronic, affectless violence typical of the times, leaving him bereft of his old vengeful strength – but not, in the end, of his humanity.

This other parable about violence and the countervailing power of love ends with a beautiful fable from physics, of time running backwards and healing the wounds, undoing the wrongs, restoring experience to innocence and infancy, a flight as perfect and consoling as the final paragraphs of Joyce's *The Dead*.

But before we settle for the consolations of art, hands up all those who know they'll find a way of *not* seriously reducing the stock of nuclear weapons this summer. Quite. So for something more recruiting, turn back to Amis's introduction, which is too anxiously hard on E. P. Thompson, but shrewd about the Reaganomics or military-industrial complexities of the situation. ('It would seem, at the time of writing, that the Soviet

Union can't afford to go on, and that the United States can't afford to stop.')

It ends with a distinctly post-modern bedtime story, a Carrollean fancy of our nuclear world as a tea party of badly behaved children who are guarded by obscenely terrifying Keepers, 'a thousand feet tall, and covered in gelignite and razor-blades . . . fizzing with rabies, anthrax and plague . . . mouthing foul threats at each other . . .

'The party has not been going for very long and must last until the end of time. Already the children are weepy and feverish. They all feel sick and want to go home.'

1 May, 1987   **W. L. Webb**

A song of the sacred land

It is now common knowledge that the people who lived in Australia before the island continent was given that name never got around to inventing the wheel because they were too absorbed in metaphysics. This could be seen as a positive argument against metaphysics, for the contemplation of the transcendental did not equip the first Australians sufficiently against the sudden arrival of technologically adept and ethically unscrupulous invaders. But Bruce Chatwin's expository novel *The Songlines* (Cape) is both a defence of Aboriginal metaphysics as a way of life and a piece of metaphysical speculation in its own right.

Human beings, Bruce Chatwin posits, are born to wander; indeed, the source of all evil is to settle down. Appropriately, the form of his novel is that of a journey. Its hero, an Englishman named Bruce, travels into the magical aridity Australians call the Centre, in order, for compelling reasons of his own, to find out what a 'songline' is. His guide is a wise young man of Cossack extraction called Arkady.

Arkady is employed to map out the sacred sites of the Aboriginals so that a proposed new railway line will not destroy

113

a single one of them. This, as he points out, is difficult, because 'if you look at it *their* way . . . the whole of bloody Australia is a sacred site'.

A sacred site, which the totemic ancestors – the grand, original wallaby, and budgerigar, and lizard and so on – once, literally, sang into existence, stone by stone, thorn by thorn; they sang into being that vast, dry, almost supernaturally beautiful country. A country which is continually being sung into existence again and again during the ritual journeyings, the walkabouts, of the tribespeople. (I hope I've got this right. It is all very complicated.)

'In theory, at least, the whole of Australia could be read as a musical score,' says Bruce Chatwin. A musical score of stunning complexity and numinous significance, of which the learning is the most imperative business in the whole world. He quotes Heidegger, from 'What Are Poets For?': 'The song still remains which names the land over which it sings.' The singing goes on and if there is no proof that it maintains the world in its precarious existence, neither is there proof that it does not.

The searcher after songlines meets and talks with strange, learned, displaced men and women, among them a policeman whose passions are weight-lifting and Spinoza; a furious old bush-crazed Communist who gives an account of the atom-bomb tests at Maralinga in the mode of black farce; a naked philosopher of the bush who gives as his occupation: 'Footwalking all the time all over the world.'

Footwalking is Bruce Chatwin's passion, too, and in the course of nearly 300 pages he investigates the significance not only of the songlines, that mythic and incorporeal map of Australia, but also of his own travels, especially those among the nomadic peoples of Africa, pulling everything together to form a grand theory of footwalking, and much more. And all this springs from an obsession with what the Eskimo calls 'the Great Unrest', a conviction that human beings, just as birds do, feel an irrepressible urge from time to time to migrate, to slough off attachments, to get on the move and stay there.

More specifically, Chatwin conjectures that 'Natural Selection has designed us – from the structure of our brain-cells to

114

the structure of our big toe – for a career of seasonal journeys *on foot* through a blistering land of thorn-scrub or desert'.

The narrative of Bruce's journey is interspersed with digressions such as a visit to a solitary priest who has carved above the door of his hut the apt legend: 'Foxes have holes, birds of the air have nests but the Son of Man had no place to lay his head.' This priest says of a friendly marsupial: 'My brother the wallaby.' Who could resist the notion of an Antipodean St Francis?

There is an equally endearing account of another visit, to the Nemadi, wanderers of the Saharan Empty Quarter, known as 'Outcasts of the Wilderness', where an ancient, deaf and dumb old lady gives Bruce a smile that lasts a full three minutes; a smile, he tells us, 'like a message from the Golden Age'. A smile that teaches him to reject out of hand all arguments for the nastiness of human nature. (As a tramp he meets outside the London Library finds out, Bruce is a very soft touch indeed; he seems to have lost all trace of cynicism on just those very roads where most travellers acquire it).

The Australian journey eventually founders in a flash flood in a remote Pintupi settlement, where Bruce finds time to unpack his notebooks of a lifetime's journeying. The remainder of the book is largely composed of sections taken from these notebooks, a patchwork of quotations – Pascale, Gautama Buddha, the Bible and I don't know what else, memories and, increasingly, speculation. Here, the fictional Bruce and the real Bruce Chatwin seem to come together.

The patchwork is assembled with a good deal of art. Rimbaud's heartfelt cry from Ethiopia, 'What am I doing here?', is juxtaposed with an account of a vile town in Brazil: 'The stucco façade is painted a pale mint green with the words CHARM HOTEL in bold, black letters. A leaking gutter pipe has washed away the letter C, so that it now reads . . .'

Bruce Chatwin discusses the nature of the murder of Abel, the wandering herdsman, by Cain, the gardener; was Cain jealous of the free spirit? He proposes the superior ethics of the hunter-gatherers; he has an aristocratic disdain for what you could call roots and quotes a Bedouin proverb: 'Raids are our agriculture.'

He recalls an interview with Konrad Lorenz, who wrote *On Aggression*, and this leads into a series of speculations on instinctual behaviour, the origins of human society, the possible origins of our fear of the dark, the nature of fear in babies, the instincts of mothers and children. When he cites John Bowlby's work in this connection, however, I felt a tremor of unease, for Bowlby's work has very largely been discredited, if not by other child psychologists then certainly by women at the sharp end of babies. And the speculation shows signs of turning into very sophisticated science fiction – science fiction in the purest sense; speculative fiction about science.

So, at last, we arrive in the Transvaal, gazing with Bruce Chatwin at the fossilized bones of the earliest members of humanity, perhaps the very earliest, for it is out of Africa that many people now believe came memory and language, the qualities that make us human. Magnificently, rather crazily. Bruce Chatwin offers us his own version of the Fall of Man. But it is not a Fall at all; he hypothesizes that at the very beginning of the human race we did not succumb to the Prince of Darkness but, instead, vanquished him.

We arrive at this awesome piece of theological revisionism thus: in those days, there roamed a Beast – Bruce Chatwin thinks it may have been some kind of giant leopard – which preyed specifically upon primates. On the conquest of this fatal creature depended the fate of Man on earth. When we invented the weapon, we overcame the forces of destruction, the terrible Beast whose memory, to this day, scares little babies and haunts our own imaginations with needless fears. 'Compared to this victory, the rest of our achievements may be seen as so many frills.' Even if the Beast bowed out of history and left us with the weapon in our hands.

When Bruce finally returns to his own narrative, it is to conclude with Arkady's wedding, but the true romance of this always enchanting, sometimes infuriating book is not that of Arkady and Marian but the one between an Englishman and the wilderness. The journey of the one within the other leads to the only happy ending the traveller can honestly aspire to, a happy death.

In the bush, Bruce and his companions visit three old men

at a ritual site; they have sung their way back where they belong. Three old men who knew where they were going, 'smiling at death in the shade of a ghost-gum'.

26 June, 1987 **Angela Carter**

Writing about the sycamores

'Seamus is going to get almost everything,' one of his fellow poets says, 'but he is never going to write a masterpiece.' A lot of people believe he already has, and he has a new book out this week, *The Haw Lantern* (Faber). Seamus Heaney's reputation has arched upward for 20 years now, bright and high as a rainbow. His undoubted personal charm is part of that reputation.

'He is remarkably untainted by anecdote,' says another poet, which in a literary world run by gossip is itself unusual. Yet despite his many public readings and the word of mouth accolades and the blessings of critics there has to be some further reason for his huge popularity. So what is it?

To some extent it depends on which side of the Irish Sea you ask the question. Few critics either side doubt that Heaney is a very good poet. Craig Raine, himself a poet and Heaney's editor at Faber, is clear enough: 'One of his greatest achievements to me is that he has an absolutely direct way with language that collapses the gap between poetry and living. Take those lines in "Field Work" [the title poem in an earlier book] about "The tart green shade of summer/thick with butterflies/ and fungus plump as a leather saddle." You know exactly what that fungus looks like and the literariness doesn't seem to get in the way.'

Over at the rival house of Chatto, another poet and publisher, Andrew Motion, doesn't have much hesitation in rating Heaney more highly than anyone else around: 'His poetry has that sensuous recall that you find very rarely . . . He does address one of the major themes, childhood, in a fabulous way. He puts the shine back on things that I did know once.'

117

And Philip Hobsbaum, the poet-academic who first picked Heaney out of the rut of undergraduates to join his writing group at Queen's University in Belfast, is equally sure: 'One reason why his work is so popular is that it is so attractive in texture. He uses language in a very tactile way, and it's intelligible.'

But there are other, less literary reasons why Heaney has become not just a critical but a popular success, and they are better understood in Ireland than in London. Though, there, his critics are sometimes wary. Heaney is a national asset, an export – he teaches part of the year at Harvard. To knock him might seem like spitting in Guinness.

'He's a splendid writer,' said one, 'but he wouldn't seem to me to be a genius. He hasn't fought the current the way Joyce and Lawrence did. We are still asked to believe in the old world, the old farm. What we get with Heaney is that the old world is still out there. It's an idealized sort of farm life: horses, walls, pumps. You don't get tractors much, you don't smell the silage. These are not our factory farms, our EEC farmers with their eye on the butter mountain.'

Heaney was born in 1939 to a large Roman Catholic farming family in Co. Derry. He grew up on the edge of two parishes. Lived in one, went to school and played football in another. 'I always had a sense, from an early age, of division. So Terminus was the God of Boundaries, and I thought I would write about him.' He won his way to a boarding school in Londonderry, and on to Queen's in Belfast.

Hobsbaum recalls that he was not seen as an undergraduate star – his friend Seamus Deane then shone brighter. In 'Singing School', dedicated to Deane (now a Dublin academic), Heaney pins the difference between them:

Those poems in longhand, ripped from the wire spine
Of your exercise book, bewildered me –
Vowels and ideas bandied free
As the seed-pods blowing off our sycamores.
I tried to write about the sycamores . . .

Heaney went to teach in a school off the Falls Road. But the schools inspector, a Protestant, was so impressed that he recommended he should be sent to 'teach other people how to teach'. Hobsbaum says: 'He is a good poet, but he is an even better teacher. I've seen him working at the teachers' training college. He listens. He could make a person talk sense simply by the quality of his attention.'

He began writing poetry around 1962, influenced by Ted Hughes and others who had reacted against the smooth urban poetry of the Fifties and sought sustenance in the backyard grit of rural life. His first collection, *Death of a Naturalist*, came out in 1966.

The timing is significant in his popularity, as some critics see it. He emerged at the beginning of ecological consciousness. And maybe more important, he emerged as the bright new young poet at a time when television was becoming important in Ireland, and he was perfectly placed by then, teaching at Queen's. 'He's very photogenic, not in the conventional sense, but he's large, he's warm, he's kind, he's a wonderful television presence – and he'd never get angry and say something silly.'

He was also the rising star at a time when people were looking for a spokesman for what was happening in Northern Ireland. He was on the edge of the civil rights movement, though he has never really been a deeply political man, and he had a foot in both the literary and the academic world.

In 1972, Heaney moved to the Republic, and it made front page news in the Irish papers. Three years later, he published *North*, the collection of poems that, as seen in England, at last confronted the Troubles. Yet that was essentially an English perception. No one in Ireland had been uncertain about his position. Though his poetry up till then had not overtly dealt with the civil strife, even his earliest collection contained references to latent violence.

'My poetry is not sectarian,' he told a *Guardian* interviewer a decade ago, 'but it has been deeply affected by the smells of sectarianism.' And later: 'There are certain humiliations available to Catholics that aren't available to Protestants.' The significant word, of course, is 'available'. No one but a writer would use it; no one but a poet could use it so deliberately.

North referred to the North of the Vikings, not directly to Ulster. The discovery of the ritual sacrifice victims preserved in bog – a central theme of the most important poems in this volume – were seen here as metaphor for the Troubles, buried in the history of Ireland. But to some of his Irish critics – including those who were trying to reflect the violent realities – it looked like Heaney once again distancing himself from the blood.

'There's hardly any Viking influence in the North at all,' says one. 'There are no bog burials there, no ritual sacrifice. This is all Nordic violence; to equate those sagas with Northern Ireland is an oversimplification.' This is in line with the other criticism: that the bogs that figure so much in Heaney's imagery are what Ireland has been trying to get rid of since the Thirties; that by the end of the war and the beginning of Heaney's childhood consciousness Northern Ireland had become even more the mechanized market garden of England than Kent, where crashed bombers had, of course, become a main crop. Tractors were flooding into Northern Ireland by then, and the old farming patterns had in most places already disappeared.

From this perspective, Heaney's early poetry already celebrated a romanticized past and *North*, the turning point in his career, took refuge in myths. *Station Island*, published three years ago, emphasized an antique Catholicism that Joyce and others had rejected, and been rejected by. 'All that guilt and breast-beating and walking barefoot on Station Island,' as one poet puts it. 'He was an altar server, and he remembers it.'

The doubts are not confined to Ireland. Motion, despite marking him top, does have reservations. 'What concerns me, and concerns me in his new book, is how that rare quality of sensuous recall is combined with his more intellectualized methods, which seem more to the fore now – and I'm not sure that's his forte. His work has become more unsettled, as though he is searching for some way to bring those two things together. It's still deeply interesting work, but I'd be sorry if the marriage of those two sides of his writing continued to be as bumpy as it is now.'

Hobsbaum, who has no hesitation in declaring Heaney 'a great man, who's not achieved his peak yet', does not feel happy about *North*. 'His main problem is a personal element. I don't think he's really cynical enough to understand politics.'

But Heaney is now an international figure. And perhaps everywhere his popularity – as opposed to his deservedly high critical standing – tells us as much about our expectations of poetry as it does about him. Poetry at the popular level is still the comforter, not the spur; the myth and not the vision.

25 June, 1987   **Hugh Hebert**

Joy and grief

Last week, I was nastily roughed up while trying to cover a political protest in Moscow's old Arbat. The bruises faded fast, but the sad thing is that I will never again be able to stroll down one of my favourite Moscow streets without thinking of that beating.

The Arbat has become for me a very real symbol of the changes taking place in the Soviet Union. First, the street itself has been preserved in all its nineteenth-century higgledy-piggledy charm. Just a hundred yards away there is the 'new Arbat', a soul-less eight-lane thoroughfare lined with high-rise buildings of dingy grey concrete. But the old Arbat is pretty much as it was in Tsarist days, except that it has been made into a pedestrian precinct. There are some pretty cafés, including a charming place for children, with miniature furniture, to which unaccompanied adults are not admitted. There is the video salon, where you can hire old Eisenstein movies and modern Russian films.

At the western end of the Arbat is the Foreign Ministry, and at the other end the Praga restaurant, still one of the best places in Moscow, where diplomats, Soviet officials and correspondents tend to lunch.

And it remains the artistic centre of Moscow. I forget how many times I have groped up semi-lit staircases to the garrets on top floors where the painters have their studios. They serve you tea and warm glasses of Pepsi as they show off the canvases they know will never be exhibited in public.

Pushkin lived here after his marriage, and so did Lermontov. The Arbat has a magic about it – one of those places that was always at its best just a few years before you got there. It is Moscow's Greenwich Village, its Left Bank, its King's Road, Chelsea. The country's music and literature is stuffed with references to the place. One of my favourite singer–songwriters, Bulat Okudzhava, wrote a very pretty melody for a song that goes:

> Oh Arbat, my Arbat,
>   my homeland is Arbat,
> You're my joys, and source of
>   all my grief.

On a summer evening, when half the city seems to be strolling down its wide paving and there is light in the northern sky until almost midnight, you hear the song hummed from every side.

And then you look at the pretty girls in their stylish dresses, watch the people watching the world go by as they sit in the Arbat cafés, see the crowds come out from the Vakhtangova theatre buzzing with the latest play, you hear laughter and music and you think that Moscow is about to take its place among the great European cities.

You think that at last, after the cultural clampdown and the years of Iron Curtain and thought police, the place has fundamentally changed. I suppose a lot of my optimism about Gorbachev and the future of this country came from evening strolls in the Arbat, from the conversations that went on till dawn in those garrets and other Arbat flats.

I remember standing in the antiquarian bookshop, where I was buying some old prints of Moscow, and getting into a conversation with a middle-aged Russian writer who knew more about the plays of George Bernard Shaw than I will ever remember, and he recited from memory St Joan's last speech as we strolled off down the Arbat to his flat.

I remember walking down the Arbat last autumn with a Soviet diplomat from the Foreign Ministry who was still thrilled by the glimmering of real hope he felt after the Reykjavik summit. He tried to overcome my scepticism at the thought of superpowers voluntarily giving up the nukes that defined their status.

And I enjoyed walking into the little courtyards, going down side streets, and turning into the wide archways that used to take horses and carriages, joining the old men playing chess under the courtyard trees, and the grannies looking after the babies.

But the courtyard I will remember now is the one that leads to the police station, the one down which I saw women being hurled like sacks of potatoes, where my TV colleagues were swatted into the gutter like so many troublesome flies.

I hope the old Arbat can work its seductive magic on me again, that the ugliness of last week was an aberration in a bumpy progress towards a better society. I can hope, but now I understand a little better Okudzhava's song about how the Arbat can also be the source of all one's grief.

16 February, 1987

Martin Walker

Playing for time at the abyss

On the last day of January 1986 President P. W. Botha of South Africa came under strong suspicion of making a joke. In an unscripted addition to his speech opening Parliament he offered to release Nelson Mandela if the Russians set free Anatoly Scharansky and Andrei Sakharov. It may reasonably be assumed that Mr Botha thought such a Soviet move so unlikely that he felt he could get away with another jibe at the Communists he blames for all South Africa's woes. Two days later, the release of Mr Scharansky was actually announced. At the time it looked as though Mr Botha must have been in on the secret, thanks to the still thriving relationship between Western and South African intelligence services, and could not resist the chance to display a touch of contrived clairvoyance, secure in the certitude that at least Dr Sakharov, of all people, would never be freed. This month, however, the joke, if such it was, turned sour when Mr Gorbachev proved himself to be rather more flexible than Mr Botha by letting Dr Sakharov and his wife return to Moscow. Mr Mandela is, of course, still inside Pollsmoor prison, and still the outstanding hero of black South Africa, after passing his twenty-fourth Christmas in captivity at the age of 68. This was not to be the only broken promise of 1986.

As late as October this year the South African regime was still placing advertisements in British publications trumpeting the changes it had made in apartheid and concluding with a plea for recognition and encouragement: 'We think we've come quite a long way in ten years.' There have been many changes indeed, but the erstwhile inhabitants of the vast Cape squatter-camp of Crossroads may find the claim that 'enforced population resettlement has been ended' hard to understand. In two bloody days, months before the advertisements vanished, more than 60,000 people were forced out of their homes by black 'vigilantes' wearing white armbands to protect them from police interference, and the bulldozers moved in. Thousands upon thousands of other Africans have been forced to move out of a good dozen other camps and townships round the country. The unctuous advertisements also said that 'a multi-racial National Statutory Council is being legislated for', to give the African majority a say in government and to draw up a new constitution. No such body exists, no law has been passed to establish it, no bill has been tabled to this end, not one black has been named as a potential member – not even Chief Buthelezi of KwaZulu, whose inclination to join, if any, must have been severely dented by the out-of-hand rejection of his plan for power-sharing in Natal. Even the Chief demands the release of his perceived rival, Nelson Mandela, as a precondition for joining such a hypothetical body.

The advertisement was headed 'South Africa: the untold story'. Since 11 December, when total censorship of unauthorized news about any form of opposition to the regime was imposed, there is another untold story. We do not, by definition, know what is is but recent events entitle us to make an educated guess. The Minister of Justice recently admitted that a total of 'from 6,000 to 7,000 plus' were being held in detention as he spoke, without charge or trial; the Commissioner of Police confessed that 256 of these were aged between 11 and 15. A string of court cases has proved the use of torture against detainees. The censorship could not prevent the news of the controversial death of a detainee from leaking out at Christmas. The best computation available of the number of deaths from political violence since September 1984 now stands at about 2,300, of whom 1,300 died in 1986 compared with 900 or so in 1985. The news blackout means that any future victims must suffer in silence; that there will be more victims seems beyond doubt, if only because the Government's excuse for the clampdown is a 'total onslaught' from within and without. We are still expected to believe that but for Communist interference the Africans would be perfectly content with their lot, and that the whites were intent on ensuring racial justice all along without any need for internal unrest or foreign pressure. What South Africa's neighbours have to look forward to was swiftly shown by the despatch of a remarkably incompetent snatch-squad into Swaziland, which the Foreign Minister said he would be just as happy to repeat in Britain if necessary.

That there was a sea-chance in Mr Botha's policy in May was proved by developments in August analogous to Sherlock Holmes's curious incident of the dog in the night-time. A special federal congress of the National Party, only the third in its history, was called, and a special session of Parliament to follow immediately, for August. The President announced nothing of note on either occasion, any more than the dog had barked in the night. The announcement of a crowning reform, such as the much-heralded Statutory Council, perhaps followed by a white referendum or election to endorse it, had been expected. Instead, the State Security Council decided to impose a new, nationwide state of emergency in time for the dreaded tenth anniversary of the Soweto uprising in June and to have no more to do with foreign intervention, even if it meant serious sanctions. The Commonwealth Eminent Persons Group initiative, which had unexpectedly promised well, was sabotaged by South African raids on three Commonwealth states. Then Sir Geoffrey Howe's forlorn hope of a Euromission, the last of its kind, was greeted with a degree of boorishness seldom

25 November, 1986

matched in modern diplomatic history. But it was the US
Congress, where the British are not represented, rather than
the Commonwealth and the European Community, which took
the lead in forcing through the kind of sanctions for which the
South Africans had been given far too much time to brace
themselves. It was the private sector and the free market,
beloved of Mr Reagan and Mrs Thatcher, which added most
effectively to the external pressure as General Motors and
Barclays Bank took to the lifeboats.

So 1986 joins 1985 as another year in which the South African
state played for time and did nothing that might have prepared
the way for a better future. Enough opinion polls have been
taken now to show that a majority of whites recognize that
black rule, or at least a black share in real power, is inevitable.
But the Afrikaner Nationalists running the state are still obsessed by the ultra-Right who believe that any concession to
the black majority means doom. Now there is a white election
in the offing. In these terms, Mr Botha's decision to receive
Mr Eugene Terre'Blanche, the convicted terrorist and former

policeman who leads the nazified AWB (Afrikaner Resistance Movement) – after his storm troopers had broken up televised National Party meetings – is his supreme political blunder of the year. So long as white politics dominate his thinking, as they have done since May, if not all along, there will be no more reform worthy of the name. As he is already 70, there is probably nothing more to be expected from him even after an election. Meanwhile South Africa has taken several more steps down the road to totalitarianism during the past year. We can only predict more of the same for 1987.

27 December, 1986   **Leader**

Some people: 2

Finished breakfast? Good. The Hippodrome, Peter String-fellow's flashy London nightclub, is not kidding when it promises a Bad Taste night next month. They're putting on a recreation of a nasty car crash, complete with seriously injured passenger and stunned survivors. This can be inspected at your leisure without some policeman saying: 'Move along now, sir, you don't want to look at this.' You can, you can! There's also 'a completely authentic hangman's lever' for you to pull, with a spy hole to watch the results.

Consolidated Goldfields, owner of 48 per cent of Goldfields of South Africa, has a motley collection of shareholders, as World in Action found out for their documentary on low-paid migrant labour in the gold mines this week. The list from March this year has Sir Michael Havers (302 shares) and David Wadding-ton (300) representing the Government. From entertainment, Esther Rantzen (242), Alan Ayckbourn (2,700), Pamela Ayres (729) and Michael Hordern (6,414); from religion, the Bible Training Institute of Glasgow (800), the Catholic Child Welfare Society, Leeds and Hallam (700), and the SPCK Pension Trust (10,700); and from the media, William Deedes (1,100) and the

Press Association (10,000). Even the Wireless for the Bedridden Society has 2,400.

Two ironic sidelights on the publication of the British Gas prospectus yesterday. County emergency planners are engaged in simulating a nuclear war, and yesterday was the moment when gas supplies were switched off to minimize the bangs. And NatWest's securities analysts are apparently telling customers that one reason for not investing in British Gas is that this is Peter Walker's Energy Conservation Year.

26 November, 1986

Stephen Cook

Hoist with his own shot foot

The Environment Secretary, Mr Nicholas Ridley, a judge ruled last week, has been 'hoist with his own petard'. This is an embarrassing condition at the best of times, and in any but the most metaphorical circumstances a potentially fatal one. Mr Ridley is by no means the first, or most famous, victim. Persillus of Athens, having built a brazen bull for Phalaris, tyrant of Agrigentum, is said to have been instructed by his master to climb inside, thus becoming the first man to be boiled alive within his invention; while the builder of the Bastille, Hugues Aubriot, shortly afterwards became the first man to be incarcerated within its formidable walls. The fate of both men predated the petard, which is not, as many suppose, some kind of flagpole – from which Mr Ridley is now flying, possibly at half-mast – but an engine of war which could be filled with gunpowder and strapped to the gates of a city under siege. This was a hazardous process in two senses, demanding operators of almost kamikaze qualities: first because the artilleryman was likely to have boiling oil poured down upon him while doing the strapping by those he was besieging, and second because petards had a habit of exploding before those who used them were able to retire to a safe distance. It is this latter calamity which Hamlet had in mind when he said after the death of Polonius: ''Tis the sport to have the engineer/hoist with his own petard.'

It is probably this sentence alone which has preserved the petard for posterity. Its working life was brief, if gory. Possibly introduced by the Huguenots in the 1570s, it was soon to be superseded by less counter-productive technologies. There are none to be bought in London today, even from the most ruthlessly entrepreneurial arms exporters. But for Shakespeare's reference, it would be as forgotten now as such other staples of sixteenth-century artillery as the esmerial (or rabinet), the pasavolonte, the minion and even the culverin bastard.

Even now, it cannot be said to have penetrated the language in the way that other, humbler items of metaphorical hardware like the wedge (thin end of) have done. Judges, like Mr Justice Taylor, or politicians, like the Labour spokesman Mr Jack Straw who quoted the judge's words at Mr Ridley this week, invoke the concept almost daily. But it is unusual to hear petards spoken of in the public bar, on the top of a bus, or on football terraces – even at the Arsenal. To customers there, Petard, if it means anything at all, suggests only a full-back who used to play for Cardiff City. The man in the street, confronted with the baking alive of Persillus or the defeat of Nicholas Ridley at the hands of Greenwich Council, sees them not so much as victims of terminal self-ignition but as the scorers of unusually calamitous own goals.

7 March, 1987

Leader

Leaders and readers

When he was a *Guardian* leader writer Malcolm Muggeridge (long before sainthood beckoned) regarded the leader writers' room as a laboratory of throbbing brains. Others imagine a gallery of skeletal drones ruthlessly winnowing fudge as they survey the drear edges and naked shingles of the world.

But there, as they are wont to write, let us pause. The current inmates seem as reassuringly bewildered by life's peripeteia as the rest of us; all the more so after being told in the first ever thesis on leader writing that *Guardian* editorials are a negotiation of value judgments in a linguistic interaction with readers.

Adriana Bolivar is a Venezuelan professor of English who has wrestled for five years (two at Birmingham University) with *Guardian* editorials to produce her 500-page paper entitled 'Interaction Through Written Text – A Discourse Analysis of Newspaper Editorials'.

Solely concerned with linguistics ('I know nothing about English politics') she was first interested to identify the kind of reader whom leader writers are addressing.

'The *Guardian* reader is a highly sophisticated person,' she says (Preen, preen). 'If you take the first leader, which usually relates to the important event of the day, very often it only alludes to the event. Unless you know what's going on you don't understand the text.'

Moreover, she found our editorials to have a complex internal structure masquerading as three basic parts: presentation, analysis and conclusions. (This might seem obvious, but Japanese papers introduce a fourth part for reasons of face – 'For instance, the leader might be discussing attitudes to women, and then brings in a car accident.')

Questions feature strongly, she found. 'Questions are important because they give the reader a chance to think and disagree. Whereas the *Times* reader expects more information and to be told what to think, *Guardian* readers expect something like, "We all know what's going on. We think this; what do you think?"'

She detects an attempt at informality through the use of conversational patterns of address, reinforced by liberal punctuation and frequent asides in parenthesis. (That's enough brackets. – Ed.)

Would she say, on the one hand, that *Guardian* editorials hedge, or, on the other, that they don't? 'The persuasion element is there, but it's indirect,' she believes. 'Your leaders use concluders like, "If we do this, then things would improve," although they often say, "Mrs Thatcher should do this".'

In her native city of Caracas the editorial in *El Nacional* consists of one sentence in a box. I put this to one of our leader-writing team. 'Abdication of responsibility,' he growled in horror.

22 November, 1986

Stuart Wavell

Rhyme and reason

Of course, as anyone who reads the *Daily Telegraph* can tell you, our classrooms are dominated by teachers who are either Marxist–Leninists or card-carrying members of the Red Army Faction. And it is, perhaps, one of the blackest marks against Mrs Thatcher's government that she has failed to uproot them all from our schools.

She has done her best to alienate them from public opinion, by persuading them to strike for the first time in their history, and she has waged a remarkably successful campaign to lower their morale to a point where a good many of them are by now thoroughly ashamed of still being teachers. She has even deprived them of resources and materials in an attempt to starve the trouble-makers out. And yet, in spite of it all, there are still teachers in charge of our children today who may vote other than Tory at the next election! Incredible, isn't it?

Under these circumstances, it can't be any surprise to anyone that the Government has finally been forced to impose what it calls 'a National Curriculum' on our schools. This means that instead of allowing irresponsible and revolutionary teachers to decide what to teach their pupils, the Government decides for them.

And why not? The Government (I'm sorry, I mean Mr Norman Tebbit, who as chairman of the Conservative Party is, of course, completely independent of the Government) now tells the BBC what it should include in its newscasts, so why not start getting public thinking into line right from the nursery?

To help in this great endeavour, I'd like to offer up a small contribution of my own. This is a politically correct Alphabet for compulsory use in infant schools, which is designed to instil the high values of the Prime Minister into the minds of our children even as they learn to read.

I'm not sure that some of it couldn't be improved somewhat, but I hope that readers will write in with their own suggestions or even complete alphabets.

THATCHER ALPHABET

A for her ABILITY (to prove black is white)
B for her BELIEF (that she's always right)
C for her CARING (when choosing her clothes)
D for her DARING (to do things one loathes)
E for her ENERGY (which is nuclear-powered)
F for her FALL-OUT (with which we are showered)
G for her GENEROSITY (when not sparing the rod)
H for her HUMBLENESS (shown only to God)
I for her INTELLIGENCE (at GCHQ)
J for her JUSTICE (reserved for the few)
K for her KNOWLEDGE (of the Westland Affair)
L for her LOVE (of a bald millionaire)
M for her MAJESTY (plain as her nose)
N for her NOBILITY (whose titles she chose)
O for her OPENNESS (to Jimmy Young)
P for her POLITICS (she reads in the *Sun*)
Q for the QUANDARY (that she's never been in)
R for her REALISM (when her underlings sin)
S for the SINCERITY (with which she hates coal)
T for her TACT (counting those on the dole)
U for her UNDERSTANDING (of what the police need)
V for her VISION (of a world built on greed)
W for her WILL (to see money well-spent)
X for the VOTES (that she won't get in Brent)
Y for her YOUTH (and their employment schemes)
Z for her ZEST (in crushing their dreams).

29 April, 1987

Terry Jones

Into the blackboard jungle

Bob and Mary's Luncheonette in Yonkers is situated a stone's throw away from where the notorious Son of Sam mass murderer was arrested. He used to come in to buy cigarettes, and when the police tracked him down to his home, there was an excellent view of the whole ambush through the luncheonette's front window. Now Bob and Mary are in a strategic position to watch an even bigger local drama – Yonkers' reluctant desegregation of its school system 26 years after even Deep South racial fortresses like New Orleans gave in.

The Luncheonette opens long before dawn, and while darkness is still hiding the Hudson River just down the hill, you can find black teenagers playing video games there while waiting to be bussed to their new schools. Bob and Mary know them all by name and much about their families and their school progress, and they have already laid down the law that games can't be played half an hour before school is due to start. On one recent morning a youth begged to be allowed to finish an exciting game because he claimed he didn't have to go to school that day, but he was firmly shown the door.

A federal judge had to order the city to begin school desegregation at the start of the school year in September, and now that the first term is over, I checked at Bob and Mary's about the progress so far. The first proposal in this blue-collar racially divided city in Westchester County near New York City was to close the huge Lincoln High School, which was 88 per cent white, and bus the students to other schools. But the school board feared there would be 'war' if Lincoln was closed, so instead Yonkers High School, a predominantly minority school, was closed and 500 of its students transferred to Lincoln, which dropped to 56 per cent white.

Lincoln is situated in an almost all-white district and the first day of integrated education there in September police officers patrolled outside in riot gear. 'There were some fist fights and minor trouble,' Bob said, 'but nothing big.' From the viewpoint of the luncheonette, the first term has passed reasonably peacefully. You hear the same from school and police officials and even the children. In the case of Lincoln, black students were transferring to a school that had a car park for students with often over 100 cars, whereas at Yonkers High the most students had had was a bicycle. 'I thought they were all rich and I'd be out of place,' said one black student, 'but I found out their parents are just ordinary people, construction workers, police, storekeepers, folk like that. Most of them moved to Yonkers from the Bronx.'

On the white side, Yonkers High had been regarded as a 'tough school' and it was thought many of the students transferred from there would be juvenile delinquents and gang leaders. In the first few weeks white and black students kept their distance, but slowly the newcomers began to take part in school activities, and integration began.

Like Bob and Mary, School Superintendent Donald Batista thinks what he calls the first phase – desegregation – is going well. That is achieved by moving students, and the bussing, after problems with timetables, has worked smoothly. Mr Batista echoed Bob and Mary when he added: 'The second phase is the hardest – integration, socializing together, living together. That's a long-term process, if it ever occurs. We're on the right road, but I wouldn't call it a raging success at this point.'

If you visit one of the integrated schools, you can see what he means immediately. Most of the white students are with whites, most of the blacks with blacks, like their parents in the racially divided neighbourhoods in which they live. One white student said frankly: 'I was mad at first because I am really prejudiced and am not used to being with so many blacks, but now it isn't that bad because I know a lot of people and no one bothers me, not even the blacks.' And a black girl gave her version: 'I hated Lincoln High School the first time I saw it and the students there already hated the integration plan, but now I feel reasonably happy there and I've met so many students from different backgrounds and cultures.'

Usually these cheerful reports come from top students who have little difficulty in adapting to new classes, but at Bob and Mary's you find concern especially for the students waiting for their buses who arrive to play the video games with no school books. 'You had no homework?' Mary asks them and they mumble something and quickly leave. 'The homes they come from, it's hard to do homework even if you've got some,' Mary says.

Bob is also concerned about the cost of bussing even with state and federal help. The city nearly went bankrupt in 1984 and had to be bailed out with a state aid package and a variety of new taxes.

Yonkers' belated efforts have also reopened the controversy about the value of bussing. A mother who had to take three buses across the city to collect her child who was ill at her new school came into Bob and Mary's with a very dim view of the inconvenience bussing caused. But in an immigrant society like the United States, one generation has to pay for the advantages of the next, as Bob knows well because his father was an immigrant from Europe.

A recent national survey of writing samples from public and private school students showed what needs to be done. It concluded that most American students can write only at a minimal level and lack the communication and critical thinking skills needed in an advanced society. ('Most students, majority and minority alike, are unable to write adequately except in response to the simplest of tasks.')

Yonkers schools like all those covered by the survey are struggling to prepare students for a changing job market dominated by computers. Even from the viewpoint of Bob and Mary's, the problems of integrating the schools seem minor compared with the task of combating growing unemployment with more education, yet the two are closely related. And on top of that, Yonkers has something else to worry about – the Justice Department has asked for the city to be held in civil contempt for failing to comply with a federal court order to establish integrated housing. Living is still as segregated there as the schools used to be. At least Bob and Mary aren't involved with that. They live in Hartsdale.

9 January, 1967

W. J. Weatherby

A law unto itself

This is a story to make unbelievers believe in divine vengeance. Antioch Law School in Washington DC is the poorest, humblest law school in America. It specializes in public interest law – the kind of law practised in Britain under legal aid, or in our threatened law centres – poor people's law, criminal and civil. Founded 13 years ago in an era when helping the poor had some official support, it is now in danger of closure.

Until this year, Antioch enjoyed a large grant from the Legal Services Corporation, the government body that is responsible for legal aid funding. President Reagan decided to close the programme and appointed James H. Wentzel to dismantle most of the services the corporation is supposed to provide. Removal of the grant has been one factor in Antioch Law School's crisis.

But a delightful sense of divine justice descended on Antioch's students and teachers when the *Washington Post* ran a story that could finish the career of their persecutor – James H. Wentzel. The *Post* told how George Pearse, a student of Antioch, was working one night as a security guard in a grocery store outside Washington. He claimed he saw a man in a smart suit acting suspiciously, and kept an eye on him. He watched him take a pack of Big Wheel snack cakes, put them in his pocket and leave the store without paying. When challenged the man was also found to have a packet of ham and a tin of succotash (mixed vegetables). 'This is going to ruin me,' he is reported to have said.

He said he was a lawyer with the Legal Services Corporation and finally that his name was James H. Wentzel and that he was president of the corporation. Pearse checked his identity by calling Wentzel's unlisted number at home to speak to his wife. He made him sign a confession and later the student identified both Wentzel and his new jeep.

This bizarre story broke the night I was visiting my friend, Shelley Broderick, Professor of Criminal Law at Antioch. She, other teachers and the students were out celebrating in a nearby bar, amid bursts of laughter. 'A tin of succotash!' they were saying to one another, shaking their heads in disbelief. Disbelief too at the extraordinary coincidence that it was an Antioch student who happened to arrest Wentzel without even knowing who he was.

Shelley Broderick is an exuberant character, as unlike a law professor as you could find. She wears old jeans and drinks a lot of beer. She is the lowest paid law professor in America. 'But I feel I'm stealing to take any money at all for this job. I love every minute of it,' she says.

She works all hours and there are always queues of people outside her door. It is hard for anyone to talk to her for more than a few minutes at a time, as her telephone rings incessantly. Will she take such and such a case? Will she provide students to act as legal observers on a demo where there will be arrests? Will she play in the college basketball game?

She talks at great speed but she also has the greatest patience with her students, coaching them carefully through every stage of the cases they will defend in court.

But however enjoyable the grocery store incident it will not help save this extraordinary law school. Antioch is the very antithesis of Harvard and Yale. It ranks the lowest on the standard ratings used by the law board that gives accreditation to law schools. Every year its accreditation has been threatened because of its unconventional methods.

Antioch's students have the lowest grades on entry to the school. Its staff have the lowest salaries. It has fewer books in the library. It has least space per person. It has rats. Housed in a curious cement-Gothic edifice, it is rundown, shabby and falling apart.

And yet Antioch's story is one of remarkable success. Its students have the lowest entry requirements because they are deliberately chosen as the kind of people no other law school would even consider. They are far older than most students – average age 28, and that includes a 52-year-old nun. Two thirds of them are black or from other ethnic minorities. They all come from poor districts around America, or from working on projects among the poor. They all come with a specific objective – to return to the underdog and the poor, better equipped to fight for their rights.

Each student has a good story to tell. Daily life at Antioch would make a wonderful television series, along the lines of *Fame*. For, unlike other law schools, from the term they enter, the students don't just learn, they actually practise law. The college has a clinic where the poor of Washington bring their cases, knowing they will get far better treatment than from court appointed lawyers who tend to urge them to plead guilty and plea bargain. The day I was there, a student from an Indian reservation, who came to Antioch to study Indian law, was shaking with nerves as he prepared his first case for court – a minor shoplifting case – but he had given it 50 hours, and infinite patience, exploring every avenue, subpoenaing witnesses all over the place. In their 13 years, they have represented 19,000 poor people and their record in getting people off is phenomenal.

Each year the college graduation ceremony is a flamboyant and bizarre occasion. It takes all day. Instead of the 150 students in decorous lines collecting their degrees, Antioch's get up one by one and confer the degrees on one another and make speeches. Their families come in great numbers, and wave, cheer and clap. The students say things like: 'I'd like to dedicate my diploma to the welfare authorities in Albuquerque. They made my Mom suffer such indignities that they made me want to go to law school to put a stop to it.' Or: 'I'd like to thank the cop who busted me when I was 16. It made me mad, it made me go to law school.' Or: 'I'd like to dedicate my diploma to the 2,000 men and women on death row. I'm going to make sure America stops murdering people.'

It brings tears to the eyes of the professors. The place is imbued with a radical idealism quite out of keeping with the current American climate. The students all have to spend at least their first week living with a poor Washington family, to make sure they all know about the inner city lives of the people they will be defending in court.

Graduates from Antioch have been a persistent thorn in the side of the Reagan Administration – which may be one reason for the college's present troubles. One case was so extraordinary that it is about to be made into a film.

It is the story of Billie Guard. She was a school teacher

in Miscogi, Oklahoma, with two children, who was getting divorced from her husband. She took a job in a census office to make extra money, where she found they were employing her high school girls. She discovered her bosses took these young girls to late night parties which turned into orgies. She complained but when nothing was done, she blew the whistle. Her boss warned her that if she told anyone, he would have her children taken away from her, as one of the partygoers was a judge. The day she blew the whistle, the judge signed an order and the welfare took both her children away.

In despair she came to Washington to get help. Antioch took up her case, fought it in court, and won. Not only did they get the children back, but they got the men involved and the judge gaoled. Billie Guard was so grateful she moved to Washington with her children and took a law degree at Antioch, so that she could help others in the same way. Now, two years later, she is working on a government accountability project in Wisconsin.

Unless there is a last-minute rescue. Antioch may close in a year. It is an off-shoot of a famous small liberal progressive university in Ohio – a university that has suffered in recent years from a shift in fashion towards the safe, establishment colleges and is now near bankruptcy. The law school is a small outpost left over from the great reforming social conscience years under Lyndon Johnson, which continued in spite of Nixon until the Reagan Administration. Everywhere funds have been cut for projects to help the poor and Antioch itself is a victim.

Its one chance is that the new University of Washington, which has no law department, may take it over and turn it into its own law school. But Washington's black mayor, with whom the final decision rests, says Antioch is not the kind of law school he wants for Washington's poor and under-privileged students. He wants a glossy, commercial law college that will project kids from the ghetto into top Wall Street jobs. Why should the poor always have to be dragged down by the responsibility of caring for other poor people?

While colleges like Harvard and Yale raise massive sums each year from their alumnus the past students of Antioch have nothing to give. They are all back in the inner cities, or poor area, struggling to keep alive civil liberties in the face of an Administration and public opinion which seem for the time being to have abandoned the poor.

24 November, 1986

Polly Toynbee

Short of a short back and sides

Menfolk in Calne, Wiltshire, who wear their thinning hair with pride, eschewing the vanities of Scargillite coiffure, have met a difficulty. The last barber in town who did a short back and sides shut down for two weeks and reopened under a new owner as a unisex salon.

Mr Bill Ponting, aged 57, walked in for his usual £2 monthly trim and was offered a £4 Cut 'N Blow Dry. 'I told them, "well I'm buggered", and walked out.' Mr Ponting said last night, 'I don't want any blow waves. I haven't got enough hair left.'

Another regular, Mr Charlie Haynes, aged 77, was invited to try a wet haircut. 'He just didn't understand,' said his friend, Mr Graham Tanner. 'He was most upset by it all.'

For 23 years they and other macho males had gone to Mrs Mavil Engel's shop in Church Street, Calne. It did a reliable cut – dry, with clippers – and they were rarely asked whether they wanted anything else as they left.

Her departure has left them almost bereft in a county whose Yellow Pages have become thick with names like Chic Unisex, Charlie Bubbles, Cut 'N Curl, and (in Calne itself) Guys & Dolls Ladies & Gents.

'It means you can't get a short back and sides in a town with a population of 11,000,' mourned Mr Tanner. The local alternatives are Lyneham, where the local RAF camp has ensured the survival of a more masculine tradition of barbering, or Chippenham, to which the bus fare is £1.35. The total cost of these excursions almost equals the price of a Calne blow dry.

Mr Steve Jones, who took over Mrs Engel's shop, said: 'They can have the cut they want but they will have to pay £4. This includes a wet cut with blow dry. I know it's unfortunate. But we do have to move with the times.'

Mr Fred Eley, ex-Mayor of Calne and chairman of the town's over-60s club, a third of whose male members are short back and sides men, said: 'There are a lot of old-fashioned people here and, of course, they are living longer. It could cause problems.'

But last night hopes were raised by reports that another Calne salon – having assessed the potential scale of custom – was prepared very discreetly to offer the older style and older price of service on demand.

13 December, 1986

John Ezard

Brainwave brings women to their feet

Women across America are responding enthusiastically to the development of a simple disposable device which could revolutionize female urinary habits.

With the help of the delicately named 'Le Funelle' women can now, like their male counterparts, pee standing up, thus avoiding the horrors of dirty toilet seats and a host of bacteria from thrush to herpes. The device is also attracting attention from women fearful of Aids, although there is absolutely no evidence that the disease can be passed in the loo.

The device is the brainchild of a German-born entrepreneur Ms Lore Harp, who lives in California and recently began marketing the device after bailing out of the overcrowded semi-conductor industry. Ms Harp said yesterday: 'I've gone from high-tech to low touch.'

Ms Harp developed the idea during her years as a high-powered business executive, when she was required to travel between 150,000 miles to 200,000 miles a year. 'I just simply became disgusted with sitting down on unhygienic toilets,' and looked for a way to overcome the problem.

Le Funelle is engineered out of one-eighth-inch-thick coated paper. The scooped end of the device is placed over the pubic area and the four-and-a-half-inch tube aimed at the toilet bowl, instead of an awful trickle down the leg. For just under $5 American women can buy a travel pack of 20 which can be carried in a handbag.

The response to her invention has been astonishing. Female newspaper columnists have described it as a breakthrough for womanhood and some 5,000 packs of the device – which went on sale by mail order at the start of this month – have been sold. Ms Lore says she is negotiating with several major pharmacy distributors so that it can be sold at the local drug store.

Market research conducted before the launch found that many women have a terrible dread of toilets in public places. Little girls are often taught from a very young age to squat over the seat rather than sit down for health reasons. 'Some 90 per cent of all women do not sit on the toilet seat,' said Ms Lore, who is president of Aplex corporation of San Mateo, California, which is selling Le Funelle.

Inquiries about the instrument have also flooded in from elderly women stricken with arthritis and other similar disorders.

'There has been a great deal of frustration out there,' Ms Lore observes. Now there is disposable relief.

7 February, 1987

Alex Brummer

The disease waiting in the wings

One can only wonder at the inconsistency of a government which promotes its anti-Aids campaign with an appeal to the people not to die of ignorance, when it is more than content to let us live with it. Indeed, the creation of ignorance is one of the few commodities still in abundant manufacture in post-industrial Britain, not the least by that most uncritical supporter of the present administration, the *Sun* newspaper. For on the very day that the crusade against Aids was launched (on which no expense was to be spared, the cost amounting to almost one-fifth of that spent on the sale of British Gas), the *Sun* carried the following 'news' item: 'Grim-faced ministers emerged from a Cabinet meeting, fearful that the killer plague Aids will spark violence on the streets of Britain. The prospect of bloodshed as terrified citizens make "reprisal" attacks on homosexuals and drug addicts is now seen as a real threat. Some gays are expected to retaliate by spreading the virus to the rest of the community through "revenge sex" with bisexuals.'

Just what this Gothic scenario is calculated to contribute to the fight against Aids is not immediately clear. Not only does the spread of superstition make it more likely that the victims of Aids will be driven to more frantic efforts at concealment, but such 'reporting' also resuscitates antique scares associated with 'smearers', those who were believed to be deliberately infecting the population in outbreaks of plague during the Middle Ages. (Indeed, the *Sun* becomes more and more medieval each day, in its style as well as its content: many of its headlines sound like a parody of medieval poetry, with their rhymes and alliterations: Princess Pushy – haughty and naughty, Naughty Night Nurse Sold Sex, Jobs Joy for Maggie, Moors Murderer Myra Must Rot, etc.).

It might seem at first an incomprehensible exercise, but it is of a piece with the purposes over a long period of much of the popular press and the so-called entertainment industries, who have set themselves up as purveyors of fantasy and horror to the people, a role perhaps more readily accepted in the vacuum created by all the ruined workplaces and the decayed and broken communities. What might have once been benignly regarded as competition in the search for sensation in order to sell newspapers is long past. It is becoming clear that the extremes of shame and degradation to which human beings are daily shown to be ready to sink, the parade of cruelties they will commit against each other, can no longer be contained in the realm of fantasy, but strain to re-insert themselves into a social reality from which it might have been thought they were securely and impenetrably separated.

What we are living through is a sustained attempt to resurrect the mob. The newspapers and the junk videos portray people, in the language of the *Sun*, as dirty rats and filthy swine, as animals and beasts; a vast human bestiary has been reinvented which systematically represents people as corrupt, treacherous and venal, in contrast to whom, in this simple Manichean world, the good is represented by money.

An admiring submission to the price of everything is the only morality known to the *Sun*: the sums commanded by pop stars, the cost of the mansion in Malibu, the details of the extravagant lifestyles of celebrities, the amount paid for the transfer of a football idol, the quantity of money earned by Bruce Springsteen in the fortnight after his new album appeared – these compel the closest thing to reverence.

The mere selling of newspapers topples over into the creation of an ideological construct, the lineaments – and the antecedents – of which become clearer day by day. An earlier, more modest, designation of people as junkies and vandals and alkies and thugs now looks relatively harmless set beside the beasts and fiends and monsters, the creatures of pure evil, who inhabit the second half of the 1980s. The saga of our social life is one of chaos and humiliation, of brutalization and breakdown, where you can't trust anyone further than you can see them; where everybody is out for the same thing – the sacred trinity of money, sex and fun, of which there is never enough to go round. In this pursuit everything falls apart, families, relationships, friendship, trust. The only repository of faith in this bleak landscape is hard cash.

In the same week as this particular Aids scare, it was also reported that crime figures have reached record levels. The law and order rhetoric of eight years of Thatcherism has failed, and it is time for a further ideological turn of the screw. Considering that the economy, as they never tire of telling us, is performing better than ever before, it can only be that we are being prepared for more lurid diversions for when we shall have fallen from this privileged state. We are living in a time of confusion, of

*we appear to have hit an Aids
commercial*

5 March, 1987

strange portents; only just short of the night of the demon,
when witches and demons and dragons stalk the land. At the
next stage the deliverer will come, St George, the bringer of
order and the restorer of things. This role, it may be remembered, is not a million miles from that which Thatcher assumed,
in a more modest way, in the distant days of 1979. (Didn't
they then call her the Joan of Arc of British politics?) Yet
Thatcherism is too genteel in its brutalities; the velvet of the
glove is too caressing a protective. When her mission is more
widely seen to have failed, that is when we shall await the
millennarian deliverance of the Strong Man, who will not only
bring forth sense out of the universal chaos, but will at the
same time restore Britain to her former greatness. Perhaps this
is why the nostalgia mills have been working overtime in recent
years, recalling a past that is safely sanitized, over and done
with, fit for recycling and for the selling of everything from

breakfast cereal to beer and theme parks; a past ripe for rehabilitation in all its mythic perfection.

The fascism that it waiting in the wings doesn't require the convolutions of David Selbourne to make it visible. A few days after the Aids scare, John Vincent wrote in the *Sun* why, in his view, the government campaign against Aids would not work. 'There are only two alternatives – the present government campaign to stop risky sex, or making sex safe by isolating carriers. The first policy is wishful thinking, the second hard to enforce and inhumane. Being British, we have succumbed to wishful thinking. This means that the disease will go from strength to strength.'

The inescapable conclusion is left to the none-too-squeamish sensibility of *Sun* readers.

When it is finally revealed what the Thatcher years have done to Britain, when not only manufacturing industry but the benefits of oil also can be seen to have deserted us, then the real asperities will start; cuts in welfare will make even the present unhappy age look like a time when the land flowed with milk and honey; the lowering of living standards will affect not just the poor and the unemployed but the majority of the people. Then will be the time of the man on the white horse, the crusaders, the merchants of deliverance with their racism, homophobia and intolerance of dissent. We can already see quite clearly the outlines of what will replace the demise of Thatcher; and it will not come from the Left.

Just as Camus' plague bacillus lay dormant in drawers and chests and papers, waiting for the moment when it would send forth its rats to die in the unsuspecting city, so the forces for which that plague was a metaphor are stirring once more, ready to work their transformation in a Britain which is increasingly unrecognizable as the familiar and loved homeplace, but looks more and more like the future site of the Second Coming of those brutalities which we went to war to defeat less than half a century ago.

22 December, 1986

Jeremy Seabrook

Tosca through a tilted glass

There in the programme Maria Caniglia, most celebrated Tosca of her day, partner of Gigli, beams out at you, the companion of the Nazi boss of Rome. If there is an obvious danger that updating the period of operas is becoming a production cliché, Jonathan Miller – as in his unforgettable *mafioso Rigoletto* – has struck again, disarming doubts with an update of Puccini's Napoleonic melodrama just as sharply specific, making you relive emotions by bringing them close to our times, most believably so.

When this new ENO co-production with the Maggio Musicale was first seen in Florence last year, one of the obvious talking-points was the inclusion of Mussolini among the worshippers in the Act 1 Te Deum scene. That distraction happily has gone, for this is not just an update to the fascist period but very specifically to the period just after Mussolini's fall, when Nazi occupation of Rome involved a terror even more intense.

That brings exactly the atmosphere of fear and uncertainty needed for this sharply structured opera, when news of victories could indeed change the situation overnight. Hence the very relevant photo of Caniglia, and a poster – also reproduced in the programme – of a saboteur slumped in a chair, executed by the rifles of the military.

The distorting lens of Stefanos Lazaridis's set goes with this. The tilt sideways of 10 degrees or so brings a reminder of the camera-work in Carol Reed's *The Third Man*, similarly evoking sinister overtones in depicting a period of violence and seedy austerity. The obvious snag is that where a tilted camera keeps figures as well as objects at the same angle, live singers standing on a canted stage seem all to be leaning into the wind, visually distracting when you get a full crowd of them.

Puccini's concept and that of his librettists is violated hardly at all by all this. The magical moment in Act 2, when the sound of Tosca singing off-stage is claustrophobically cut off by Scarpia shutting the window, is totally destroyed, but there is little else to worry about, and the company's main problem

147

now is to get a musical performance that will do full justice to a potentially powerful production.

Act 2 is already electrifying. That is largely because Neil Howlett as Scarpia is so much the dominant figure. This is a sauve, handsome police chief, spruce and immaculate in his double-breasted suit, preening himself behind his Clark Gable moustache.

The voice matches this picture, firm, dark, fresh in timbre with no worn edges, and he acts with it splendidly. So Scarpia smilingly sips his coffee in preparation for delivering his *coup de grâce*, revealing to the tortured Cavaradossi that he knows Angelotti's hiding-place and with it revealing Tosca's betrayal, a moment to relish just as the villain so obviously does.

Opposite him in Act 2 Josephine Barstow is powerful too. Last year in Salzburg she gave a commanding performance as the distraught heroine in Penderecki's new opera, *Die Schwarze Maske*, and there is much of that same intensity, hysteria barely suppressed, in her portrait of Tosca, particularly while Cavaradossi is tortured.

Eduardo Alvares from Brazil, who sang Radames in the ENO *Aida* last year, is Cavaradossi, and we were asked indulgence. He was only just recovering from a serious face wound received in rehearsal when in the execution scene he flung himself off his chair. ('Try to fall correctly,' says Tosca in Edmund Tracey's translation, adding insult to injury.)

There are some commendable vignettes among the incidental characters, a baggily disorganized Angelotti strongly sung by John Connell, a slimy, bespectacled Spoletta from Stuart Kale. In the pit Jan Latham-Koenig was making his ENO debut, as yet lightweight, ruining the ominous coda theme of the final execution at too fast a speed, but already bringing out the wind-based sharpness of Puccini's orchestration rather than any opulence, rightly with this production.

Costumes, like the sets, by Lazaridis, are authentically drab for wartime. Before this *Tosca* matches the success of Miller's *Rigoletto*, the musical side will have to be tightened up, but the ingredients are there.

15 January, 1987

Edward Greenfield

Decline and fall of a parish

Parish councils are the smallest units of elected government, and the one of which I am a member must be one of the smallest in the country. Our electorate is only about 200 and we have a job to find sufficient people prepared to serve as councillors. Even so our elections are as scrupulously supervised as parliamentary ones.

One year we all failed to get our nomination papers to the town hall on time, as a result of which nobody was elected and we had to have another election. At the last one, I received (if I remember rightly) 12 votes. I was very touched by those 12 votes. Since the parish council has five members and there were five candidates I can't see why anyone bothered to vote at all.

Our powers are not enormous, but they do exist. We set our own precept, for example. This year it is 2p in the pound, which raised us the mighty sum of £390 on the rates.

By definition the duties of a parish council are parochial. If you want to know what is meant by parish-pump politics then come along to one of our meetings. (I only wish someone would.) None of us represents any political party, and our decisions are usually unanimous.

Our minutes show that over the past 10 years three main issues have taken up most of our time in the six meetings we hold each year.

One was what best to do in the aftermath of the catastrophic Dutch elm disease which dramatically altered our landscape and robbed us of what the late Sir John Betjeman considered to be the finest collection of elms in the country. We own, and are responsible for, various small parcels of land, so we had to have dead trees felled, and choose what species to replant them with.

The second issue was a dispute over the ownership of the village well. Naturally we argued that it belonged to the village, but we were unable to prove our claim since an earlier council had not got round to registering it. After many years of argument the matter was amicably settled by our agreeing that the well did not belong to the parish council, whereupon the owner sold it to us for £1. Perhaps national and international politicians could learn something from parish-pump politics.

And then there was the extension of the village hall. We committed what we could from our meagre finances, and the rest was made up by a grant, various generous gifts, a raffle here, and jumble sales here, there and everywhere. The whole thing cost a few thousands, but eventually we got it done, and I don't mind saying we were a little bit proud of ourselves. Indeed some philanthropic body recognized our efforts with an equal second prize and a cheque for £500.

Now that we've dealt with the trees, the well and the village hall, we don't really have a great deal to do. We discuss a footpath, or the verge of a road, or a spot of litter, but to tell the truth most of our time is taken up with reading the minutes of the previous meeting. Then we chat about this and that, such as the state of health of old so-and-so. We usually manage to spend quite a lot of time discussing the date of our next meeting. There's very little Any Other Business, which is just as well since our coffers have been emptied by the village hall and the maintenance and insurance of the village well, which has turned out to be an expensive thing, but our own.

What crops up fairly frequently are applications for planning permission. We are in a Conservation Area and an Area of Outstanding Natural Beauty, and all that kind of thing, which means that you practically have to have planning permission to get your hair cut.

We usually give these applications our approval on the grounds that at present the population of the village is too small. I have heard it said that the population of English villages is now lower than at any time since the Black Death. Certainly our population is much lower than it was in the living memory of our older inhabitants.

Modern farming methods mean that there are only a fraction of the number of agricultural workers that there were in the past. There used to be a forge, a school, a carpenter's shop, a butcher, baker and candlestick maker. All have gone.

We are lucky in still having a village shop and sub post office, and no fewer than two pubs in the parish. But we have a declining and ageing population which includes some weekenders.

Few people earn their living by working within the parish boundaries. If the village is not to die (or to survive at best as a pretty picture postcard) then we need more people and we need local employment. This is why, when the parish council is asked for its views on a planning application involving an extension to an existing building, or the conversion of a disused building into a dwelling, we usually say yes. And if we say yes, the district council usually says no.

Let me give some examples. In 1978 there was an application to replace an unsightly and decrepid Second World War Nissen hut with a bungalow. This would remove an eyesore, increase the population, provide some local employment, and contribute to the local economy. We supported the application; the district council turned it down. The result is that eight years later we still have the eyesore and have not had the benefits of local employment or increased population.

Example 2: on the Downs there is an old and rather fine timber-built barn. It is dilapidated and unsightly. Application was made to convert it for domestic purposes. Same story. In January 1985 the parish council's minutes record that we regretted that our opinion had been disregarded and that the barn will now probably fall irrevocably into disrepair which will mean that it will have a far more detrimental effect on the beauty of the landscape than would a well-renovated, well-maintained dwelling. A year later the minutes note that the parish council seemed to have been justified in its attitude. The building was now very nearly beyond repair.

I recently discussed this building with Paul McMahon, Newbury District Council's Director of Planning Services. He said that it had been the opinion of their architectural adviser, a specialist in listed buildings, that the barn was so far gone that a complete rebuilding of the structure would be needed. Therefore it was effectively the same as applying for a new building on a new site. Therefore, no. Instead it should be allowed to dilapidate and fall down of its own accord.

How long, I asked him, did he think this would take? He said that the architectural expert had said about two years. But the architectural expert said this a good bit more than two years ago and the building still stands.

These people don't seem to know very much about old timber-framed buildings. They are extremely difficult to knock down. The roof may fall in, but the timber structure will stand for centuries unless someone gives it a helping hand. Anyway, the upshot is that the district council's concern for conserving the outstanding natural beauty of the parish has provided us with another eyesore for the foreseeable future, and delivered its death warrant to a building that was well worth keeping in some shape or form.

Example 3: in the centre of the village is the Ebenezer Primitive Methodist Chapel, built in 1864. This is a building both of architectural and historical interest. When it was built there must have been a considerable number of Primitive Methodists around to raise the money for this substantial brick building: comparatively it must have cost many times more than our extension to the village hall.

However, there are not many Ebenezer Primitive Methodists in the community now. In fact, as far as I know, there are none. The chapel has been used as a store for many years, its windows are broken and it is in a bad state of disrepair. Same story. Application was made to convert it into a dwelling. We supported the application. The district council turned it down. So it looks as though we have to put up with yet another eyesore until eventually it falls down, or is knocked down, and another interesting building has gone.

The minutes note that the parish council is 'at a loss to understand the attitude of the planning department to these old and treasured buildings'. In an attempt to understand the district council's attitude, I spoke to the Director of Planning Services. I was told that so far as our village is concerned the policy of the district council and the county council is 'geared' to 'inhibit growth'. He went even further. He said that the policy was to 'foster decline'. Ye gods. It seems that eighteenth-century romantic notions of picturesque decay are alive and well in the Newbury District Council. Foster decline, indeed.

What the district council thinks is good for us is at odds not only with those who actually live in the village but also with the policy of the Department of Environment. In his speech to the Oxford Farming Conference in January, William Waldegrave welcomed the idea of increasing rural populations and said that as planners 'we must not let Green Belt or wider rural planning policy block the small-scale additional housing and the conversion of redundant farm buildings for the light industry which will be needed'.

On 30 April this year, the then Environment Secretary, Kenneth Baker, said that new uses could be found for redundant agricultural buildings to help the rural economy. He spoke of the need to diversify the rural economy by encouraging new types of environment and enterprise, and said that redundant agricultural buildings can provide very suitable accommodation for small firms or tourist activities, or can be used for individual residences, without detriment to the Green Belt and to the benefit of the local community, especially where the buildings are of attractive appearance. Apparently this message has not yet got to the Newbury vandals.

The latest communication the parish council has received from Newbury district council's development services committee has to do with the Local Government (Access to Information) Act 1985. Students of double-speak will not need to be told that Access to Information means less access to information. Sometimes in the past parish councils would be invited to a meeting on site to discuss an application. The news is that these 'site meetings' to which we used to be invited are to be replaced by 'site visits' to which we will not be invited.

From my own first-hand experiences of one very small area I conclude that conservation policies are being applied rigidly, unimaginatively, unsympathetically and destructively, and that far more weight should be given to the views of people who actually live in the place rather than those of bureaucrats. In other words, the views of the parish council rather than those of the district council. I know whose decline I would like to foster. As Butch Cassidy said, who *are* these guys?

30 August, 1986

Richard Boston

A Country Diary: Northumberland

We are bobbing in the swell which laps the rocks of the Longstone; our coble *Glad Tidings* has dropped anchor to allow its passengers to watch the seals. The Farne Islands host thousands of these mammals and there has always been conflict with the fishermen. Billy Shiel, our helmsman, told us that the seals can be seen jumping up to catch the struggling salmon while they are being netted. On Holy Island, the net-fishermen fire guns over the heads of the seals to scare them off. Feeding on their regular diet of codling we saw several large seals tossing the fish up and skinning them. Heaving themselves about on the rocks, the bulls resemble lethargic slugs, but the cows and calves are more graceful and many swam quite close to our boat, curious to see us. We land on Staple Island which hosts avian high-rise flats: 11,000 pairs of guillemots nest here during the season. Shags build nests in extraordinarily precarious clefts and the warden told me that if the chicks moved even a foot from the nest, the mother wouldn't feed them. So, there is a certain amount of infant mortality. The wardens record nests, watch and count birds and, where necessary, collect gull eggs, because the gull population needs to be controlled. Gulls will kill lesser birds and eat their eggs. Last month, there was an interesting sighting of a fall of 35 blue throats (a North European robin) which paused on the Farne Islands for several days. 'I watched them practically night and day,' the young warden said. 'It was a marvellous sighting and I know experienced ornithologists who would have given anything to have been here.'

26 June, 1987   **Veronica Heath**

Always the right script

Did she truly – one night at Clarence House when the footmen were late bringing her nightcap – phone to say, 'I don't know what you two old queens are doing down there, but this old Queen is dying of thirst'?

Did she genuinely say, in 1940, when the first of seven bombing raids damaged Buckingham Palace, 'I'm glad. Now at last I can look the East End in the face'? And did the policeman she was talking to really remark, of the German pilot's low-level approach up the Mall, 'A magnificent piece of bombing, ma'am, if you'll pardon my saying so'?

Did Queen Elizabeth the Queen Mother, who today celebrates the 50th anniversary of her accession to the throne, actually reply when it was urged that her daughters should join the flight of other rich children to Canada, 'They will not leave me. I will not leave the King – and the King will never leave'?

That, at least, is the tabloid press version of this vow. A more scholarly version, which the *Guardian* will use in her eventual obituary, goes, 'The children will not leave unless I do. I shall not leave unless their father does; and the King will not leave the country in any circumstances.'

The answer to all these queries is that 'there is just no way of telling any more', according to the Queen Mother's press spokesman, Major John Griffin. She wouldn't precisely remember words she spoke 40 years ago; and everyone to whom she said them is long dead.

With her, still ploughing exultantly through 120 public engagements a year at the age of 86, affectionate hagiography reigns supreme. Some of the unusually bountiful quotes attributed to her read as if scripted by her actorish friends, Ivor Novello and Noel Coward, or by Laurence Olivier in his younger Agincourt mode. For historians and a few of the rest of us, obstinately anxious to distinguish between real person, valid legend and candy-floss, that is vexing.

In fairness, she always has been not only wittier than her bland manner would suggest but the cause of wit in others.

And, whatever she said, the point – which is also part of the basis for the depth of feeling behind the hagiography – was that she and King George VI did stay in London with the girls, exhausting themselves in travels totalling tens of thousands of miles to bombed towns. A Canadian woman sent her a poem: 'Be it said to your renown/That you wore your gayest gown and stayed in town/When London Bridge was falling down.'

She was Queen for less than 15 years until her husband's death in 1952 – a role which, like the acclaim she has enjoyed ever since, was unthinkable when she was born as Elizabeth Bowes-Lyon into a minor Scots aristocratic family with its seat at Macbeth's castle, Glamis.

Her father, disgusted by the philandering and drinking of the Prince of Wales, declared, 'If there is one thing I have determined for my children, it is that they shall never have any sort of post about the Court.'

In 1922 the Duke of York sent his parents the most pathetic telegram ever wired by a royal prince: 'It's all right! Bertie.' He meant that Elizabeth had accepted him, stammer, depressions, apparently hopeless diffidence and all, after several rejections. She was, like everyone who has married into the family since, 'afraid never, never again to be free to think, speak and act as I really ought to'.

When the abdication brought what she called the 'intolerable honour of being Queen', she told the children, 'We must make the best of it.' And, although she must have a negative side which will emerge in posthumous biographies, no one in 59 years has seriously suggested she ever did less than that. Strength of character, and the resolutely uncomplicated faith of many women of her generation, got her through.

With her husband and King George V, she is one of the great moulders of the twentieth-century monarchy, successfully establishing Bagehot's notion 'that it is natural to have a virtuous sovereign'. Her private keepsake, from deeper reading than the hagiographers suggest, is a phrase of William Blake's: 'Labour well the Minute Particulars, attend to the little ones/ and those who are in misery cannot remain so, long.'

Her early impact was colossal as the first princess this century to smile in public. Her real successor is the Princess of Wales.

Watching Diana last month flinching at the relentless hours of exposure to cameras during her Gulf tour, it was natural to think of her husband's grandmother and wonder, How can any girl face the prospect of 50 years of that?

The answer is, with difficulty. But if you survive it with your heart and your marbles intact, and with little except a yen for gin-and-tonic, you become a legend.

11 December, 1986

John Ezard

Male-ordered

She will not grow old as we who are left, etcetera. Alive, she never really grew much older than Norma Jean Baker, little girl lost. Kept Norma Jean's baby face and baby whisper, added some pounds of delicious flesh, discarded a first boy-next-door husband, called herself Marilyn Monroe and with a seductive wiggle or five set off for the rainbow land of Hollywood, there to turn all men into her missing Daddy and some few stout-hearted women into her missing Mom.

And arrived bang on time. The war was over and the men were home again, hungry for pretty girls in or on their arms, in or out of wedlock but not, repeat *not*, in their jobs or in their way. Who better to represent postwar womanhood, the dames there is nothing like, than soft marshmallow Marilyn, so transparently in need of returning heroes, the fairest of the fair that only the brave deserve? Marilyn, who offered sex without a string in sight, who promised the pushover pleasures of gaol-bait without the gaol. No wonder strong, challenging women like Joan Crawford, Bette Davis, Katharine Hepburn temporarily lost their lustre.

Gloria Steinem, all-feminist American and founder of *Ms* magazine, has collaborated with George Barris, who photographed Marilyn just before she died, to produce *Marilyn*, the latest of the forty-odd increasingly necrophilomanic books on

157

the candy floss phenomenon, who always made more money for others than she did for herself and continues to do so from the grave. Ms Steinem, however, is donating her share of the proceeds to a children's fund in memory of Norma Jean and she writes of her subject with a feminist hindsight and a nice maternal warmth 'for the endlessly vulnerable child who looked out of Marilyn's eyes'.

In Marilyn's heyday, the Frightful Fifties, few women were secure enough to be so generous, dependent as most of them were on male approval and male earnings. Many found the ice-cream-soda star more threatening than other celluloid beauties: if they possessed a spark of rebellion her compliant image reproached them, if they felt even faintly uneasy in the clinging male-worshipping feminine role she made them feel worse.

'I always had a talent for irritating women,' wrote Marilyn, irritatingly. 'Sometimes I've been to a party where no one spoke to me the whole evening. The men, frightened by their wives or sweeties, would give me a wide berth. And the ladies would gang up in a corner to discuss my dangerous character.' That comment was a near cliché in those women-fear-women days, combining as it did an anxious siding with men, a nervous glee in female jealousy and, underneath, loneliness: a lot of that.

Gloria Steinem likens those women's feelings, quite rightly I'm sure, to 'a black moviegoer watching a black actor playing a role too passive, too obedient'. She is too kind, too American-sisterly, to mention the names blacks called those 'too obedient' blacks: Stepan Fetchit, Uncle Tom and other nastier ones. She defends MM, born too early to draw courage from the women's movement, and perhaps she is right. But she can't have it both ways.

If Marilyn had the intelligence she claims, albeit untutored, then Marilyn knew who buttered her bread, knew very well it wasn't the women made awkward by her dumb-blonde stereotype, rendered more than ever vulnerable by her cartoon vulnerability. The feminine mystique was in full and depressing swing anyway – women could have done without its personification at every neighbourhood cinema. Marilyn was solely male-ordered from her gold-dyed curls to her wiggly walk, so much so that she more resembled a female impersonator than a flesh-and-blood woman – or perhaps, poor lamb, simply an adult impersonator.

This year, MM would have been sixty and, in the distinctly unyouth-obsessed 1980s, might still look good. Certainly, George Barris's photos of her at thirty-five show a woman of infinitely more delicate beauty than the rubbery pin-up features of Norma Jean.

However hard I try, though, I cannot believe with Ms Steinem that, given the opportunity, she might have become a student, lawyer, artist, defender of animals, rancher, home-maker, sportswoman, rescuer of children, serious actress or wise comedienne. Dreams may come true in Hollywood but only on the screen. Off-camera, drugs, alcohol, night terrors and movie moguls with all the sensitivity of hogs at the trough quickly put paid to them.

More convincing is Ms Steinem's portrait of a simple, kind-hearted, essentially honest woman with the instincts, if not the stamina, of a fighter. She worked hard for her fame, did what the hogs expected ('I spent a lot of time on my knees,' she told a friend once) but made every penny of her own money and was beholden to no man. And she always sympathized with the underdog.

Of Lincoln Steffen's autobiography she wrote, 'He knew all about poor people and injustice. He knew about the lies people used to get ahead and how smug rich people sometimes were . . . I loved his book.'

When her publicity department asked her to list the ten greatest men in the world, expecting sex symbols no doubt, she put Steffen's name at the top, to be hastily removed by said department as 'too radical'. And when Arthur Miller was in trouble with McCarthy's UnAmerican Activities Committee, she stood by him and helped to pay his legal costs. A brave act in those witch-hunting times.

But in the end, after all sympathy has been given for the oh-so-well-documented tribulations of Marilyn's life and all credit for her triumphs, after every suitable and unsuitable adjective has been employed to describe her appearance and her character, after all the shock-horror-sensation of her luminary lovers and mysterious death has been disinterred and mulled over, one question remains and every author asks it, in one way or the other.

Not so much 'Why does Marilyn continue to haunt us?' or 'What is the secret of her enduring legend?' More, 'Why am I writing this book about her?'

People who are turned into myths for no very obvious reason have one thing in common – a vacuum where a self should be, a blank space upon which any one of us may project anything we feel. So books on Marilyn Monroe are not so much about her as about the authors. Using that yardstick, Gloria Steinem is an unmercenary, warm-hearted woman admirably ready to praise and defend, reluctant to dwell on faults, secure, not given to envy and fond of children.

Marilyn? She, I'm very much afraid, will always be many other stories.

2 February, 1987

Jill Tweedie

High spirits

My wife was worried. I had got home late from the office, partly because it was so cold it took a long time to start the car, and also because the drive home was treacherous and slow.

'The hot water has been off for three hours, and now the heating pipes are cold,' she said. The flat was cooling fast. I kept my coat on as I checked with neighbours that their heating had also gone off. I rang the Russian caretaker, who said that the emergency services were working on it.

What about our children? Keep them in bed, well wrapped up, and put their fur hats on, was his advice.

Outside, it had just hit minus 40 degrees Centigrade. That is very cold indeed. In our all-electric flat we could not even turn the gas taps on . . . I remembered what Russian friends had said about the last big freeze, when whole blocks of flats were evacuated.

But then there was a groaning in the pipes and the warmth began to return. I felt like cheering.

Normally, I relish the approach of a Moscow winter. I have taken up cross-country skiing since arriving here, and have learned to love the Russian landscape under snow, the astonishing radiance of the winter sun filtered through the bare birch trees, the taste of cold vodka after a long run, the sweet pain of warming myself at a picnic fire deep in the forest.

This year it has not been like that. We had our first snow in September, which lasted for two days and then gave way to an Indian summer. In November and December, we had snowfalls that melted in sudden thaws. It was wet and cold and nasty.

The *babushkas*, the all-powerful and all-knowing Russian grannies who really run the country, began to prophesy last summer that this winter would be the coldest and most fearsome for years.

The squirrels began collecting their nuts early, and in unheard-of quantities, they said. The red berries in the forests were two and three times more plentiful than usual, an infallible sign that Mother Nature was preparing winter food stocks for the poor birds.

Certain kinds of mushrooms were thick on the ground this autumn, they said, and I forgot what it was the pine cones were said to be doing, but this was another reliable sign that this winter was going to be a real stinker.

Forty degrees Centigrade below, the *babushkas* cackled, and then they poked me hard in the chest and said, 'Don't let me see you or your children going around without a good fur hat, young man.'

Forty degrees below freezing, I last came across that kind of temperature when I was in central Siberia, about a thousand miles north of Lake Baikal. And there I heard the mystical, marvellous sound that the Russians call the 'whisper of stars'. It is the rustling and crackling noise your breath makes as you exhale, and the water vapour instantly freezes into ice crystals and falls tinkling to the ground.

Siberians are quite mad when it comes to winter. Having listened to the whispering of the stars I was quite ready to get

30 March, 1987

back into the jeep and cower around the heater. My host insisted on an open-air picnic.

I was put in charge of the spirit, a Siberian super-vodka that is as near pure alcohol as makes no difference. In my view, spirit explains the success of the Soviet space programme – rocket fuel cannot compete.

I nursed the spirit, while my hosts built a fire, piled snow into the cauldron, and began to whittle flakes of deep-frozen fish into what became a delicious stew. Some salt, some potatoes and dried herbs, a few slugs of spirit and we became a very merry party.

Then it came time to take a pee. I trudged through the snow to a discreet distance, and began a long process of unbuttoning several layers of garments. Finally, all was ready. And I watched in disbelief as a thin but sturdy stalagmite of quick-frozen urine began to ascend towards me.

At moments like this, your entire past life tends to flash before you – or at least those bits where knowledgeable people told you about frostbite, what it did to the affected part, and whether the damage was reversible. At this point memory failed me and panic ensued.

I began to flounder slowly backwards, away from this growing pillar of ice. It followed me with obvious menace. I retreated further, stumbled, tripped and fell, just as Siberia's rival to the Leaning Tower of Pisa collapsed on to the snow and lay there in the shape of a large question mark.

Understandably shaken by this experience, I hurried back

162

to the campfire, where my friends had become so hysterical with laughter that one of them fell over and knocked down the last bottle of spirit, which was probably just as well.

12 January, 1987

Martin Walker

Spiritualists seek happy medium

Britain's spiritualist mediums are suffering a crisis of over-popularity, brought on by an apparent national urge to get in touch with the Beyond. The Spiritualist Association of Great Britain is finding it impossible to keep up with the demand from local churches for experts with access to 'the room next door'.

The result has led to a second crisis for novice mediums, who face a similar fate to young officers and men sent prematurely to the front in the First World War. Muddles over dark strangers, incorrect leg wounds or the colour of a departed one's favourite cardigan are bringing increasing complaints from congregations.

The president of the association, Mr Terry Gordon, acknowledges in an interview in today's edition of *Psychic News* that standards are falling. He laments: 'The standard of mediumship has declined everywhere. I am very concerned that as mediums like Nora Blackwood, Ena Twigg and Doris Stokes pass on there are gaps to fill.'

The recent deaths of Mrs Stokes and other experienced mediums has worsened the problem, according to the association's general secretary, Mr Tom Johanson. 'There's no decline of interest in spiritualism. Quite the opposite – and that's the problem,' he said yesterday. 'There's been a fantastic demand in the last few years and it's put a lot of pressure on mediums in training. They've allowed themselves to be coaxed away from their classes. They're often inexperienced, not fully trained and not used to working in front of an audience, and of course it shows.'

The association is doing its best to get new mediums through their training quickly but without missing out on essential details about auras, kundalini and other telepathic nuts and bolts. In emergencies, trainees are sent officially to deputize on platforms but only if the congregation is told beforehand that their training is incomplete.

The association's headquarters in Belgrave Square, whose immensely valuable lease is one of the British spiritualists' main material assets, has meanwhile raised its number of weekly 'medium development' classes to 14. More than 150 would-be mediums are in training, and the association is permanently on the lookout for 'naturals' who could become the next Doris Stokes.

'We are always looking for up-and-coming mediums,' said Mr Gordon, who is 72 and runs a spiritual healing centre in Wimbledon. 'If we think they are good enough, we will give them a chance.'

27 June, 1987   **Martin Wainwright**

A passage from India

'Please, Mr Silver,' the motherly receptionist at India House beseeched me just before I left London three years ago, 'please write something nice about us sometimes.'

Well, madam, I tried, but India didn't always make it easy. What with the assault on the Golden Temple, the assassination of Indira Gandhi and the pogrom that followed, the Bhopal gas disaster, the disappointed hopes in Rajiv Gandhi, the proliferation of communal and ethnic violence.

It was soon after the army flushed the Sikh gunmen from the Amritsar shrine that India flattered me with my first death threat. I answered the telephone to an unfamiliar, apparently drunken, voice. The man trapped me into giving my name and confirming that I was the *Guardian* correspondent, then droned: 'I am Babar Singh. I am going to kill you.'

After the appropriate expletive, my instinct was to dismiss it as a bad joke. After all, I had written nothing particularly offensive to the Sikhs. But everyone I consulted – the British High Commission, the head of the government press office, a Sikh writer–MP long on the terrorists' hit list – said: 'Whatever you do, you mustn't ignore it.'

The local Nizamuddin police station sent a genial sub-inspector, who assured me he was used to the foreign press. He'd just wrapped up the case of an American agency correspondent found dead (of natural causes, as it happened) in his flat. He, too, urged me not to treat Babar Singh's threat lightly.

Thank you, but what were the police going to do about it? 'What do you want us to do?' How about a spot of protection? 'Right,' the sub-inspector promised, 'I shall send you a *jawan*.'

The constable turned up at our gate 15 minutes later, a drooping, shabby figure of indeterminate age, armed with a bamboo *lathi*. He didn't look much of a deterrent, but we assumed his superiors knew what they were doing and went back to our lunch.

After another hour the friendly sub-inspector phoned to inquire if we'd had any more calls. No, we said, looking out of the window, but what happened to our *jawan*? Ah, the officer explained, there was a riot due outside the BBC a couple of blocks away. All able-bodied men had been summoned to protect Mr Tully. The next morning we hired a *chowkidar*.

'You haven't exactly fallen in love with India,' an old friend and colleague, a son of the Raj, reproached me in the newsroom when I came home for my first leave. I had to plead guilty, but with mitigation.

Tourists or backpacking seekers after wisdom may fall in love with the romance of this exasperating giant of a land, but no one living and working here can be indifferent to the daily frustrations – the telephones that die on you, the power cuts that leave you sweltering in summer temperatures of 110 degrees Fahrenheit, a timid bureaucracy that works by the book and insists on the last non-word. I'm still waiting for my multiple entry visa to be renewed six months after the last one expired. 'No problem, sir,' they say. 'You'll be hearing from us.'

But the lady at India House was right. You miss a lot if all you do is moan. So do your readers. I had been prepared for the negative side, not just the personal discomforts, but also the casual cruelty of Indian to Indian, the enormous gap between rich and poor, the tenacity of caste even among those who had sought an escape through conversion to Islam, Sikhism or Christianity, the underlying racialism of the old Hindu divisions (parents advertise for a marriage partner of the right 'wheaten' complexion as well as the right sub-caste).

James Cameron and V. S. Naipaul had written it all. The one-big-public-lavatory view of India, the betrayal of Mahatma Gandhi's vision, the compromise of Pandit Nehru's. Eric Newby, whose intrepid *Slowly Down The Ganges* is rich with the smell and hawk and spit of India, offered a text for survival: 'In India you can win every argument, except the last.'

But, as Cameron knew better than most, that is not the end of the story. What I was expecting least was the vitality of India. Hindu fatalism is not dead, but it is a much over-rated drag on initiative. For all its abiding poverty, its debilitating climate, its cycle of flood and drought, India is not an international basket case.

It is a land with resources, physical and human. India has its share of minerals – oil, coal, ores precious and useful – gems and spices. In the present decade it has become self-sufficient in foodgrains. That is, of course, relative. People are still sleeping in the streets, but they are not dying in the streets. The majority remains under-nourished, and thus vulnerable to disease, but fewer Indians are starving.

The explosive danger, as a Sikh building contractor argued over his Black Label whisky, is that the expectations of the poor may not be fulfilled. The new prosperity is unevenly distributed. The rich are getting richer. For all the pious socialism of the ruling Congress, India's mixed economy tilts towards the haves. And the poor are ill-equipped to grab their share.

India is a split-screen society, living simultaneously not just in different centuries but in different millennia. The man sweeping the road outside the space research centre in Bangalore has still to invent the broom handle. The young scientist inside, a man at the leading edge of his field, wears a fresh Brahmin pooja mark on his forehead.

The government discriminates in favour of underprivileged castes, classes and tribespeople in education and public-sector employment, but 70 per cent of India's children drop out at primary school level. Indian scientists know how to make an atom bomb, but only 6.4 per cent of homes have modern sanitation.

The population is growing slightly more slowly, but it is still growing. No one can tell you for sure whether there are 700 million Indians or 800 million (a margin of error bigger than the entire population of Britain). It is a Hindu-majority state with the third biggest concentration of Muslims in the world.

Education Guardian phoned me not long ago to check a story that 80,000 teachers had been gaoled in the South Indian state of Tamil Nadu a few months earlier. It rang no bells, but I phoned an Indian reporter in Madras. 'Yes,' he said, 'of course it's true. In fact it was more like 100,000.' But how many gaols did they have in Tamil Nadu? 'Not that many,' my friend replied. 'They just packed them in tight.'

About 20 of the teachers died in custody. The 80,000 had been striking for more pay. They were imprisoned for a month after defying a state government order to go back to their classrooms.

India's vigorous, but flawed, democracy gives you a chance if there are enough of you in any given place to constitute a 'vote bank'. But that in turn has reinforced a tendency to identify with your group, be it caste, religion, language or region, rather than with Mother India. Group competition can, and often does, degenerate into mayhem.

I may not have fallen in love with India, but after three years you begin to feel you belong. What shall I miss? First, the friends we made and shall keep. The hospitable Indians, warm, earthy and articulate, who remember only the best of the Raj and still take the British as their role model.

Then the barrack-room lawyers of the Indian press, independent and bloody-minded, sprouting new titles as fast as Fleet Street. And the joys of Indian English ('the miscreants are absconding, but the sleuths of the Delhi CID are busy seeking

167

clues'), matched only by the fantasies of official signwriters, who seem to believe that every problem can be solved if only you can devise the right slogan.

Our first landfall in India was Calcutta at midnight. We drove into town on an ex-servicemen's bus through row upon row of pavement-dwellers, wound in bedrolls like corpses after a natural disaster. We stayed for two days, but never quite got over the initial shock. Driving back to the airport we were sent on our way by a municipal hoarding that thanked us for 'visiting the city of intellectuals'.

The other day I spotted a sign printed the full length of a Delhi transport bus, which read: 'Service without humility is nothing but selfishness and egotism.' Delhi bus drivers are notorious for killing more than 300 people a year on the roads of the capital.

We shall miss our white Hindustan Ambassador, the 1954 Morris Oxford still rolling off the Calcutta production lines in defiance of all the laws of economics, engineering and Japanese infiltration.

But we shall not miss the trial by ordeal of Indian roads. Driving in Delhi is like auditioning for *The Keystone Cops*. There are no rules, or if there are they are not enforced. You take the shortest distance between two points, without signalling and often without looking. If another driver can see you, it's his responsibility not to hit you.

There is, of course, a slogan: 'Lane driving is sane driving.' But the only law is the survival of the fittest, which usually means the biggest. Pedestrians give way to cyclists, cyclists to rickshaws, rickshaws to cars, cars to lorries, and everyone to buses. Everyone, that is, except the dirty-white, hump-backed Brahmini cows, who yield to no one.

Mostly, it's been fun.

14 April, 1987

Eric Silver

They shoot Roos, don't they?

Let us look at the facts. The Australian government sets a quota for the slaughter of kangaroos: last year, it was 2.7 millions. Yet conservationists estimate that between four and six million kangaroos were slaughtered. And unaccounted for was 10 to 20 million kilos of kangaroo meat.

In 1981, the Woodward Royal Commission looked into the substitution of kangaroo meat for beef which was going into the US hamburger market. But, though the press made a meal of it and the Woodward findings were published, no one was charged and no action taken.

Kangaroo meat still goes somewhere, a lot into pet foods and much for human consumption. (This carries a risk, as there is a high incidence of salmonella bacteria.) In Australia, the meat is rumoured to appear illegally in dim sums, salamis and a range of junk food products.

Anyone interested in its taste can eat a kangaroo steak at the Hilton in Adelaide. Not that the kangaroo is killed just for its carcass; that is a by-product. Its skin is the most valuable part, and is made into rugs, toys, cushions and coats. Its feet are used as doorstops; its paws as bottle-openers; its head mounted as a wall display. You can buy an inexpensive kangaroo-skin coat at Sydney Airport.

After all, these animals are not farmed; they are shot in the wild, on the run. The ones to aim at are the bigger animals, the adult population. There is an 80 per cent mortality rate in baby kangaroos. A kangaroo mother gives birth once a year, carrying her one offspring in her pouch. Until the pouch is free, the next tiny embryo, already in the womb, is not expelled to climb up its mother's stomach and crawl into the pouch. So, mothers are often slaughtered with two offspring in the making.

A bushranger from the Balranald area of New South Wales told me: 'In the Fifties you could drive along the Great Plains and see Great Roos. Some of the Big Reds were nearly eight feet high. Now they are gone. The area is over-shot. The Western Greys are in serious trouble. I think all the roos will be extinct in the district in four to five years.

'A few weeks ago, I drove through the area. I counted three hundred roos between Menindee and Ivanhoe. They were all youngsters. They travel in mobs; the shooters have killed their mothers and left them to take their chances. They haven't got any parental guidance. They lack the aloofness of properly reared adult animals. These pathetic creatures are helpless.

'The trouble is that country towns are dying economically. State and federal governments are turning a blind eye to the legal and illegal killing of wildlife because, if they didn't, proper solutions would have to be drawn up for these places. The shooters aren't bothering with the code of practice. They want to kill as many roos as they can, so they're shooting them in the spine, in the chest, anywhere to bring the animal down.'

But it is not just a question of state and federal government turning a blind eye; the plot thickens and grows murky here. I was told that because the exported skins are not physically checked by Customs (fauna in bureaucratic terms take a low priority), the skins are used to conceal drugs and arms.

Australia, because of its uninhabited vastness, is a smuggler's paradise. There are 900 airstrips in the Northern Territory alone. Customs officers work from nine to five and have no training to identify fauna or, indeed, the aboriginal artefacts which are also illegally exported.

All this is making millions for someone, possibly quite a few, and it is more likely to be a cartel with representatives in state and federal government.

The Kangaroo Advisory Committee meets every year to decide the quota of animals to be slaughtered, which always rises as the population further dwindles. It has no representative from a wildlife or conservation group. The Australian Senate Standing Committee on Animal Welfare has been sitting for two and a half years. Recently, they heard evidence from Sue Arnold, representing a conservation group, Australians For Animals. She took the lid off a complex web of federal and state illegalities which make fraud in Wall Street or City insider trading look as fresh as the archbishop's tea party.

The out-of-control trade involves unlicensed wildlife processors, out-of-date import and export licences, and anonymous import licences – the company's name is left blank. In the state of Victoria, there is an illegal refrigeration plant, hardly any law enforcement staff, no government prosecutions of companies breaching the Wildlife Act, backdated permits and licences. Incestuous company structures in the rest of Australia which help vested interests make the illegal trade a nightmare to halt.

Arnold's evidence made the headlines. A leader in the *Canberra Times* entitled 'An Industry in Chaos' said: 'It is all but impossible to believe that anyone knows who is shooting how many kangaroos of what species each year, where those animals are being sent to and processed, how many are going overseas and how many are ending up in pet food cans. In fact, can anyone have much faith in statements about the size of the kangaroo population or the extent of the damage they are causing farmers?'

Whenever you mention slaughter of wildlife, whether it is kangaroo or our own species of deer, the reply is the same muttered yet defensive 'The damage they do . . .' The Senate Committee has used two studies to support the contention that kangaroos are killed to contain agricultural damage. Arnold points out that these are merely a survey of farmers' perceptions without the benefit of objectivity, regional conditions, climatic changes and population studies. One of the surveys questioned 300 farmers by post. There has been, she pointed out, no attempt to quantify the damage in a scientifically objective manner. (Nor, I might add, has there ever been such a damage report on our own native deer.)

Only if the EEC banned the import of the wildlife products would the kangaroo industry sustain a real blow. The environment committee has recommended such a ban. They meet to discuss the subject this spring. However, if such a ban came into existence – and the US would hopefully follow such a lead – in Australia one is up against something deeper: the Ocker nature.

The Queensland Cattlemen's Union has called Arnold's lot 'traitors' and 'terrorists' – an understandable statement when you consider that a weekend in the country in Queensland means that guests are encouraged to leave doped food out on the porch so that the bush turkeys become drunk and can be shot more easily. Or – the real sport, this one – shooting herds of wild horses from a two-seater aeroplane, leaving the dead while the maimed run on in a frenzied herd until many drop dead from exhaustion.

10 March, 1987   **Colin Spencer**

The man who . . .

In this week of silly bicentennial attempts to sail old boats from Portsmouth to Botany Bay an important Antipodean anniversary has been under-celebrated. A hundred years ago, that is to say exactly a hundred years after the first 759 British convicts set sail for their new prison, a very funny thing happened in Australia. H. M. Bateman was born in the one-kangaroo town of Sutton Forest, New South Wales.

What is it about the Antipodes that produces so many outstanding British comedians – Low, Dyson, Humphries, James, Rodney Hogg? In Bateman's case he couldn't get out of the place quick enough. By the age of 18 months he was in London; 18 years later he had published his first cartoons. Five years after that he was the richest and most popular cartoonist in Britain – and there was still a decade to go before he even invented 'The Man Who . . .' series.

Pre-First World War Bateman's speciality was the social caricature. His approach was the traditional Australian approach of sneering at the Poms, particularly the rich or artistic ones: men with long hair, fat women in thin dresses, opera singers, billiards players, antique dealers, concert pianists – all were sniffed out and caricatured in that jolly but somehow merciless way of his.

Nice, quiet, polite, timid Mr Bateman had a dingo's nose when it came to detecting self-importance. Policemen, tax collectors, museum attendants, tennis umpires, bank managers, minor clerics, all the Jobsworths of Edwardian England had the stuffing comprehensively caricatured out of them. When the war started it was the sergeants and the colonels who took the brunt. But it was all bouncy and well-meaning stuff. Wasn't it?

Of course it wasn't. In these post-Freudian times it is difficult not to recognize the deep worries of social inadequacy and the hatred of authority figures that propelled Bateman. His life was classically unhappy. The little cartoon man who made the social gaffes that brought H. M. Bateman unparalleled wealth and fame (in the early 1920s he was already getting £200 per cartoon from the *Tatler*) was clearly some sort of self-portrait.

Cursed with a domineering mother who wanted him to become a serious artist, Bateman had his first nervous breakdown at the age of 21. During the First World War he turned out to be, in his own words, 'a hopeless dud' as a soldier. He spent the war years as a civilian and an invalid.

This did not stop him producing nasty cartoons ridiculing those 'splendid fellows who are unfortunately debarred from meeting the Germans', conscientious objectors, artists, vegetarians and the like.

Seriously disturbed by the war, he retreated into a suburban loneliness that was to last another 50 years. There was a marriage but it came late and did not last. Retreating further and further from civilization he spent the last half of his life succumbing finally to his mother's wishes and trying to become a serious painter. He died alone on the Mediterranean island of Gozo in 1970.

I do not know of a cartoonist who drew more funnily than H. M. Bateman. There have been more perspicacious, more savage, more clever, more ambitious, more moral exponents, but none who could inspire in me a louder belly-laugh.

He had the timing of a great stand up comic, always arriving on the scene at exactly the right moment of greatest embarrassment, greatest confusion, greatest unwanted drama. Like all the best comics, he often went that little bit too far and moved into the realms of surrealism.

'The Debutante' shows a tennis novice on the Centre Court at Wimbledon who suddenly becomes aware that every big eye in the place, thousands of them, unnaturally large and bulging, belonging to ball-boys, linesmen, photographers, her opponent, the spectators, rows and rows of them, have all swivelled in her direction. And the ball is just coming over the net . . .

'The Bull That Was Colour Blind', 'Discovery of a Dandelion on the Centre Court at Wimbledon', 'A Ventriloquist at Christie's' – merely to catalogue the titles is to catalogue a sequence of irresistibly funny situations.

Mark Boxer, in his new collection of *The Best of H. M. Bateman* (Bodley Head), makes an astute comparison between Bateman's little man – the one who lit a cigar before the royal toast, or, masquerading as a cad, was improperly dressed on the Lido, or who, as a young curate, lost his temper with his bishop and kicked him hard during high tea with the parishioners – and Charlie Chaplin. The pathos of the situations is certainly Chaplinesque. And if you watch the little man and his aghast audience you are definitely watching some very skilful mime artists at work, their eyebrows madly twitching, their hair standing on end, their hats flying rocket-style from their heads, surprised jaws dropping like guillotines.

Fifty years of Bateman-inspired cartoon antics have made this comic body language familiar. But, before Bateman, cartoons stood still and let the captions do the talking.

My own favourite in the cluster of shows and books that have appeared to mark the centenary of Bateman's birth is *The Boy Who Breathed On the Glass* in the British Museum.

Having performed the dreadful act and been caught by an officious museum attendant, the boy is sent to court and then to prison, where with wonderful Batemanesque timing he becomes a young man, then a middle-aged man, then an old man, then a very old man, until finally he is let out. Hobbling straight over to the museum he breathes on the glass again and drops dead.

16 May, 1987　　　　　　　　　　　**Waldamar Januszczak**

174

Ring of no confidence

The M25 opened yesterday, all of it, at last. It is the London Orbital, that is to say a ring road round the capital. It has taken 14 years. In all, there are 120 miles of it. Yesterday I drove right round and shall set out my thoughts on first encircling London.

First: how beautiful the countryside is, particularly to the south and west, in Kent and Surrey. From an unfamiliar road I saw it anew, as if it were a foreign landscape. Second: well, the road is there, but how can a common or garden motorway, of that short distance, take so long? Third: it's absurdly too far out from the centre, which must be obvious even to those bicycling protectors of disused allotments and the like who ensured by their protests that it should not be closer in. And fourth, and sadly: London still has the worst approach roads of any big city in the Western world.

Mrs Thatcher, opening the last seven-mile segment yesterday, had a hack at those who carp when they ought to be congratulating Britain and beating the drum for Britain all over the world. I am quite happy to beat drums, and I loathe the sociological cant already being written about this motorway – mutterings that it encloses 90-odd Conservative constituencies, as if that were not coincidence, and questions about what it does for the north-east, as if that were germane. But, with respect to the Prime Minister, and I assert that I mean that, this is no matter of beating drums for Britain. It is a matter of asking what possible excuse there can be for a single tat-tat-tat for the timidity of politicians and engineers that brought about this motorway.

For a start, first find your motorway. I started out yesterday from Clapham, just south of the river, and, on roads I have known well for 25 years, drove 14 miles and took 51 minutes before I saw so much as a sign to it. I drove 20 miles before I met the M25 just south of Dartford, and turned westwards, circumnavigating London clockwise. Wonderful countryside. Some bridges elegant, but most – like those where four roads cross each other at four levels, near Gatwick – pretty ordinary. The only striking piece of engineering I saw all day was a brick-built, nineteenth-century railway viaduct south-east of Rickmansworth, before exit 17.

And were the exits always numbered? I got on at exit 3 and, though I looked for the signs, saw no other numbered until exit 12. That doesn't help. It's easiest to be able to say, 'Get off at 15,' or whatever, which is the American practice.

And who did take the trouble to learn from the American practice when this road was being built? This is the obvious place to look, since they've had roads like this for 40 years. The engineers now seem to be surprised that so many users of the new road aren't travelling long distances but simply come on at one junction, stay on for a few miles, and then filter off two or three exits along. The most casual observer would see that this happens on the Connecticut turnpike all the time. At rush hours, its principal users are long-distance trucks and women in Volvo estates taking their kids to school or going shopping in the next town.

Anyway, by the time I'd got to exit 21, the next stretch still wasn't to the public. Mrs Thatcher had cut the ribbon an hour before, but they were said to be still dismantling the podium. But, just after 1 pm, I set off again on an evidently brand new stretch of road, with fine particles of builders' sand rising up from the wheels of the cars in front, and small crowds waving from the bridges.

Then on to the older, northern and eastern, stretches of the road, where the road signs are faded, and so on to the Dartford Tunnel. After that, I came off and drove west, back to London. The 120 miles of the M25 had take me 2 hours 20 minutes. In that time I had seen only five police patrol cars, but then I saw no example of dangerous driving either.

Having left the London Orbital, you next have to find London. I make a slight detour, in order to come in on the Dover road. Can it be 25 years since I talked to the Irish navvies making the M2 which was to join Dover and London? And can it be that this same M2 has still not even got as near to the capital as the new Orbital, which is here almost 20 miles out?

It can be, and it is. To get to London you have to follow the

A2, and you come in over Blackheath, then through New Cross and then along the Old Kent Road, which in parts is in a state of boarded-up decay. Then to the Elephant and Castle, a horrible example of 1960s planning, a wretched thing which I remember Sir Keith Joseph citing as an example of how to get everything wrong with the best of intentions.

That is the dismal route that most traffic from Europe and most visitors from Europe must follow. Of all approaches to London it is the worst. But then I would argue that there is only one good one – that followed by the M40, which does at least bring you in near Euston, near enough to the centre of London. And in London itself, the only decent roads for traffic are the Thames Embankments, which are mostly Victorian. The Victoria Embankment itself was completed in 1870.

Today you can drive conveniently and fast across or around Paris, and I do not think the Periferique has taken much from the beauty of that city. You can get out of Manhattan, to New Jersey or Long Island, with reasonable ease. On highways running up the east and west sides of Manhatten you can get out fast into lower New York State and New England. A man called Robert Moses built better roads for New York in the 1930s and '40s than we have today. The Connecticut turnpike, which I mention again because I have driven up and down it so many times, and know its exits and entrances, is better and wider than any motorway in England.

And this is all the sadder because it was England in the nineteenth century that was the home of great and audacious engineering. The English (and the Scots) built the railways of England, and of half the world besides, on a scale that would now amaze us. The London to Birmingham railway was built in four years, and is full of mighty works bridges, viaducts, cuttings and tunnels – which are not demanded of a motorway engineer today. Cars can easily climb hills and take curves. An early locomotive could do neither, so the railway had to be flat and straight. The railway from London to Bristol, which is known as Brunel's billiard table, has a mean gradient of 1 in 1,380.

Now we have built a motorway round London, of only three lanes, and miles from where it is needed. And what is principally astonishing about that is the mangy poverty of our present expectations.

30 October, 1986

Terry Coleman

A Country Diary: Keswick 2

I saw a fine gander in a farmyard yesterday and was reminded of one I saw just a year ago on a much colder April day. Then I was waiting for friends in a small lonnin near Buttermere. Time did not drag; a wren fossicked in the lower hedge and a flock of ewes and their tottery new lambs were gentled down past me by a quiet dog. That was all very peaceful but beyond the upper hedge a fierce, grey gander watched over his two subservient white geese cropping the grass beside him. He kept a hard, agate eye on all that passed and on me, too. I would not have gone into his field for anything. I avoid some ganders as I do playful cows and athletic pigs. A herd of these last once chased me and my growing children across a rough field, squealing loudly – the pigs, not us, we had no breath for that – until we gained a welcome fence. I have been menaced by red and roe deer. The red was a stag, met accidentally at rutting time in the Thirlmere woods. His blood was up and he lowered his head, antlers too near for comfort, for what seemed an age before giving a half roar and turning firmly away. The roe, so much smaller, was equally combative with lowered, pointing tine and pawing hooves. I found I was near to a roe-ring in blackthorn – his place not mine. Sheep may stamp at sheep trial dogs (who would not?) but that is all. I wonder what it feels like to be savaged by a sheep?

20 April, 1987

Enid J. Wilson

178

A town like Victor

In the Place du Tertre, behind the Sacré Coeur which dominates the northern skyline of Paris, dozens of painters display their canvases of the Seine, the Notre Dame, the boulevards. Cheap, kitsch and in real oil paint. Not entirely insincere, however. The intentions of poor art are simply kinder than those of great art. One or two tourists occasionally buy a canvas, but the more interesting trade is in portraits.

Strolling between the café tables of the little *place*, other painters politely accost the foreign and provincial visitors. A drawing while you wait in charcoal or conté. The price may be as high as £50. A surprising number of tourists agree, stand on the street corner for a quarter of an hour to be drawn, pay up, and go away happy. Why?

The answer has to lead us to another question. Why do people visit art galleries all over the world? Art appreciation? I don't believe it. People really go to the great museums to look at those who once lived, to look at the dead. By the same token, the tourists who pose, standing still for a long quarter of an hour on a sidewalk in the Place de Tertre, believe that their likeness, if 'caught', is already being preserved for the future, their old age, their grandchildren. Fifty quid to be there when the angels come marching in is not so expensive.

What of course is derisory in this commerce is the carefully encouraged hint that the portraits being made in the Place du Tertre have somehow been 'authenticated' by Renoir, Van Gogh, Utrillo, Picasso and all the other great painters who, half a century or more ago, worked and drank and went hungry in the same quarter, within shouting distance of the little *place*. This, however, is an art-critical point, and has little to do with the ontological wager that a likeness, once caught, carries the mystery of a Being.

The mystery of Paris. How can I draw a likeness of the city? Not the official one, stamped on the coins of history. Something more intimate. The date of my birth shows that I was conceived in a hotel somewhere between the Madeleine and the Opéra.

The Madeleine was much admired when it was built in the nineteenth century because it resembled a bank more than a church. It was a monument to worldliness, keeping a proper distance from the original Madeleine's washing of a preacher's dusty feet. Today, inside, it is like a half-empty warehouse for every sort of broken public promise.

I prefer to think that the hotel in 1926 was nearer to the Opéra. Perhaps where today, two storeys down in a basement, there's a tea dance every afternoon. The strobing coloured lights gyrate in a circle; the mirror wall along the side of the dance floor reflects the turning dancers. The music is retro – waltzes, tangos, foxtrots. It's an old-fashioned Aladdin's cave of glitter, where time, dates, age, are put aside (not forgotten) between 4 p.m. and 7 p.m.

Men of a certain age in well-cut suits come to relax and dance with women they've never met before. The women, younger, genteel and a little disappointed with life, come in the hope of meeting a kind widower. They are not tarts. They dream of becoming wives or understanding mistresses. There's a bar but scarcely anyone drinks. The first pleasure is dancing, and everyone dances exceptionally well.

Both the women and the men pride themselves on being experts in life without illusion. In this expertise there is a typical Parisian fastidiousness. A chic. What is touching is that, entwined with the music, between 4 p.m. and 7 p.m., an unreasonable hope still intermittently flickers and persists there.

In 1926, when I was conceived, I was a hope without any expertise, embalmed in sweet illusions, for my parents were not Parisians. To them the city was a simple honeymoon. To me it's the capital of the country in which I've lived for 25 years. Yet what distinguishes Paris from any other city has perhaps not changed so much. How to draw its likeness?

Take the first metro from a suburb early on a summer morning. The first swallows flying. The dustbins under the trees not yet emptied. An incongruous small cornfield between apartment blocks. The suburbs of Paris demand a portrait to themselves. Among them you find the only remaining details from the world as painted by the Impressionists.

They are anachronistic, make-shift and look as if they've been constructed out of contraband. They were marginal – long before the word became fashionable. A man sleepily clipping the hedge of his tiny front garden, still in his pyjamas. Beehives. A take-away hamburger counter, not yet open, but with the smell of yesterday's oil. Rich Parisians don't live in the suburbs: they live in the centre. Take the train.

There's little traffic there yet. The cars parked along the streets are like silent toy ones. On a corner the smell of fresh croissants wafts from a patisserie. Time to get dressed. In a greengrocer's shop two men are arranging fruit and vegetables as if they were millinery. An uncle in a café is looking through a magnifying glass at the stock prices in the morning paper. He doesn't have to ask for the cup of coffee which is brought to him. The last street is being washed. Where's the towel, *Maman?*

This strange question floats into the mind because the heart of Paris is like nothing so much as the unending interior of a house. Buildings become furniture, courtyards become carpets and arrases, the streets are like galleries, the boulevards conservatories. It is a house, one or two centuries old, rich, bourgeois, distinguished. The only way of going out, or shutting the door behind you, is to leave the centre.

The vast number of little shops, artisans, boutiques, constitute the staff of the house, its servants, there, day and night, for its hourly upkeep. Their skills are curiously inter-related; hair-dressing and carving, needlework and carpentry, tailoring and masonry, lacemaking and wrought-iron work, dressmaking and painting. Paris is a mansion. Its dreams are the most urban and the most furnished in the world.

Sufficient to look at Balzac's study. (Now a museum in the rue Raynouard, 16ème). The room is not extravagant. Far from it. But it is furnished, enclosed, papered, polished, inlaid, to a degree that would make anybody but a Parisian very claustrophobic. Yet this is highly appropriate to the city's imagination: Balzac's novels are about property, the human heart, destiny, and the natural meeting place for all these forces in Paris is the *salon*. The battlefields are beds, carpets, counters. Everything made in Paris is for indoor use. Even the marvellous silvery light of the typical Paris sky is like a framed skylight.

Who lives in this mansion which is Paris? Every city has a sex and age which have nothing to do with demography. Rome is feminine. So is Odessa. London is a teenager, an urchin, and, in this, hasn't changed since the time of Dickens.

Paris, I believe, is a man in his twenties in love with an older woman. Somewhat spoilt by his mother, not so much with kisses as with purchases: well-cooked food, fine shoes, after-shave lotion, leather-bound books, chic envelopes. He discusses everything, he is handsome – perhaps, for once, the word debonair is the right one, and he has a special courage. Life is enacted on a stage and he wishes to be exemplary, whatever the risk. His father was his first example of an Expert. Now he has become one himself. There's a complicity between the two men, but also a slight anxiety, for they risk having the same mistress. She also is Paris, and if every city has its own unique smile, in Paris it is hers.

I try to think of a well-known painting containing such a smile but cannot find one. Walking in the city you see it often. The boulevard Charonne is working class, hot in summer, without shade. A large woman in a floral dress with hefty arms is drinking a beer on the sidewalk at a café table. Under the table is a black mongrel dog with pointed ears to whom she feeds peanuts.

A neighbour passes, stops at the table. The woman goes to the counter to buy her friend a lemonade. She's pretty, your Maman! says the neighbour to the dog. When the woman comes back with the lemonade, her friend, laughing, says to her: 'I'd be happy to be guided by you – so long as the lead wasn't too short!' And the woman in the floral dress, who must be in her seventies, smiles that inimitable smile of indulgent but lucid experience.

Often cemeteries are unexpectedly revealing about the life of the living. And this is true of the Père-Lachaise. One needs a map, for it is large. Sections are built like towns – with streets, crossroads, pavements: each house is a tomb or a mausoleum. The dead rest there in furnished property, still protected from the vast exterior. Each tomb has a licence and a number:

Concession Perpetuelle Numéro . . . It is the most urban and the most secular cemetery.

Where, for example, would you find a father's grave with an inscription, ordered by the family, declaring: 'President of the Society of High Class Masculine Hairdressing. World Champion. 1950–80'?

A shrine of property this cemetery, certainly. But also one of popular heroes: the last 147 Communards summarily shot against a wall here in 1871, Sarah Bernhardt, Edith Piaf, Chopin. Every day people come to visit them and to listen to their silence.

There is also another, more mysterious shrine, which is our reason for coming: the grave of Victor Noir. In 1870, Prince Pierre Bonaparte, cousin of the Emperor Napoleon III, wrote an article in a reactionary Corsican journal attacking the good faith of the radical Paris paper called *La Revanche*. The editor sent Victor Noir and another journalist to ask the Prince for an apology. Instead, Pierre Bonaparte seized his pistol and shot Victor Noir dead.

The popular outrage provoked by this murder of political pique transformed a relatively unknown young man into a national hero, and the sculptor Jules Dalou made an effigy for his tombstone. Life-size, cast in bronze, it shows Victor Noir – 22 years old – dead on the ground, an instant after the pistol shot had been fired.

Dalou was a realist, making in sculpture works whose vision had something in common with Courbet's paintings: the same kind of fullness in the bodies and limbs depicted, the same close attention to realistic details of costume, a similar corporeal weight. The two artists were friends and both had to go into exile after the fall of the Commune, which they had actively supported.

Victor Noir lies there with the abandon of the two girls in Courbet's *Demoiselles Au Bord de la Seine*. The only difference being that the man has died at that very instant – his blood still hot – whereas the girls are overcome by drowsiness and the langour of their daydreams.

An elegant tall hat lies on the ground beside him. His handsome face is still proud of his own courage, believing it will be rewarded by the love of women. (Each generation of young men knows that, from time to time, the mansion is transformed into an improvised theatre, on whose stage history is played out – often to the death.) His coat is open, the top button of his tight trousers is undone. His soft-skinned, well-manicured hands lie unclenched, expecting to touch or be touched only by what is fine.

The effigy is moving and strange in its integrity, for it gives the impression that the death it shows has somewhere been selected with the same fastidiousness as the shirt or boots.

Beneath the sky of the cemetery the bronze has turned a dull green. In three places, however, the metal is shiny and gold-coloured where it has been polished by innumerable caresses and kisses. For Paris, Victor Noir has become a talisman, a fetish, promising fertility, potency, success, continuity. People come all the while to seek his aid, to touch his example.

The three places where the bronze metal shines are his mouth, the pointed toes of his superbly elegant boots and, most brilliantly of all, the almost imperceptible mound which his sex makes against his tight trousers.

Perhaps a likeness of the city of Paris begins there in the south-east corner of the Le Père-Lachaise cemetery?

27 March, 1987

John Berger

How art can bowl you over

At least once a month, the art treasures of Florence claim another victim. In the presence of a Caravaggio, a Raphael or more likely Michelangelo's statue of David, the world spins and a foreign tourist is observed to collapse with acute mental bewilderment. They then spend two or three days resting in the psychiatric ward of the Santa Maria Nuova hospital.

'These people were apparently healthy when they left home,' reports Professor Grazielea Magherini, whose hospital team has been documenting the Stendhal Syndrome, a phenomenon experienced by the French writer in 1817.

'In eight years we have had 107 victims of the syndrome. That is not a lot statistically but it is certainly interesting from a medical viewpoint.'

A study, to be published next year, is building up a revealing profile of the tilting tourist. 'More than half the patients came from European countries, whereas the majority of tourists until 1986 came from outside Europe,' she says. Italians, it appears, are completely immune, as are Japanese, whose tight schedules allow no time for dizzy spells.

Variations from the vertical have been recorded in Venice (and no doubt Pisa), but Florence has cornered the Stendhal market. 'Because the Santa Maria hospital is the only one in the city centre, all tourists in need of emergency care are automatically brought to us, whereas elsewhere they would be dispersed and a trend would become less noticeable,' she told Reuters.

She now divides foreign tourists into three psychological categories. 'The bulk of tourists who come to Florence, like many other cities rich in history and art, are in fact well defended against art because all they want to do is write postcards home and sit and eat pizza.'

The next group comprises a minority in search of an experience similar to that of Stendhal, who wrote: 'On leaving the Santa Croce church I felt a pulsating in my heart . . . life was draining from me.' However, this category remains rational and upright.

The tiny, most vulnerable group are those who have difficulty adapting to changes in their environment and who attach a particular, overwhelming significance to an event. 'Those people with certain characteristics, not intellectual but sensitive and easily susceptible to emotions, when faced with the impact of this city, can succumb to a complex crisis that can lead to catastrophe.

'There is no direct cause – people carry many factors with them – but Florence can be the catalyst.'

5 May, 1987   **Stuart Wavell**

Sunflowers in Provence

Looking back on it after some months, now the wounds have healed and the scar tissue looks less angry, I wonder what exactly it was that we did wrong. If ever there was a family holiday that was properly tailored and buttoned up this was it, and yet it all came apart at the seams.

It began with an exchange scheme, whereby we were first hosts to a French teenager, then would carry him and our own sprig for the second leg in Nice. Duty done, we would retreat into the hinterland of Provence for a general immersion in Cezanne country.

To this end we contracted with Vacances Franco-Britanniques, who always come out top of the customer-satisfaction polls conducted by *Which?* for a villa in the vineyardy ridges below the Sainte Victoire range, near Aix and about 150kms west of Nice, handy for the eventual pick-up.

VFB did everything their reputation implied with exemplary fastidiousness, including insurance, booking of hotels en route, and pictures of the property with directions on how to find it. When our knees wobbled under the accumulation of disasters, the VFBosom proved amply reassuring, which is all anybody could expect of a bosom heaving 1,000kms away in Cheltenham.

On a Saturday evening in August, the pieces on the Provençal board were all in place. Our cub seemed to have taken a shine to Nice, and we preened ourselves on a neat performance, though but for a bank holiday running into the weekend, we might have had a better stock of francs.

The villa, a self-contained annexe to the owners' house, framed imaginary Cezannes back and front – vines and winding route below, and a slope of dense maquis and needle-dripping conifers behind. The book for guests' widsom was full of tips on climbing to La Croix de Provence, parking in Aix and shopping in Trets village. Tish and Babs apologized for burning the oven instructions, and warned everybody not to start a forest fire with the barbecue.

We had had a good meal under an awning in a *ruelle* amid

the charm of old Aix, and taken a circuit of the higher ground along the zig-zagging *route des vins* to look seawards over the valley, then came in to be told by the villa owner that the phone had been urgent with bad news from Nice.

The cub had had a pain watching football – nothing to do with the game – and at the party afterwards refused to eat – nothing to do with the food. In short, an appendix. But the GP wanted the second opinion of a surgeon.

The surgeon, soon found, concurred. He was brisk, but understanding: he could operate at his clinic in the morning, or the patient could be despatched to London. Against the latter was the probability that he would, on whatever plane, reach London too late.

Since there could be only one answer, we were told to report at the clinic at 8 a.m. We complied, finding first a garage that would take a credit card, when the tank was all but dry. He was a laconic man, that garage manager, but by the end of the week, when we'd refilled six times and driven 2,000kms, he was vouchsafing an entire sentence. And when I said it was the last time, he smiled.

In the meantime our stricken student of French, who would in the next few days acquire an unforgettable skill in a special corner of the language, had been visited by the technician of an extramural lab for a blood sample, and in the clinic by another outsider called a *cardeologue*, with a sphygmoman-ometer, whose function is exercised in British hospitals by nurses. My deposit of £300 having been paid, it wanted only the collaboration of a further freelance, the anaesthetist, and the op was under way.

No problems. Brilliant surgery. Cut so low it could have been used to explore a kneecap. Appendix available for a bracelet if desired. In the euphoria there was only a smidgen of ill omen: when we'd wanted to discuss payment the surgeon had gleamed over his half-glasses at me and said in shocked tones, 'Ah, M'sieu. Medicine today, papers tomorrow.'

There were no papers on the morrow, nor on any day until the end. Each morning we drove into the rising sun from villa to clinic, to keep our cub company, each evening we drove back into the setting sun.

It was fiendishly hot and dry, and the mistral blew. The symbol of the heat that sticks in my mind is the butterflies swarming to drink the moisture from the washing as we hung it on the line by the villa. In the clinic there was no air-conditioning, and the door was closed against the wind. Drinking water had to be fetched from the basement and paid for. Except to deliver meals, the attendants mostly kept to their little office. 'How hot is it!' they repeatedly exclaimed. 'How hot it is!' they said in the shops. Nice airport reported the record equalled.

Each of those medical technicians put in his own bill, and the clinic two more (care, plus extras). The anaesthetist came back daily and scared his patient rigid again, by demanding an £80 supplement. The surgeon's was the seventh, a bill to be settled in his consulting room at a separate address.

Now the clinic, we knew in advance, was *conventionne*. That is to say, the state takes care of the bills. We had our own Health Service's E111, and we had private insurance. When the supplements showered down, we sought advice from the Caisse National in Nice. They were indignant on our behalf, but powerless. There are too many clinics, they said, which are hybrids of private and public practice. The most you can do is insist that on each *feuille de soins*, the basic charge and the supplement be set out separately.

We did that. It wasn't liked, and in two cases the supplements disappeared. The total charges, by the way, amounted to £820. The surgeon would take only cash, and waved away the Paris telephone number of the insurance company. 'I am a surgeon, not a garage mechanic,' he said.

To collect his cash, we went to American Express. Despised by restaurants and garages, the card now did a useful job. I came back down the road of a baking city too choked with traffic for business or pleasure with two ice creams, and we ate them reflecting that our experience was a defeat for the E111. With our son briefly released into the sole custody of his French hosts, we trailed back to the villa.

And were violently ill that night. The ice creams, I suppose. The salmonella held complete sway for 48 hours until, gutted like fish, we were able to creep into Aix for a restorative stroll among the fountains. It was lovely, lots of elegance about, and we drove back to the villa feeling braced to collect the cub from Nice next morning and make the best of the last few days.

We were level with the peak of La Croix before it really became obvious that smoke at the base of the mountain was only part of a huge gusher, with great flames seeming to seek their freedom from their black casing, all being whipped along from ridge to ridge by a wind that reached 80 kph. In and out of the beastly confusion, little glinting planes dashed bravely with their pathetic cargoes of fire retardant.

The fire marched, trotted, cantered and broke into a gallop. Of the many fires in Provence last summer, started by fire-raisers, or empty bottles left in the maquis, and in this instance apparently by a young German backpacker who thought he would get a lift from vehicles that stopped to see the spectacle, it was not the worst, nor the least. Before it was reined in, it would cover 14 kilometres of our valley, and kill four people.

From the villa we watched the march with Madame the owner. She had seen not a few, and reckoned there was no need to pack, as the wind was bearing it away from us. All the same, we surreptitiously packed. When the wind was in our faces, the fire made short work of the four-kilometre interval, leaping lightly from ridge to ridge and ignoring the hollows, taking out the fancy villas on the high ground, and sparing the houses below.

There is something both appalling and compelling about the progress of such a fire as it comes near. It moves up a ridge in a series of little leaps. Each time there is first a puff of white smoke as the undergrowth catches, which turns black as the trees give in, and the roar of resin exploding, then the process is repeated.

The fire came behind us, on both sides, in a horseshoe, closing all the roads but one. Down this we fled. We were told to find lodgings in the village of Rousset, where it was raining ash, but it was already congested with people and cars. They let us break east for St Maximin, where we'd touched before for dinner, and were lucky to get the last room, though such a windowless cell by the dustbins would not have been luck any other time.

With the cub we went back next day to the villa, in a new landscape of smouldering ash, the maquis quite gone and those trees not dead obviously moribund. The fire had lapped the house on all sides and filled it with ash, but neighbours and volunteers on the roof had drenched it all night, and it was whole. We were thrilled for Madame, who'd helped us such a lot, and even wanted the next hirers to be alerted in case they wished to cancel.

The next night the long-awaited rains came. Unhindered by maquis, the waters drenched away the red soil of the slopes, created a lake and buried the tomatoes in sludge. There were floods all over. Time for Cezanne to come indoors. 'You have very active holidays, M. Hamilton,' remarked Madame.

11 March, 1987

Alex Hamilton

Hockney at fifty

Mulholland Drive twists and lurches up and down the Hollywood hills like a gorgeous scenic roller-coaster. High above Los Angeles it climbs, above the freeways, above the urban scrubland, above the smog line, up on to a lush green hillside that smells of dew and flowers.

Clinging with some difficulty to the steep slopes is an interesting assortment of lopsided houses. Most of them are inhabited by film stars and painted white. David Hockney's is bright red and blue. The garden chairs arranged on his big veranda are bright yellow. His chronically inviting pool, twinkling below, is the colour of Paul Newman's eyes and looks amazingly like a Hockney painting. Indeed, on closer inspection, that is what it turns out to be, a faded signature on the floor of the shallow end revealing that DH added the bluest ripples in 1982.

Rather like Andy Warhol, whose funeral he had just attended, David Hockney when he quietly materializes by my side at the pool gives the impression of being an after-image of himself. Born a brunette, he has since the age of 24 been a strikingly pale man with peroxide blond hair and a taste for light white cotton clothes. His skin remains a Bradford cream, not a Californian brown. His handshake is little more than a soft stroke of the palm. His accent combines Bradford vowels with Californian consonants in a fashion I imagine to be unique.

'There was a Watteau exhibition in Paris last year. I went to see it. Beautiful painting.' He responds firmly to my query about the obsession with funny perspectives and jigsaws of photography that has characterized his work over the past half-decade.

'There's a painting of a lady in it called "The Intimate Toilette". The lady is sitting in her chair with a kind of negligée on, a servant girl powdering her. Beautiful painting. It kind of reeks of perfume. And I'm looking at it – I was with Celia actually [Celia Birtwell, Hockney's long-time confidante and model] – and the next day we went to the Beaubourg to see the Kahnweiler Gift, about 20 Picassos. One of them was a small painting of a girl. But you could see the front and the back of her.

'Now, I tried to point out to Celia, you're looking at it in a different way. The Watteau is as though I'm looking at it from here through a door. If in the Picasso you see the front and the back, you are in the picture. You're not outside of it. You're in the world in a sense. Not outside of it.

'I don't know, I tend to think, well, no wonder, we might blow ourselves up if we keep all these images when we're not in it. We're not in space. It's like stereoscopic photography. Certainly you get a strong illusion of space. But you're not in the space. You're outside looking in, aren't you? Well, where are you if you're not in space? You're nowhere. You aren't anything. And wouldn't all this be doing something to us . . . ?'

This summer David Hockney will be 50. The boyishness that is as integral a part of the public persona of Britain's most popular artist as his bleached hair and owlish glasses does not seem to stretch very comfortably to 50. To be David Hockney, and middle-aged, seems somehow a contradiction in terms. Even the huge hearing aids he now wears, comprehensively blocking off both ears, look suspiciously like some exotic flesh-coloured personal stereo system on which he is probably listening to Mozart while his interviewer prattles on.

'I became aware that I was losing my hearing – they said it's hereditary, my father, my sister both have it – I became aware of it in 1979 when I went to teach in San Francisco just for a week. And there was a seminar in a kind of big room. And I realized – anybody talking back I couldn't hear at all. I went to have my hearing tested and they told me I'd lost 20 per cent.

'Then I realized it was getting worse. And what happens is you avoid crowds, because it's too difficult to hear. It's like being in a fish-tank. So, slowly you get very anti-social, I think, if you don't do much about it. I avoid noisy restaurants. And most of the restaurants here are noisy. So I go to really lousy restaurants because there's hardly anybody there. Actually I stay in most of the time.'

Where, from my experiences of a long warm afternoon in the Hockney household, the whole world comes to see him. The phone never stops ringing. An assortment of males, young and old, secretaries, workmen, assistants, biographers, hangers-on, visitors from abroad, people doing books, people who make the tea, people who look after Hockney's two noisy little dogs, gardeners, college friends from Bradford, and me – all of us buzz around the lopsided house clinging to a hillside like drones around a hive.

I am led into a studio built on a tennis court that came with the topsy-turvy house which Hockney acquired eight years ago to end 15 years of nomadic LA life. He grins shyly and informs me that he did not even know the large tennis court came with the property when he bought it. The Almighty's unconditional love for artists never ceases to surprise me.

Inside the studio is a strange black construction resembling a Bedouin tent. Inside the tent is an impressive clutter of audio equipment, a miniature stage and a musty settee which I am invited to share with a large, loud and vaguely familiar man who turns out to be the restauranteur Peter Langan, come up into the Hollywood Hills to drum up support for a new LA eating house.

We are treated to the sad long finale of Wagner's *Tristan and Isolde*. Hockney manning the switches and re-arranging the props conjures up an amazing night sky in which the stars sparkle like Elizabeth Taylor's torso at the Oscars. Slowly the night sky turns into a new dawn. Director Jonathan Miller, he tells us, was really excited. So were Peter Langan and I.

Scheduled for only six performances in Los Angeles, Miller and Hockney's *Tristan and Isolde* is, he insists, his last opera. 'Collaboration means compromise. In the theatre you have to do that . . . And I think my hearing's very affected. But it did occur to me, you know, hearing is spatial. You make space with sound as well. You locate yourself with sound as well. It did occur to me that maybe if this happens you might develop a more acute sense of visual space to counteract it, just as a blind person probably develops a more acute hearing in space. I thought maybe that made me notice things and I think probably started me off on all that photography . . . Piano tuners are often blind, aren't they? I don't know if it would ever happen but it sounds plausible to me.'

David Hockney moved to California in 1963. Even before he set eyes on America he had painted imaginary Californian interiors inhabited by the showering, suntanned beach boys who had replaced Cliff Richard – drooled over in a wonderfully secretive series of Royal College works – as the main object of the artist's erotic fantasies.

The imaginary Californian interiors were based on photographs found in Physique Pictorial, whose LA offices he quickly visited. A wish fulfilled, he has stayed ever since. And will never go back. In private David Hockney refers to the English as 'downers'.

Those first few months in California were, according to his autobiography, the only truly promiscuous months of his life. They resulted in the creation of an unmistakable world, a towel-dried poolside playground that most observers still assume to be a reflection of his real life.

At the centre of this painted world is a bright blue expanse of water, just like his own, glittering and beckoning in the Californian sunshine. Around the pool a selection of nude young men, pretty, blond, sullen, go lazily about the business of doing nothing much. Occasionally they swim. More often they go indoors and shower. Always they pose and appear wrapped up in their own thoughts. They are being watched.

It is 20 years since the poolside paradise ceased to be Hockney's principal subject. But it is far too memorable a creation to disappear quickly from his audience's image of him, a symbol of its times as instantly recognizable as the mini-skirts of Mary Quant and, according to his fiercest critics, just about as shallow.

Should D.H. live another 50 years and effect completely the transformation into a slightly eccentric philosopher–artist concerned with the mysteries of time and space that he now seems to have embarked upon, he will still remain in most people's eyes the jolly poolside decadent of the 'Bigger Splash.'

In fact during the Eighties Hockney has hardly painted a thing, concentrating instead on a series of curious and, to me, rather batty technical experiments, most recently with colour xeroxes and most famously with collages made out of complex arrangements of colour photographs.

'I think collage is one of the most profound inventions of the twentieth century, actually. And there's more and more of it around. I'm putting together a lecture and I've found lots and lots of examples of how collage is deceitful. Stalinist collage I call it. My example was – Stalin made a collage when he removed Trotsky from a photograph. He took one layer out. His intention was to deceive, to make you think that Trotsky was not at Lenin's side at whatever the moment was. Stalin is basing the technique on you thinking it's all the same time. He doesn't show the glue from the collage, therefore he can deceive you. That's the intention.

'Well, now I've got wonderful examples where computers can re-do photographs. The examples I found were amazing. You can see a picture of a man looking out of window and he's looking out over the Thames, at St Paul's. And in the next picture, the same picture, they've moved the furniture around, yet it still looks like the photograph, only he's looking out of a temple in Bangkok. This is in a leaflet demonstrating what these computer techniques can do. And I look at it and I think: "Aha. This is Stalin again. Because there's no evidence of the collage."

'Now, if there's no visible evidence of the collage the intention is to deceive. That means even police photographs could be doctored. You can superimpose anybody into a riot. Into all kinds of things. Well, so long as we know that, they won't be very powerful. We have to know that these kinds of things happen. Therefore these technical leaflets should be spread around . . . a lot more.' And he laughs the thin unexpectedly conspirational laugh of a student agitator.

'I'm rather thrilled with it because it will mean that the photograph is going to lose its authenticity about reality. I tend to think images are powerful enough to make us see the world in the way they are. We think the world's like a photograph now, don't we? And it's not.

'I mean, I tried to tell the Royal Academy when they voted me in – and I've never been there. I've never exhibited there. I don't really care about them at all. I didn't really know what to do when they said I'd been voted in – I said this to Ron Kitaj, I pointed out that the trouble with the Royal Academy is that, like all Academies, in the end its aim is to defend itself as an institution, not to defend art, which is what it was made for.

'And I pointed out that in the eighteenth century, if Parliament had been discussing Depiction, Joshua Reynolds would have had a lot to say to them. Today, when Parliament discusses Depiction, it wouldn't listen to an artist. Would it?'

The chances of today's Parliament discussing Depiction are, I mutter, slim.

Inventive playfulness is clearly an essential component of his talent. Outside his living room a series of cut-out fish, painted in day-glo colours, dangling from threads in the breeze, turn his windows into the walls of a giant aquarium. Asking me to sit down he strides off to play the piano and sounds very impressive. A giggle alerts me: he's winding me up with a wind-up piano.

I wonder if the advancing years have filled him with any great desire to deal in more obviously serious subject-matter than swimming pools and Cairo hotel rooms, and thereby refute the common charge that he is irrevocably an artistic lightweight. Hockney sighs a weary sigh.

'I've always thought this: everybody is touched by tragedy.

Every human being. And every human being knows about it. Unfortunately not every human being knows about comedy. The comic in life. To have only one side is, I think, unfortunate. Tragedy, of course, is a literary concept. Not a visual one.'

What about the charge that he plays too much to the gallery in his role as Britain's most popular artistic hero and Granny's favourite modernist?

'Art is for everybody, really. When I was doing this opera I read a few things on Wagner. He had an argument about art. In 1850 the concert-makers of Europe said: these concerts are cultivated and people need to be cultivated to understand and appreciate this music. And Wagner's argument was this: he said this denies the power of music to go very deep into you. Deeper than cultivation is. I think that he was right.'

So do I. And it is surely the gap that exists between David Hockney's splendidly articulated ambitions for his work and the lack of nerve-gas in the work itself which has caused critics to judge him so harshly, earning him Douglas Cooper's shrivelling assessment as 'an overrated minor artist'.

Hockney's talents are obvious and hardly negligible. The thin dry line with which he has immortalized friends and lovers in drawings and etchings over the past 25 years is one of the more pleasing inventions of post-war art. So quiet and yet so certain.

Not many artists can claim to have put their name to a colour, but use the description 'Hockney blue' and your audience knows what you mean – a particularly clear and luminous azure that represents both water and sky. It comes complete with matching mood, an introspective cocktail hour when the day is at its laziest.

From England the poolside paradise can seem unforgivably vapid subject-matter. Sitting by his isolated pool in California it is easier to see it as a confrontation with reality rather than an escape from it.

But while Hockney's various diversions into pool-painting, theatre, photo-collage are all in their ways impressive, and usually pleasing, none of them provides the echoes of profundity by which one wants to judge the truly important artist. He gives the impression of a talented truant, messing around with various amusing distractions in order to avoid the exam for seriousness. Certainly he has never dealt in any resonant way with the loneliness he claims for himself in his autobiographical writings.

'I love seeing. I get excited seeing.' He waves, exasperated, at the various optical jigsaws scattered around his studio, multi-directional photographs of the Mojave desert, colour xeroxes of landscapes and still-lives set in eye-boggling bendy space.

'And I think as you get older it's like – have you been to Madrid and seen the Goyas? Until he's 45 they're all wonderful – joyful, silvan glades, pretty people dancing, lovely paintings. But then, he went deaf at 50, didn't he, Goya? Stone deaf. And something happens. You can see it in the Prado because there's a sequence of so many. I was really impressed. All those screaming people . . . silent?'

Does he believe in God, I inquire, detecting new whispers of mysticism in his voice?

'My attitude actually is that I've never really had much conventional religious thought. I think I'm a bit oriental in my thinking there. I think actually we're all part of one thing. I believe in wholeness, really. It's all one. And therefore we're just bits of it. And if we can see it right we can see something very different and realize in a sense that we are God. We're only parts of the whole.'

How far has he reached in these philosophical experiments with photography and perspective? Far enough, he sighs, looking like an old alchemist who has just boiled his last toad. There will be no more photography. No more theatre. No more collaborations. He feels, he says, ready now to begin painting – at last.

21 May, 1987   **Waldamar Januszczak**

To Russia with love

As an accurate document *Blunt* (BBC 2) leaves some room for an eyebrow to rise.

My favourite communist hooted like an owl that has heard a good one when Burgess, a Soviet agent, was seen to carry a party card. I prefer to take my stand on etiquette. If a royal equerry says 'His Majesty would be pleased to have you dine on Thursday the 24th' you *never*, like Blunt, check your diary to see if you have a prior engagement. Even if you are busily organizing the headlong departure of a couple of dear friends to Moscow on the 25th, you do not hesitate. You indicate that you will be charmed to share the royal pie and mash and you make a point of being particularly attentive to the Queen Mother, who is known to be tiresome about treachery. 'The one thing I cannot stand is a traitor,' she said after Burgess and Maclean's flight.

As a play, *Blunt*, by Robin Chapman, is highly entertaining, funny and taut. It could equally be called *Blunt and Burgess* being, according to Chapman, the story of a long love affair and its final betrayal when Burgess escapes and leaves Blunt to face the music.

If it was so, they are a strikingly ill-matched couple. Anthony Hopkins makes a cheerful meal of Burgess, a hail-fellow, what-ho, what's–yours charmer, who first appears crowned with a sea scout's hat–'The train was packed with sea scouts. Managed to get through three before Basingstoke'–and disappears into the distance backfiring like an undependable but lively car. 'Cheerio. Love to everybody. Hugs to the kiddiewinks. Bye.'

He seems to explode out of his jacket like a Christmas parcel; his handkerchief bursts from his pocket like a rabbit. This is the man who hid a copy of Kinsey in Ernest Bevin's room at the Foreign Office, judging it to be the safest place, and laid in a stock of Old Etonian ties before leaving for Moscow, where they are known to be in short supply. It must have been quiet in London after he left.

(Anthony Hopkins was appearing simultaneously on *The South Bank Show* (LWT) as the only King Lear I have seen who, while complaining he was a poor, old man, could clearly have wrestled a bull to its knees.)

Ian Richardson's Blunt, perhaps from Burgess's habit of referring to him as 'dear old Ant', irresistibly suggested a maiden lady of high principles, wearing a virginal grey cardigan, his silver hair corrugated like the roof of a particularly strict chapel. He could have gone on as Lady Bracknell without rehearsal. When he removes all the incriminating correspondence and pictures of Lenin from Burgess's flat, he does so in Fortnum and Liberty carrier bags and incinerates them in an elderly boiler called Britannia. Talking of elderly boilers, all the protagonists look rather older than one would expect but then they had led difficult lives.

A visit to Goronwy Rees (Michael Williams) offered the visual treat of the Thames Valley in a particularly exuberant spring. Everything was green as if the willows were leaking colour into the river, except for one huge meadow which was thickly buttered with buttercups. How, you think, looking at this green and gold, could Burgess bear to go. Here, playing with the Rees children, he fished for minnows: 'Have you caught him . . . yes, he's there . . . look, there's another one. Missed him.'

There was a fine, shining performance from Rosie Kerslake as Margaret Rees, a Silver Shred-coloured girl with the smooth, bulging forehead of a baby and a child's gift for asking unanswerable questions. 'Guy's a spy? So you are a spy too? I think knowing someone's a spy and not telling makes you one too.' 'Report one's best friend?' said Goronwy Rees, horrified. 'Spies can't have friends,' she said. Friendship seems to be the stake which skewered the whole crew like so many kebabs and when one turned they all turned and when one burned they all burned.

When Blunt was exposed in 1979 the BBC was showing *Henry IV* Part One. A minor character, never noticed before, leapt into the spotlight. He was called Blunt. Blunt was very busy on behalf of his friends. 'Here is a dear and true industrious friend. How now, good Blunt, thy looks are full of speed.'

Blunt's activities were cut short at Shrewsbury – 'A gallant knight he was. His name is Blunt' – giving Falstaff the occasion for some acid remarks on the subject of honour.

12 January, 1987

Nancy Banks-Smith

Steel and stone

By an extraordinary chance, two early, virtually unperformed Eugene O'Neill plays have opened simultaneously in London. Peter Stein's Schaubühne production of *The Hairy Ape* (1921) weighs in at the Lyttelton at close on four hours in a display of epic Expressionism; Patrick Mason's production of *Desire Under The Elms* (1924) at Greenwich Theatre gets through its business without an interval in two hours. Art is not a competition. But while Stein's production boasts images that sear themselves on the retina, Mason's seems closer to O'Neill's tragic rhythm.

Whatever my reservations about Stein's production (which had a technically nightmarish first night), I am delighted to see it on the National's stage: not only because it re-introduces us to a great director but because (like so many shows in the old World Theatre Season) it widens our experience of world drama.

O'Neill's play is astonishing because of the way it theatricalizes alienation. Its hero, Yank, is a stoker on a transatlantic luxury liner. The daughter of the President of the Steel Trust pays a visit to the hellish, fiery furnace of the stokehole, during which Yank confronts her in all his 'unknown, abysmal brutality'. Vowing to get even with her and her kind, he returns to New York, provokes a fight with the Fifth Avenue capitalists, gets thrown into jail, thrown out by the Wobblies and ends up in the zoo changing places with a gorilla who kills him.

It is not, as the best American critics have realized, a social drama about the heroic prole versus the wicked capitalists. Edmund Wilson pointed out that 'the *Hairy Ape*'s ultimate struggle for freedom takes place within the man himself'. Harold Clurman added that the play 'articulates the basic loneliness or alienation of the American worker'.

I would go even further: I would say it is about the profound isolation induced by the industrial process. The dominant verbal image of the play is of steel. And it is no accident that Mildred, the Steel President's social worker daughter, sees herself as redundant as Yank. 'I'm a waste product in the Bessemer process – like the millions,' she says, emphasizing the industrial dehumanization that Chaplin (O'Neill's future son-in-law) seized on in *Modern Times*.

Stein's production and Lucio Fanti's mammoth designs grasp this vital fact. From the first image of the stokers, cramped and huddled in the fireman's fo'c'sle like animals in a steel cage, we see what mechanization has done to man. Stein realizes O'Neill's Expressionist theatricality: nowhere more brilliantly than in the stoke-hole scene where the stokers rhythmically swing open the furnace-doors like toilers in Dante's Inferno. And when Mildred (looking like Lindsay Kemp with her white face, white dress and cloche hat) is confronted by Yank, it is like the meeting of polar social opposites but spiritual kin.

Viewed singly, each of the eight scenes is astonishing: Stein's archaeological eye for detail is apparent in the scene in the Wobblies' office with its high Dickensian desks, tasselled stool and improving radical literature. But that is the problem: each scene becomes a monumental single event. When you read the play, Yank's progress to the zoo seems propulsive and inevitable.

But here Stein and Fanti have broken O'Neill's headlong rhythm in a combination of hyper-realism and Murnau Expressionism. You gasp as each scene is set before you – Fifth Avenue is a mirage of angled black towers, the jail offers a receding perspective of cages with white hands fluttering through the bars like doves – but you lose sight of Yank's dizzying trajectory. It's a heck of a long time from the opening sight of him trapped in one steel cage to his final enclosure in another.

Rolan Schafer himself is superb as Yank: a lost, marooned, animalistic version of Rodin's Thinker. The company also do a heroic job moving from coal-blacked stokers to choreographed capitalists to studious unionists and chattering simians. I am grateful to the National and the Festival of German Arts for bringing us this production. But I feel that Stein and Fanti (having given us a dominant single image in their Welsh National *Otello*) have here fallen prey to the kind of epic mechanization. O'Neill himself condemns: you feel that backstage it must be a bit like the liner's stokehole.

Down in Greenwich, Patrick Mason and designer Joe Vanek have also taken an Expressionist line with *Desire Under The Elms*. This is, in a sense, Greek tragedy (the Phaedra–Hippolytus story with touches of Oedipus thrown in) transposed to a New England farm in 1850. Ephraim Cabot, stony, proud, old and lonely, brings his new bride, Abbie, back to the farm. Abbie, dispossessed young widow, wants the land. But even more she wants, and gets, her stepson Eben.

To prove the point, she murders the child they have illicitly had and which one day will reap the inheritance. Abbie and Eben end up united in passion: Ephraim has the land and the chill satisfaction (as he sees it) of God's vengeance.

In Mr Mason's production you get plenty of desire but no elms. He ignores O'Neill's very precise stage-directions with their description of two overshadowing trees with 'a sinister maternity in their aspect'. Instead he and Mr Vanek frame the action inside an enormous V-shaped hangar-like barn with Mick Hughes's footlights throwing looming shadows on the back wall. It is a daring device but it works partly because it removes the taint of Cold Comfort Farm rustic melodrama and partly because it reminds us how much the early O'Neill deals in dominant themes and images. In *The Hairy Ape* it is steel and solitude; in *Desire Under the Elms* it is stone and solitude.

The latter is a less good play because you sense O'Neill straining for tragic effect (the murder of the child is abrupt and implausible). But, in Mr Mason's production, the farm takes on symbolic overtones of America where acquisitive ownership battles against shared love.

And there is an extraordinary performance from Tom Hickey (whose work I have often praised in Dublin) as Ephraim: a stiff-gaited old pentecostal puritan capable of sudden bursts of manic vitality. Carmen Du Sautoy catches both Abbie's land-hunger and her sexy langour and Colin Firth's Eben is suitably guilt-ridden and Oedipal.

But what is astonishing, seeing Mason's and Stein's productions back to back, is the raw theatrical power of Twenties O'Neill and his ability to capture poetically the doomed loneliness of American life, whether on a New England farm or in the concrete canyons of New York.

13 May, 1987   **Michael Billington**

Potter beats the old conundrum

Doctors are also detectives, private eyes are in private practice, patients have things done to them and are in the condition of children. It's as plain as the diagnosis on our faces. Dennis Potter's *The Singing Detective*, which ends tomorrow night, is both a quest for the causes of Philip Marlowe's sickness and an exploration of the power of the imagination to overcome the body's ills and pain. Except that you can rarely parcel up Potter's work as simply as that, and you certainly can't do it with this one.

Aside from the way he parodies two or three different genres, each episode has revealed new strands of an ever more complicated story whose core remains the oldest theme in the thriller business: betrayal. Writers right wrongs. What Marlowe most needs and least wants to know is whose or what treachery has made his body betray him.

Am I right, or am I right? It's a joke quote from private eye pulp that Potter uses as a refrain. And he doesn't just mean right in his detective deductions. In the Puritan conscience that still nags Potter, to be right is to be saved; and to be saved is to be right. His refrain is not an idle or a rhetorical question.

But there are other questions underlying everything. Marlowe enters a belligerent dialogue with those who care for him, either in the personal or the professional sense: doctors, nurses, the psychiatrist Gibbon, his ex-wife Nicola. It's a mode of communication he learnt from his mother and his fearsome schoolmistress, women who blame and punish and deceive. The underlying question is always Why me? What have I done in my ordinarily blemished life to deserve this?

From the third episode on, the heart of the story has been the boy Philip Marlowe's childhood experiences, which the adult Marlowe, with half his mind, believes are the psychosomatic causes of his illness. We know that some of his guilt is – not very believably – traceable to the child Philip betraying the backward boy Mark Binney in his class at primary school.

What we don't know, and Potter always leaves us with this kind of conundrum at the end of every episode, is whether his wife Nicola is cheating him in some way he *hasn't* imagined. And whether the fingered Mark Binney really did deposit the turd on the teacher's table.

It doesn't seem enough, does it, even if it turns out that Philip was, after all, the guilty coprophile? Nor is spying on his mother in her illicit pleasure in the concealing forest. Not enough to justify or explain Marlowe's 20-year martyrdom to his body. There has to be something more. Did something really bad happen to Mark Binney? Or to Philip's mother? That's what we have to find out tomorrow.

Maybe I'm a little disappointed that it has proved such a very personal quest. And yet, in the year of Aids, it has picked up a public resonance that perhaps even Potter did not envisage. As the schoolmistress metaphorically rubs the boy's nose in that offensive turd, you couldn't help thinking of Chief Constable Anderton and his cesspool.

Some of the set pieces have a wonderful theatrical unreality straight out of B movies; like the shooting in the night club, and any other scene that contains those murderous broker's men in trenchcoats. The only thing that I'm still unsure of is the use of popular songs again.

Initially, the effect was, if anything, more lapel-grabbing than the same device in *Pennies From Heaven*. By any standards its first appearance in *The Singing Detective*, when the doctors and nurses break into 'Dem Bones, Dem Bones', is a hugely effective production number, an explosive release from the pain and humiliation we've just shared with Marlowe at the hands of these bizarre, insensitive medics.

The device still works but its power to surprise has diminished, even if Potter's has not.

It would have been easy to make a complete hash of a script as rich and complicated as this one. In fact it has been brilliantly realized by Jon Amiel's direction and Ken Westbury's camera. Order a dozen bouquets for the whole cast from Michael Gambon down. Just as important, the diamond-pointed editing (Sue Wyatt) has made it possible to move in and out of Potter's involuted time warps with a total assurance that carries the audience over the gaps.

What's the scarecrow's significance? Why, every time we see the drowned woman fished out of the Thames – a dominant, recurring image – does she seem to have a different face? Shall we know in the end who she really is? Marlowe's relations with women are heavily distorted anyway.

These are quibbles. Try naming another writer who could weave a spell as strong as this out of such a tangle of over-used, often parodied material: sub-Chandler crime fiction, hospital drama, childhood sex traumas, daft psychiatrists, Bing Crosby . . . Am I right, or am I right?

20 December, 1986

Hugh Hebert

The stars in their galaxies

In Times Square, a few years back, New Yorkers were alarmed by a gigantic poster that asked, in large white letters on a black background, a somewhat unsettling question: PATHETIC HUMANS, WHO CAN SAVE YOU NOW? A couple of weeks later, the answer went up in the question's place. It read: FLASH GORDON.

Hollywood always did see us as pathetic humans, didn't it,

as lesser breeds in need of the profane demigods up there in VistaVision, Todd-AO or CinemaScope. Our place was a seat in the dark, from which we could look up to the stars and watch them shine. Banality made our lives unreal; *they* were the ones who were fully alive.

So we munched our popcorn and grew confused about reality. As the modern city became the negation of nature, so the movies were the perfect metropolitan form, mythologies of the unreal, and they came complete with a new religion: fame.

'Fame! I wanna live forever,' runs the song. The game is, has always been, immortality. Once you had to be a Roman emperor, a prophet, a hero, or at the very least, a genius, to qualify for that particular curse. Hollywood pretended to democratize deification. If you were Lucille LeSueur, you could step away from your sleazy, poor, unhappy past, say the magic word, and shazam! There you were: Joan Crawford.

But the cinema is the least democratic, most hierarchical and status-ridden of worlds, and Hollywood has always been a place of despots (Goldwyn, Thalberg, Cohn), Kings (Gable) and Queens (Pickford). Of course the stars were snobs. Of course they wanted to be aristocrats. But maybe they never quite believed they really truly were, because when Rita Hayworth married Aly Khan, she cried, 'I'm so excited, I can hardly think, I'm sort of lost in a dream world.' And when Grace Kelly married Monaco's Rainier, an even dizzier pinnacle had been attained.

Debrett Goes to Hollywood* sets out to chart the dynasties of Golden Age Hollywood, offering us both family trees and 'webs' at whose heart the sacred monsters sit: Elizabeth Taylor of the six husbands, Constance Bennett, Howard Hawks.

It's a bizarre book, its nose at once high in the air and deep in the dirt. Its author, Charles Kidd, seems torn between the posh genealogical delights of revealing the connection between Tyrone Power and Evelyn Waugh, and the pleasures of gossip-column scandal-mongering.

That isn't surprising. Scandal and Hollywood were always difficult to separate. Maybe we always wanted the stars to fall. We wanted their divinity tarnished. So when Charles Kidd

* *Debrett Goes To Hollywood*, by Charles Kidd (Weidenfeld).

evokes 'an age of glamour never to return', he conjures up the Bennett sisters, who 'totalled twelve husbands, eight divorces and twelve children. Their stories include an unsolved mystery, the tragedy of mental illness, and a scandal that nearly ended a career.'

If that's glamour, his book is full of it: alcoholism, syphilis, suicide. 'Unhappy Sapphic affairs' were the undoing of one Pepi Lederer. Heterosexuality didn't have much better results. 'I hope they blast the living daylights out of that Elizabeth Taylor,' murmured Debbie Reynolds' mum after Liz ran off with Debbie's Eddie, whom she later ditched for Dick. 'Everyone knows exactly what she is.' Take *that*.

Who are the really pathetic humans, I thought more than once as I read; and who can save them now?

One of the (unintentional) revelations of *Debrett Goes to Hollywood* is, after all, that stars do dim, fade and go out; that, except in a very few cases, fame isn't for ever, and the promise of immortality was a con. Many of the 'legends' in this collection no longer seem quite so legendary. Does it interest you that Joan Bennett's daughter was once the sister-in-law of Gloria Swanson's daughter? How much do you care about Franchot Tone? Who on earth were the Rankin and Davenport dynasties? Sic transit Gloria Grahame, even if she does turn out to be descended from Edward III.

Many of the old-time stars whose immortality still seems assured are missing. No Mae West, no W. C. Fields, no Keaton. Even Monroe only rates a photograph. It's significant, too, that the two most interesting connections Charles Kidd has managed to unearth catch the eye because they are links between the movie world and famous people from the 'real' world.

One of these connections is that between Humphrey Bogart and Princess Di (Bogey's mother was an eighth cousin of the Princess's great-grandmother; pretty close, no?). The other is even more startling. Groucho Marx's wife's sister's husband's ex-wife's ex-husband's ex-wife's husband was Randolph Churchill, whose father was, of course, Winston himself. Thus are two of the world's greatest cigar-smokers joined by indissoluble (well, sort of) ties.

Very few stars, nowadays, can generate enough power to

dazzle us. TV has made them smaller than we are. We no longer go to their darkened temples; no longer larger than life, they visit us instead. We channel-hop while they kiss, we push the fast-forward button on our videos when they bore us.

But maybe Hollywood gets the last laugh, after all. The stars may no longer command our devotion, but the religion whose first deities they were has conquered the earth. In *The Big Room*, Michael Herr and Guy Peellaert's portraits of celebrity revealed that the real stars, today, can be gangsters (Meyer Lansky), gamblers (Nick the Greek) or hoteliers (Conrad Hilton). They can be used-car salesmen like Richard Nixon, or, like John Fitzgerald Kennedy, they can be Presidents of the United States.

When murderers start becoming stars, you know that something has gone badly wrong. When ordinary folk queue up to submit to the diverse humiliations of game-shows just to get their five minutes in the spotlight, you realize how far the disease has spread. And when the techniques of starmaking, of image and illusion, become the staples of politics, you understand: we are all idolaters now, and there don't seem to be many iconoclasts around.

At least the old movie stars, flickering up there at twenty-four frames per second, were gods who knew themselves to be false. Come back, Flash Gordon; all is forgiven.

28 November, 1986

Salman Rushdie

Yielding to a hard master

No film by Andrei Tarkovsky is anything other than a daunting prospect. He yields up his secrets slowly, massively, and with the utter conviction of a film-maker who knows he is out of step with his times and does not regret it. You have to draw a deep breath and plunge into his world with as much concentration as he has fashioned it.

The Sacrifice, which looks more and more like his testament, is no exception. Filmed in Sweden and using mostly Swedes both behind and in front of the cameras, it will inevitably seem like an incursion into Bergman territory. But, in fact, it is so Russian that it almost hurts, in its warning thunder, its call for sacrifice, and in its final intimation that there could just be hope.

This is a world we all secretly dread, on the very edge of nuclear disaster. It is part of our corporate nightmare. And, as in a nightmare, where you are falling and falling, there is the half-waking feeling that something can stop the descent if only we could will it strongly enough.

That something, in Tarkovsky's terms, is faith, which can only be obtained by blasting through the dream into reality and then having the courage to change everything. Faith heals only with the most intense effort. Spirituality triumphs over materialism only after a bloody battle.

In *The Sacrifice*, a middle-aged intellectual, celebrating his birthday with family and friends at his isolated home by the sea, faces the prospect of the holocaust with them and strikes a bargain with the Almighty. He will give up everything, including his cherished son, in return for the chance to start again.

After burning the house down, he is regarded as mad and taken away, but his son, a deaf-mute, finds his voice and survives to water the tree his father had planted. Perhaps it will bear fruit.

The film is 145 minutes long and full of those lengthy, intricate and virtuoso takes that, with symbolism as well as heightened realism, seek to post a stage in the argument. Erland Josephson plays the writer with utterly dogged concentration, moving like a man wading through the water which rushes and trickles through most Tarkovsky films.

Susan Fleetwood as his wife and Allan Edwall as the local postman provide the fire with which to melt some of Josephson's ice, but there is little real warmth in the film, because that is not what Tarkovsky is after. Perhaps he should have been, since it is a kind of love that makes the sacrifice possible. Such a stern prophet, however, will not give us anything that smacks or sentimentality, or posits an easy way out.

Needless to say, it is supremely well-fashioned, Sven

Nykvist's cinematography brilliantly matching Tarkovsky's mordant, merciless and stretching vision. There is so much to see in it that, if only we have eyes, the whole argument can be relived again and again, almost without recourse to the sub-titles.

Exceptional works of art like this are seldom flawless but equipped with so defiant a sense of their necessity that, even when you are bored, you feel it is a fault of concentration and not of what is actually up there on the screen. They trample you half to death with their superior strength of will and single-mind-edness of purpose. They can also fire the imagination and enliven a dead fish. In that way, *The Sacrifice* is a classic.

If you can even begin to cope with it, the dividends are immense and lasting. And even if you can't, there are whole sequences – such as the burning of the wooden house – which will hold you like a vice. But for his death last week, I would have said that no one in the cinema at present can begin to compete with Tarkovsky at this level. And now there is a huge void.

We have lost a hard master, but a master he was. It would be stupid to tell you that you must see this film. But, if you don't, it could be your loss.

8 January, 1987

Derek Malcolm

The holy ghost of the Revolution

'Life is not about the *Workers*, it is not about the *Cause*, it is about living!' This is the voice of Rosa Luxemburg, who in life and death held two generations of European socialists spellbound.

She was screaming at that 'angry man . . . with no natural impulse to love', Leo Jogiches, a man obsessed with power and his mother, who ran the Polish Social Democrats with her, who had launched and sustained her, but who could not give her what she wanted. 'Can't we go for walks, to the opera, have a nice flat with nice furniture,' she cried . . . 'perhaps even a baby, a very little baby?'

Nor could she give to him; as she grew in stature, he shrank. Yet they stayed locked together to the end. He was to bring on his own death in his relentless pursuit of her killers.

Not that she had better luck when she turned her all-engulfing passion on the much younger Costia, son to Clara Zetkin, no less obsessed with his mother, a young aesthete and Adonis with the mind of a child – 'What is my Niuniu doing? . . . is baby learning his Marx?'

Life became a drama when a jealous Leo started to make frightful scenes, one of them in a London restaurant, with the orchestra playing *Carmen*. There was, in truth, something operatic about Rosa. In one photograph here, she looks the very image of Madame Butterfly; she called her cat Mimi. That loyal and perceptive creature used to sidle up to Lenin, tentatively lascivious, only to rear and roar like a tiger when he touched her!

Wherever this little woman limped, with her big head, big nose and blazing eyes, men keeled over like ninepins. Yet she never found any peace. When she went on her triumphal progresses and fought those battles which have created the lost, libertarian tradition of European communism – the fight against revisionism, for the mass strike, against Lenin's kind of revolution – she was utterly wretched.

'What is this life about? What is it for?' she wrote to Jogiches when his mother died. 'Is it *worth living*?'

Two-thirds of the way through this hypnotic book,* I got the distinct impression that much of the pre-1914 leadership of central European socialism had just been interviewed by Anthony Clare.

Elzbieta Ettinger, a woman from Poland who is now a professor at MIT, has already published a brilliant edition of Rosa's letters to Leo. Now, armed with much new material, she is so remorselessly 'perceptive' on every shift and naunce

* *Rosa Luxembourg: A Life*, by Elzbieta Ettinger (Harrap).

of human relations that, in the end, one has to jib. Surely not even an author as talented as this can 'know' quite so much?

This is unjust. What Professor Ettinger does – and most memorably she does it – is to locate the objective Rosa of text, oration and action in the subjective reality of Rozalia Luksemburg.

She certainly proves her point that it was Zamosc and Warsaw, nor Zurich and Berlin, which shaped her. In the little Jewish girl with the limp, who lived through a Polish progrom and was passionately devoted to Poland's great Romantic poet Adam Mickiewicz, the woman is foreshadowed.

Rosa was to scorn her Jewishness and to treat her parents abominably (to awake crying in the night, too late). Trapped among 'Huns,' 'Asians' and the chauvinists of her native land, she rejected all forms of nationalism as she did any 'women's movement'. Yet what Elzbieta Ettinger demonstrates as no one else has done, with skill and sympathy and in superbly readable prose, is that Red Rosa, the Jewess, was a Polish Romantic straight out of the Mickiewicz tradition.

And what a woman she was! She must have been dreadful to live with, but at our safe remove, all that passion, intellect, anger, the cultivated mind, the loving kindness, seem the more entrancing for being doomed. This sense of a grace which is damned is not mere hindsight. The spontaneous and creative Revolution of her generous imagination has sometimes happened, but if the great days are Rosa's, the long, dread mornings-after are something else.

In her last prison, she seems to have felt it herself. Reading Cervantes, she turned against the Germans as she had long turned from their socialist leaders. She had good reason. She came out of jail to be dragged into the doomed rebellion of her Spartacus league in the Berlin of January 1919, rancid in its paranoia and inhuman hatred of Jews. It led directly to her bestial murder.

'The old slut's swimming now,' her murderers exulted, after they'd tipped her into the Landwehr canal. They lurched off, to be duly rehabilitated not only by their rotten Reich which rotted Europe, but by the Federal Republic of Germany in 1962.

I knew an old Spanish steelworker who organized a branch of the Spanish Socialist Party in Dowlais, south Wales. His second daughter was born the year Luxemburg was killed; he christened her Rosa. When last I knew her, she used to sit at attention during the Queen's Christmas broadcast.

Rosa lives as legend. She is not Kautsky, not Lenin, not Stalin, not Trotsky. She is the True Revolution which never happens. She is the Holy Ghost of the Revolution.

The account of her last day in Elzbieta Ettinger's sparse and stark prose is unbearable. We have seen millions of unrecorded Rosas go since, but there is still something unspeakable about that final scene in which a small, doomed, grey-haired woman limps bravely through a sick mob of braying brutes. It kills hope.

'Cursed be peoples,' wrote her Adam Mickiewicz, 'that murder their prophets.' Are we to go on cursing for ever? What is this life about? What is it for? Is it *worth living*?

8 May, 1987

Gwyn A. Williams

A copper of character

One reaches the end of this remarkable tale told-out-of-school much in agreement with PC Daley, and certainly much in awe of a man who managed to go his own hedonistic way in such a situation.*

Accepting early on that society was something to be seen through, he came to judge it with a strong mixture of disrespect and affection. He was easily unimpressed, unambitious and logically accepting of the fact that if he didn't bother to wear a mask at all times, he would collect the usual brickbats.

These were often more hurtful than he expected them to be. He was acutely sensible, rather than sensitive and thin-skinned,

* *This Small Cloud: A Personal Memoir*, by Harry Daley, introduction by P. N. Furbank (Weidenfeld).

213

very large by the standards of his malnourished day, and highly vulnerable. His lover Morgan Forster found his forthrightness appealing but also a bit reckless. The novelist and his circle have no place in these recollections and without P. N. Furbank's witty Foreword the only suspicion that the author must have had a closer contact with culture than what could be achieved in a Carnegie library lies in the excellence of the writing.

Daley died in 1971, having made this candid memoir his own 'act of contrition or self-habilitation', as Furbank describes it, although few will find much that he should have been sorry for. Rather the reverse, in fact. His peculiarly English form of subversion strikes one, at this distance, has just what the old country needed – ours too at the moment. Harry, thou should'st be living at this hour.

The hard rational side of him, part of his East Anglian inheritance, convinced him early on that, there being no reason for or possibility of denying his homosexuality, he might as well enjoy it. His 'small cloud' was all too visible to his mates at the police station, but there it was, hanging over him, attracting pleasures and brickbats for life.

Being so exposed himself made him take a close look at what other people took such a lot of trouble to cover up. His conclusion was similar to that of Joe Orton, who wrote in his diary, 'The whole trouble with Western society today is the lack of anything worth concealing.'

A considerable portion of Daley's soul-baring is taken up with stripping away the protective covering of his contemporaries. His attitude is one of 'we're all in it together,' as he surveys humanity's follies and decencies in penurious Lowestoft, comfortable Dorking, but most mercilessly from the matchless vantage point of the inter-war Metropolitan Police station. Dreadful rooms full of dreadful folk in dreadful situations. And a dreadful Edward Burra-like insouciance and gaiety flowing through it all.

How did a nice lad like Harry, music mad, head always in a book, tolerate it? The answer is because it was all so fascinating and because of the perks. These ponderous and hard-worked coppers of the jazz age could, if they wished, take plenty of what they fancied, although after the Goddard case few of them took bribes.

Daley took a shine to the ordinary, broke, occasionally criminal, essentially innocent male of his time. What he preferred to the prissy affairs of 'Bloomsbury' was an emotional mateship carried on in the municipal swimming bath with some costermonger-turned-god once he had left his clothes in the cubical. Although Daley's sex life dominates the book, it also manages to integrate itself most successfully with an astonishing piece of social history which links us, with no particular wish on the writer's part to do so, with the London, Home Counties and Suffolk coast of Dickens.

The Suffolk chapters have a classic quality. Daley was born in Lowestoft in 1901. His father, an orphanage boy from Poplar, was the skipper of the *Geneste* and his mother a parlour-maid from Blundeston. The herring trade was at its zenith and he was reared close by a harbour crammed with shipping and stinking fishyards, and among 'children of exceptional beauty and ferocity'.

There was dire poverty and a profound innocence like that possessed by the 'characters in an early Victorian book'. And there was an ignorance to match. One of the first things which Daley saw was how little his teachers knew. After his father was drowned and he and his brothers and sister qualified as September Gale orphans, his mother took in lodgers and the small, masterly pictures which he gives of these are a prelude to the great range of wonderfully observed types which fill his pages.

There is a key-hole view of a group of Scottish fisher-girls and their sedate boyfriends, which is perfection. Young fishermen make love to Harry and initiate 'the real beginning of my happy life'. This period is immersed in the sepia regret of an old judge's postcard. 'Keep your boots clean and say "Yes Sir" and "No Sir" smartly and you'll get on in the world all right,' he was advised.

In the middle of the Great War the family moved to Dorking – 'the best thing that could have happened to us' – to share the house of a sister whose husband had been in France, and 'thus I saw the tail-end of a world that was about to die'.

215

It was the England of Elgar, Vaughan Williams and Butterworth, says Daley, with 'stillness and sorrow' hanging over the gently rotting scene. Abinger, with no hint of the future, lay just down the road. Assorted monsters inhabited the great houses, Beaverbrook, Marie Stopes, Lord Ashcombe, Mrs Greville. In between ran the rather tumbling territory (everybody called up) of the maiden ladies, the liberal intellectuals and the modest old gentry, all of whom were sweet to the hefty teenager collecting orders for the local grocer.

Daley's assessments and observances are those of the novelist. He doesn't miss a thing. His size provokes the stock response – 'You should join the police force.' If anyone recommended a different prospect because of his way with words, he doesn't mention it.

In 1925 he did join the police, and loved it. First Peel House, then Hammersmith ('mildly and cosily corrupt'), then Vine Street and finally Wandsworth, a quarter of a century of British turpitude and fecklessness, most of it erupting from poverty and ignorance. A London seething with prostitutes, Grundys, mini-gangsters, the unemployed, Mosleyites and Bright Young Things.

How a largely uneducated police force coped with it all, how it lived and what it thought, fill the remaining chapters. Daley's colleagues run the complete gamut from fair to foul, from unbearable to most welcome, as do elements of the old police system, and as do the malefactors – few of them at all ghastly by 1980s' standards. His enemies were the forever moralizing politicians, judges and parsons of the day, the life-spoilers. Daley is a great gossip, a great give-away, a not very great believer in the rules.

20 February, 1987

Ronald Blythe

'Love that suit!'

Can intellectuals be lonely, too, just the same as you and I? With all those books to read, plays to see, music to hear and thoughts to think, are intellectuals out there in the night in empty rooms writing to Miss Lonely Hearts? Of course they are.

Up a very swish alley in Knightsbridge on a bright and breezy Saturday morning I called on Mrs Zelda Fischer of Boston, Mass, in the newly opened British offices of Gentle-people Ltd, her spreading dating and mating agency for the well-heeled, 'professional people' they call them in the US, to separate them from us amateurs and, I suppose, angels down on a visit.

Madame Zelda, the Matchmaker, could very well be something out of Thornton Wilder, although she is much too quiet and ladylike to be played by Barbra Streisand. 'Stan,' she said, dropping the fussy formality of the Old World, 'I love that suit!' I hastily mumbled that it was off-the-peg, but I could see the practised eyes looking for missing buttons or other tell-tale signs of a live one, a bachelor.

What makes Madame Zelda's lonely hearts different is that it costs a lot of money. She is charging £500 at the bottom end of love and £1,500 at the top. For one you get to meet people with common interests, that is Chopin and Schubert; it's rather toney stuff. For £1,500 you get 'the full international research', all the runners and riders, maybe even a dope test. You go out to dinner, to the theatre, the opera, concerts. Suddenly, it is a social and cultural whirl and it is, said one of her clients, a handsome female tax lawyer from Boston, Mass, who was in London to meet some Englishmen, such a good time one actually doesn't want to give it up to get married.

Zelda, a tiny, 59-year-old, redhaired mother of three grown-up married children, apparently, wandered rather absent-mindedly into matchmaking for money five years ago after a lifetime of doing it for fun, 'because it came to me naturally'.

She had an old male friend who suddenly decided he wanted

to get married. Zelda had been fixing up people since she was in her twenties. He said get me a wife and I'll fix you up in business. 'Then he took two whole years to find the right woman.' This was unusual. Most men aren't fussy in that way.

'They think they know exactly what they want. They say five feet eight inches tall, blue eyes, long hair, a good cook. A woman will say, "I want a good man. An honest man. A man who is kind."' Zelda laughed at this weakness of her sex. 'Some of these men who come to me are high-powered businessmen used to making quick decisions and they will propose to a woman right away.' This, she said, was male foolishness.

Two of the American women who came to London to meet some Englishmen were with Zelda in her office. One was a tall, dark beauty, like a film star, and very well dressed in an American *Vogue* sort of way. Oddly enough she was shy about talking of love and romance to even a tweed-clad old buffer from the *Guardian*. The other was a very pretty 29-year-old with that sort of Fergie red hair. She looked like a Cavalier's girl and was that night going to go out with a rich Scotsman who was coming down from Scotland to meet her. Zelda said, in that American way, that she had 'titled people' on the books.

It was nice to think of the rosy Cavalier's girl going back to her roots with a laird in a castle somewhere, but I was just being romantic. There is something very American and Businesslike about this sort of matchmaking. We do meet people in the most haphazard way.

'Have you been married, Stan? Have you had long-standing relationships?'

'Oh, yeah, three.'

'And where did you meet?'

'Huh, ah, in bars. Three times I met them in bars.'

This, however, is not so disastrous as meeting at work. There is, of course, the common interest. But what happens when they break up? The lawyer lady had 'gone with a man from the office' for four years. Never, she said, again. And what about two doctors talking about doctoring through life, two accountants putting themselves to sleep? Or the financial thin ice of two actors? It all has its practical side, and there is life after work, the common cultural interests of 'civilized people – I don't like the word "intellectuals", it's so open to misinterpretation.'

How did she find England?

It was a complete surprise. She had always thought Englishmen so reserved, but they are so funny. What senses of humour Englishmen have! She was completely sold on Englishmen. On England also. What a wonderful country, full of, well, intellectuals, what a marvellous educational system it must have, so many people interested in the arts. But! But all these bachelors! 'I've heard of so many men, 40, 50, 60, and they aren't married. They never have been married. They're old bachelors!'

There were, I offered, bachelors and there were bachelors. But, no, she said, these were bachelors. Like Watson and Holmes, Professor Higgins and Colonel Pickering. They were the grist for her mill and at the same time The Enemy.

'In America,' she said, 'a man of a certain age almost always has been divorced, but not here.' It was obviously a challenge and she was up to it.

This England full of crusty old Professor Higginses seems rather a revelation, but Zelda says it's true. With about two of her people a week getting married (she has, by the way, *not* yet had one single divorce!), she must spend an awful lot of time going to weddings.

Zelda laughed. 'I never get invited to the weddings,' she said.

What, I said, after all this careful research and businesslike effort she had done in getting Miss Right introduced to Mr Right?

'Well, you see,' she said, 'they like to pretend they met in an elevator.'

5 November, 1986

Stanley Reynolds

A thrice-cursed people

Patrick Campbell, who would never have thought of himself as anything but Irish, said the word suggested to him vainglorious shouting and the sound of breaking glass.

Clichés are truths that have been around a long time. According to their sorely tried neighbours, pre-Christian Celts were given to garrulousness, good with horses, religious, vivid, fond of a drink or two or three, boasters and braggarts, fine though undisciplined fighters. Celtic combat – a clash of heroes cheered on by the ranks – strongly suggested to one archaeologist in *The Celts* (BBC 2) a football match trying to get out.

Only the tiresome fact that they had no glasses prevented them breaking it with brio on a Saturday night.

The persistence of the stereotype is breathtaking. Time that blunts the lion's paws has not chipped a corner off the Celtic character.

Frank Delaney, who wrote and presents this series, says they were wiped out by an insulting stereotype and yet he is incapable of using one word where three will do. 'They scratched, clawed, fought their way up the ladder of existence. They were tribal, familial, hierarchical. They were known, respected and feared. They were swift, warlike, fierce and lethal.' I'd have thought that went without saying. Warriors are rarely slow, affable and ineffectual. They find people point at them in the street.

Caesar noted this habit of doing things in threes and smartly divided Gaul into three thus throwing the Celts into permanent confusion.

You can see the essence of Celtic extravagance in the death of a Celt, Pete Marsh, dug up a few years ago in what Delaney calls Cheshire, England. He was hit with an axe, garrotted and stabbed. Not Delaney – Pete. Though that too is a possibility if he keeps saying Cheshire, England.

This sort of thing shows a sneaky hope of selling *The Celts* to Cheshire, Massachusetts or Cheshire, Connecticut. Or Bohemia, Belgium and Budapest, all mentioned in the first episode. *The Celts* is a coproduction with Ireland, Wales, Austria and Brittany so *they'll* take it, and it was filmed in France, Switzerland, Germany, Canada and so forth so *they'll* nibble.

A Celtic curse descends on stuff like this. They are, as Delaney might say, blighted, jinxed and banjaxed. At the very name of Boadicea critics take to the hills. It is the Curse of Vercingetorix. All those actors in long wigs and short nighties hacking away with their swords and quaffing from their skulls.

I remember Billy Connolly playing Vercingetorix, King of the Gauls, in a series for Channel 4 called *Scotland's Story*. He spoke at length in a high wind about liberty and not being in it for the money, which is more than many TV producers can say. Between us, I enjoyed it. When you have seen Billy Connolly as Vercingetorix all other imitations pale.

Celts are not history's only persistent cliché. In a war game Delaney confronted Brigadier Peter Young across opposing armies of toy soldiers. The brigadier wore a mulberry smoking jacket matching his complexion, his white moustache was sharpened to a fine point, his manner affable. 'Well, Frank, my old Celt. I see you've reduced your tribal hordes into something approaching military discipline.'

The Celts attacked, scratching, clawing and fighting their way up their ladders. You did feel they might have done better just to climb them. The brigadier pushed them off. 'We'll take a few of you with us,' cried Delaney. 'Can't make an omelette . . .' said the brigadier. It all seemed somehow familiar.

15 May, 1987

Nancy Banks-Smith

My Gogh!

Many people must be wondering why I decided to buy one of Vincent van Gogh's seven sunflower paintings for £25 million. Obviously this is not the kind of thing you rush into blindly, and before making my successful bid I gave lengthy consideration to other ways in which I could get rid of the cash.

I could have splashed it all on about 15,000 rolling acres of English agricultural land, or rather more than 100 million Mars bars.

I could have paid for three Clore galleries for the Tate Gallery (£7.8m a throw) and have plenty of change to buy paintings to put in them. I could even have bought the *Guardian* at 25p a day for 320,513 years.

I could have bought Queens Park Rangers three times, or Watford Football Club eight times. Ian Rush I could have bought eight times over. But I am less interested in sport than transport. I could have bought 100,000 return tickets for Britain's longest train journey, Penzance to Wick, and still have plenty left over for a British Rail breakfast.

I could have built a couple of miles of urban motorway or five miles of three-lane rural motorway, or spent the money on low-cost engineering schemes to eliminate accident black spots. The Department of Transport has identified 250 such sites in London and reckons that some £8,000 spent on each would prevent more than 1,000 accidents a year.

Were I in warlike mood I could have bought two Harrier jump-jets, or a Tornado for £17 million and with the change run a Leander-class frigate for a year, and still have £1.5 million left over for a Challenger tank. I could have bought my own flight of 16 cruise missiles with warheads.

I thought about education. A few months ago my £25 million could have solved the teachers' dispute, but I missed the chance. I could have founded a post-graduate Oxbridge college. Mr Bakero has asked industry to put up £1m a time for 20 inner-city Technology Colleges. So far only one of those millions has been forthcoming (from the Hanson Trust).

I could have done the other nineteen and still have enough to keep the Royal College of Art going for a year (£5.7 m). Since I'm so fond of painting I could have provided 1,000 artists with £25,000 a year each, which should cover their studio and materials and absinthe or whatever it is that artists drink nowadays.

Or I could have gone into films – for £25 million I could have financed four of this year's Oscar-nominated films: *Platoon, Hannah and her Sisters, Room With a View*, and *Children of a Lesser God*.

I thought of charity, but the best that War On Want could come up with for my money was 1,235 specialized tractors for Algeria, or 1,547 quality control pharmaceutical laboratories for Eritrea, or the digging of 24,000 shallow wells or 3,000 deep wells in that unhappy country.

I could have covered War On Want's budget for four years – £6 million a year for projects and administration. And since I'm so keen on sunflowers, I could have bought 33,000 tons of sunflower seeds which when grown as a crop would have meant an enormous amount of oil-rich flowers. They would cost a lot less each than the £1,650,000 a bloom I paid for van Gogh's painted ones, for which van Gogh, the living artist, was never paid a single franc.

I could have done any of these things, but I didn't. I bought the painting, and I can tell you that when it's hanging over the mantelpiece it's going to look really GREAT!

1 April, 1987

Richard Boston

A hard Lucca story

Italians are agog this week at the spectacle of the squabbling contenders for the estate (which includes the rights from his operas) of Giacomo Puccini, who died 62 years ago last month. Claimant number one is the illegitimate daughter of Puccini's own illegitimate son, Antonio. Last year, after 12 years' litigation, she established her legal right to be known as Simonetta Puccini – and she is not going to let anyone come between her and the estate.

But she has a problem. When Antonio Puccini died in 1946, he left his father's money and property to his wife, a Milanese baroness. When she in turn died, without children, the Puccini estate went to her brother, the Baron Livio dell'Anna. Now the baron, a Riviera socialite, has died in a Milan hospice, bequeathing everything to no less a figure than his lifetime butler. So this latterday Figaro now becomes the owner not only of Puccini's possessions (including his villa at Torre del Lago in the Tuscan coastal pinewoods) but of the rights to his operas, including *La Bohème*, *Tosca*, *Madame Butterfly* and *Turandot*. And, if that were not enough, a third claimant has now entered the competition. The Puccini Foundation, which thought it had the rights to Puccini's birthplace in Lucca and to the composer's villas and which exists to perpetuate his memory as a musician, is also anxious to protect itself against the granddaughter and the butler. As a result, a Lucca court on Tuesday sequested the entire contested estate, pending a final decision as to which of the three claimants should triumph.

It could make a Puccini opera, and it would not be the first time that the composer's extrovert lifestyle found itself influencing his work. Not so long ago, a production of *Turandot* in Glasgow transferred much of the action from Imperial Peking to Torre del Lago in order to point up the connections between Gozzi's cruel play on which the opera is based and the domestic scandal which engulfed Puccini in 1909 when his servant Doria Manfredi committed suicide after allegations of a relationship with the composer that went beyond the call of duty. But the most striking parallel is already there. Puccini's one act comic opera, *Gianni Schicchi*, is precisely about a will. It tells of the anguish of the relatives of a recently deceased Florentine when they discover that he has willed his entire fortune to a monastery. They call in Schicchi, who agrees to impersonate the dead man and to dictate a new will, leaving the estate to the relatives. That isn't quite what Schicchi has in mind, of course, and he duly wills the valuables to himself, leaving the house to his daughter and her lover. Somehow, we suspect there may be a Gianni Schicchi alive and active in Lucca in 1986, too.

11 December, 1986

Leader

Scotto voce

What exactly is a diva? Renata Scotto smiles the beatific smile of a goddess and spreads her hands knowingly. 'She is an image, a dream, untouchable like the moon. But off stage,' and here her voice drops, 'she is a *woman*.'

A diva also has a very pushy American press agent who travels everywhere with her and phones all over town night and day, exerting every pressure he can to show her he's earning his pay.

'Miss Tony-Bee? I want you to know that Renata Scotto is a mother first, a woman and a mother. That's the angle that would go down great for your page, the woman's angle, right? I mean I've known that woman turn down important interviews because of some event at the kids' school. That's the kind of mother she is, right?'

Scotto has been singing in the great opera houses all over the world since her debut in Milan in 1953. She was perched on a sofa in the Savoy, with a carnation in her hair, her press agent at hand. She is promoting her recently published autobiography, *Scotto – More Than A Diva** – a rags to divadom story, full of backstage rows and long quotes from triumphant reviews.

She is a tiny figure, lithe as a ballet dancer, whose every phrase is matched by an elegant gesture with the hands. 'I used to be *fat*,' she says and the earlier photographs in the book bear that out. 'But there is no reason for singers to be fat. It is a great effort for me to stay slim. Some people worry that losing weight might hurt the voice and I say Nonsense. This is a myth to protect the fat singers.' She lost 40 pounds in 1976, after she was horrified at the sight of herself in her first televised broadcast of *La Bohème* from the Metropolitan Opera, New York.

She was born into a poor family, daughter of a policeman in Savona, Italy. The book's description of her childhood reads just a little like the well-polished chronicle of a saint. Her first concerts, she writes, were sung as a child from the window of her family's apartment, when passing villagers threw her gifts

* *Scotto – More Than A Diva*, by Renata Scotto and Octavio Roca (Robson Books).

of candy for another song. During the war the family all but starved.

She learned arias when out fishing with her uncle in his boat, and it was he who took her to her first opera when she was 12, to hear Tito Gobbi singing Rigoletto. She went home, made a hunchback out of cushions and went round the house singing Gobbi's part. 'It never occurred to me to sing Gilda,' she says.

At 14, her parents sent her to work in a convent in Milan. To earn enough for singing lessons, she skivvied all week, something much disapproved of by the nuns. She won a major singing prize which gave her, at 18, her first role, as Violetta in *La Traviata*. Even while she was first singing in the opera, she still lived and worked in the convent, in her brown uniform.

'I am,' she says, 'very superstitious and deeply religious.' She has believed herself guided all her life by a long-dead diva, Maria Malibran – heroine of the romantic era of the 1830s – who died young when thrown from her horse while pregnant. Renata Scotto went to a seance in Milan in 1956 where, she says, Malibran appeared.

'She talked to me, saying I must sing what she sang. She said that I must sing for her, that I must sing her roles.' The medium signed Malibran's name and, Scotto says, the signature perfectly matches Malibran's own.

But she had famous run-ins with a diva of flesh and blood – Maria Callas. Her first major breakthrough came when she had to stand in for Callas at the last moment at Edinburgh.

'Callas had other plans – a party at Elsa Maxwell's – and she had no intention of singing,' Scotto writes, somewhat cattily. But it gave her a chance to sing two major roles, to rave reviews. Callas had swept out of the opera house telling reporters: 'I am leaving the role to a younger colleague who will cover herself in glory.' And she did.

But the first time she actually met Callas a few days later was at a recording session when Callas praised her extravagantly and then tried to get Scotto's only aria cut out of the record. Ferocity between the two was carried to absurd lengths. In 1970, Renata Scotto opened a new production of *I Vespri Siciliani* at La Scala that had not been performed since Callas sang it in 1957. Callas, by then retired, booked herself the first

226

box for the opening night. A claque of Callas fans were in the house, too. The moment Scotto entered the stage, before she had opened her mouth to sing a note, the claque started shouting 'Brava Callas!' and 'Maria, Maria!' all through the evening.

It destroyed the performance and afterwards Scotto stormed off the stage and snapped at reporters: 'Let them get Callas to come and do *Vespri*, if she can sing!' The claque kept it up through the remaining performances.

It happened again in New York when she sang Verdi's *Luisa Miller*. Just as she was about to begin the opening aria the mysterios 'Brava Callas!' cries started. She had the pleasure of singing back at them in that opera with peculiar energy, 'Punish me, O God, if I have offended You, but do not abandon me to the wrath of these barbarians!'

Then there was an equally well-publicized row with Pavarotti, over the curtain calls of a world-wide live televised opera from San Francisco. She and Pavarotti were in conflict throughout the rehearsals. The crunch came at the final, carefully rehearsed curtain calls, when Scotto says he pushed everyone out of the way and insisted on taking unscheduled solo calls.

A backstage television documentary was being made of this performance. Scotto refused to take any more curtain calls, and marched away shouting about all these *'gente di merda'*, shitty people, right into the television cameras.

Rows permeate her life story – a break of many years with La Scala over their failure to publicize sufficiently her performances in Moscow and a break for a while with the Metropolitan Opera that led to headlines in New York, 'If the Met won't sing her tune, it's goodbye Scotto.'

She grumbles: 'The press is fond of exaggerating the temperament of singers.' But from her own life, she seems to have gone from one well-publicized row to another. Why does it happen so often? 'I love my art so much,' she says, spreading her hands expansively, 'so very much that I feel it deserves all of my attention. What I do up there on the stage is so very difficult that maybe it makes me difficult. It requires temperament.' And indeed the sight and the sound of a great singer in magnificent flight is an awe-inspiring experience, enough to explain and justify all manner of extravagant passions.

But I have always thought a truly ingenious press agent would struggle to keep an aura of mystery and miracle surrounding a performer. When it comes to interviews they are so often much worse than mundane. A sublime lack of self-awareness, a taste for stating the banal with crushing aplomb and a complete ignorance of the normal human rules of modesty so often leaves great stars not just with feet of clay but encased in it.

Likewise, I would steer them away from writing auto-biographies. Renata Scotto has some interesting things to say about the art of singing, about the training of her voice, and her approach to the many roles she sings.

'My book has had a very beautiful success in the United States,' she says with one of her dazzling smiles. But it is also full of paying off old scores and reprinting rave reviews: 'The greatest singing actress in the world,' says the *Washington Post*. And of directors' comments: 'The wonderful thing about Renata is that she comes to you every time as a virgin.'

Her husband, Lorenzo Anselmi, was first violinist at La Scala. Of him she says: 'The biggest decision that a man can make is to give up his own career to dedicate himself to his wife's.' He is now her singing teacher, manager and adviser. They have two children of 14 and 17, whom she used to take with her, with a retinue of nannies, all round the world.

She has now launched out into a new career. She is the first woman to direct herself in an opera at the Met in New York, with her production of *Madame Butterfly* this year. Next year, in Verona, she is directing the same opera in the vast 35,000 seat Roman arena. This is not unknown for a singer but it is rare. Madame Butterfly is probably her most famous role and she has performed it more than 600 times.

She takes the art of directing seriously and says she has always been careful not to become one of those international singers who fly in for a performance to give *their* Violetta, or *their* Butterfly, regardless of the director, the other performers or the particular production. She insists on ten days' rehearsal, however often she may have performed the role before. She also insists on helping to design her own costumes.

We turned eventually to what her agent thought should be the purpose of the interview – the Diva as La Mamma. 'I am

a better singer for being a mother,' she says, with a small sigh. Her children could never bear to watch the last acts of her operas, as she usually dies. She says motherhood has made 'life' more important than opera. Then she adds with a certain venom: 'If tenors could be mothers they would not be the way they are.' True, certainly, but not altogether self-explanatory.
8 December, 1986

Polly Toynbee

The princess and the bison

A Question of Sport (BBC1) is one of the few programmes I watch for pure amusement. You don't have to pay me, it is my pleasure.

It's a sort of *My Music* with muscles. The team captains, Emlyn Hughes and Bill Beaumont, have the look of bison which, starting at either end of America, have charged towards each other and collided with a frightful crack in Kansas. They shake their heads a good deal in a bewildered fashion.

I assume, therefore, they are rugger players. If they are ice dancers, I apologize, but knowing about sport is not crucial to enjoyment of the game. Bill Beaumont is the less ebullient or more deeply concussed of the captains. His endearing moustache has the look of something that has been wrenched off in the scrum and re-applied at random. Emlyn Hughes is the star turn. He effervesces like a bucket of bubbles. Extraordinarily like Colin Welland in *Blue Remembered Hills*, a small boy who has grown amazingly large but still acts exactly like a small boy. In a grown man his passionate desire to win would be embarrassing. They are, by chance or design, the archetypal double act and so successful that last night's show was the 200th.

Which is where Princess Anne comes in with her handbag. One has always wondered, don't you think, about royal handbags. Why the Queen insists on clutching one on all occasions when she doesn't carry money. Spectacles, speeches, aspirins for other people's speeches – all these things could be handed to her as required by the Mistress of the Handbag. Surely she doesn't carry a gun? The purpose of the royal handbag is, one now sees, primarily offensive. It is very handy, for instance, for hitting Emlyn Hughes.

A couple of weeks before the 200th edition Emlyn Hughes had mistaken a picture of Princess Anne, completely chocolate-coated with mud, for a male jockey. Her appearance on *A Question Of Sport* was, therefore, partly a tease for Emlyn. Teasing Emlyn almost *is* the game.

He behaved towards her as if she had just scored a difficult try. 'Well done, mate. You can come back again,' he beamed, bouncing up and down. 'Good stuff, brilliant,' he cheered, slinging an arm irresistibly around her. 'Whee,' he wheed. 'Woo,' he wooed, having a repertoire of whoops only normally seen in *Beano*. 'Tell 'em, pal,' he crowed, and Princess Anne brandished her handbag a bit.

Almost any man is better at horseplay than a woman, even a horsewoman. Nigel Mansell, for instance, whom you would expect to have eyes of flame, turned out to be one of the world's great gigglers with a tendency to bang his head on the desk.

Princess Anne did, however, score one notable first. I have never heard anyone else on the programme start a question: 'Can one ascertain . . . ?'

6 February, 1987

Nancy Banks-Smith

Flood, sweat and tears

Further to being a university without a Chancellor, Oxford is now faced with the oarsome prospect of being without a crew. Lay persons may be forgiven for wondering why nine grown men – average age 26 – cannot see their way to sit in a boat together to practise for a race they want to win on 28 March, or why it matters.

As college porters stoically answer calls from Fleet Street searching in vain for rowers, and photographers snap anyone within a mile of Carfax wearing a sweatshirt, the air is thick with No Comment while the atmosphere is charged with opprobious epithets. It was even rumoured yesterday that Mr Terry Waite may be on his way to rescue the hostages of fortune.

The giants of the oar, post-grads almost to a man, spend their afternoons on ergometers, fearsome machines whose dials show you how fast your life is passing while you work up a sweat, and their evenings holding council behind closed doors to persuade their president, Donald MacDonald, to deliver himself from their boat and manage their affairs from the bank.

Mile Spracklen, the best rowing coach in Britain, meanwhile twiddles his thumbs at Marlow without a crew to coach, while MacDonald calls cabals of coaches and Oxford rowing heavies to investigate the data of ergometer readings and individual contests to determine whether he or the Californian Blue Chris Clark is the best man to sit in the sharp end of the boat.

After last year's defeat, an event to which Oxford is unaccustomed, Clark vowed to return and 'kick Cambridge's arse' with the help of American friends. True to his word, he is here with three other American oarsmen and a cox, and finds himself at the centre of a storm which he has partially brought upon himself by his good-humoured, abrasive approach to winning the race.

Furthermore, he cannot see the way out. The word on Tuesday was that even if he dropped away, the lads would not allow it. They want him on stroke side, which is the other side of the boat to the one the coaches have had him rowing on. They think he may be a better boat mover than their president, and seem to have forgiven him for peccadilloes like throwing a cup of soup across the room during a chat with Dan Topolski, himself almost a sage by now, having been Oxford's chief coach and mouthpiece since 1973.

So, making up a cox and eight is not a simple matter. You need calm men to counter head cases and socialists to counter anarchists, apart from right and left-handedness with brawn, sinew, and the will to win.

Oxford has not been without a crew since 1850, the war years apart, although there was a mutiny in 1959 and there have been presidents who've taken to the bank from illness or design. Oxford's Jock Lewis did so against the advice of his coaches in 1937 and his crew broke Cambridge's longest run of 13 wins. Last year, Cambridge's Quintus Travis courageously made himself unavailable to stage-manage the end of Oxford's run of ten victories.

By failing to gauge the mood of his men before vesting selection in his coaches and getting their agreement to sack Clark last Sunday, MacDonald has dug a pit for himself. The 31-year-old Scot must rue the day when life was reading English at home with his wife and three baby sons. He still awaits the US cavalry to extend the oar of loyalty.

Meanwhile, the cavalry and their British comrades talk of the coach-crew meetings as a kangaroo court, with loyalty sewn up in advance pledges to the old heavies, ordained before hearings commence. And the 26-year-old Californian says that everything's gotten out of hand, can't believe anyone cares as much as they do, including himself, and gets on with his social studies in a quiet corner of his college – between work-outs, that is.

Topolski, usually such a good psychologist in crew matters, will be kicking himself for not reading the omens last autumn. But his mind is on other matters, because his actress *companiero* is due to produce an heir before the Boat Race.

On the whole, being merely Chancellor of Oxford University looks like a ticket to a quiet life.

29 January, 1987   **Christopher Dodd**

Down and out at Molineux

Wolves v. Preston in the Cup. Ah, romantics would relish the ring of such a fixture. This afternoon, Wolverhampton Wanderers might indeed have been playing Preston North End in the FA Cup. But Preston are meeting Chorley, who beat

Wolverhampton in the first round. Chorley 3, Wolves 0! Where or what is Chorley? Chorley some mistake?

Dark days in the Black Country. You wander round Molineux, famous home of a famous club, and all you get is the feeling of one of those ghostly deserted ranches which cowboys came across in the West. Signs creak wonkily on rusty hinges, shrubs grow out of gutterings, ancient graffiti mocks faded dreams, paint peels. It is the colour of sad, yellow ochre, self-scorning the celebrated old gold shirts made famous when Wolves were men and they blazed trails across the world a quarter of a century ago.

'It's a desolation now,' says David Potts, local reporter, who has missed covering only two Wolves matches since the end of the war. Triumph, decline and fall. 'It's so shabby and neglected, it grieves me terribly,' says John Richards, sharp-shooting centre-forward in the gold for all of 14 years. 'Quite frankly,' says Stan Cullis, centre-half, manager and co-founder of the very legend, 'when I go there now it's like going to a foreign place.' No, he adds, he hasn't been there yet this season. 'I expect it's even worse now, the atmosphere, the drabness.' You tell him it is. Some ancients can't even talk about it: one-time 'saviour' of the club, Derek Dougan, is relieved now to be putting all his considerable drum-banging energies into the Duncan Edwards Sports Injuries Clinic in Dudley. He was away this week organizing Pat Jennings's testimonial. 'Don't upset him,' said a friend, 'He never speaks about Wolves any more.'

The team with the legendary name, out of the Cup and wandering aimlessly around the Fourth Division, play in pale lemony jerseys now – money for which, incidentally, the club only scraped together 48 hours before the season started. That's nothing; last year the team minibus could not set off for a match because there was no money for a gallon of petrol.

The club's younger manager, Graham Turner, finds it hard to talk about Chorley. 'It was just deeply humiliating for all us,' he says. Before the match, the Chorley manager, Ken Wright, had gone to Molineux to spy on Wolves and their support: 'It was so dead, it was like listening to a fishing match on radio.'

The most mockingly forlorn feature of Molineux is the extensive new grandstand, set back from the pitch and yet to see a rousing match. The rest of the ground accommodation is pretty well closed to the paying public – or would be if there was any. A gate of 5,000 men and a few dogs is a multitude now. In the not too distant past, one Wolves chairman, Jimmy Baker, boasted: 'We can't get less than 45,000 even if we try.'

David Potts first took his pencil and notebook to the press box for the opening League match after the war (Wolves 6, Arsenal 1). 'There might have been 60,000. In those days no working man in Wolverhampton would go home when the Saturday lunchtime hooters went. They would all take their sandwiches and queue to get into the ground from 12.30 and wait happily two hours for kick-off. Local manufacturing was reliant on Wolves – no joke, if the team won you could guarantee production would be up the following week, and down if they lost.'

The romance of Molinuex then was dramatic, as it stood, like some sort of medieval cathedral, four square and proud at the very heart of the town, the very centre of the community.

Such an attribute has helped cause the downfall, for the area is a prime site for redevelopment as a shopping complex. The council meet next Thursday week and the probability is a public inquiry in the New Year.

Sure, the same sort of thing is happening all round the antiquated Football League. But Wolves isn't your Swansea, deep in rugby union country, or your Halifax, ditto in rugby league. Wolverhampton Wanderers grew out of the very bed-rock of the English game and it is not too fanciful to call them a national institution.

Wolves were founder members of the League in 1888, having been formed eleven years before by the board-school urchins of St Luke's. Molineux was built for the club by its first sponsor, Northampton Breweries.

Wolves were pioneers. They took pigeons to away matches to send back scores to the club, where thousands waited. The first, still-born Players' Union was started by their brave goalie, W. C. Rose in 1893; and, eat your heart out Watford and Wimbledon, Wolves also 'invented' the long-ball game in April

234

1889. As *Athletic News* groaned: 'Wolves' long kicks and individuals' rushes compared unfavourably with Preston's short passing and combined attacks.' Wolves v. Preston, in the Cup Final. Yes, 97 years is a long time in football.

Wolves were still making the long-ball game pay when the team of Stan Cullis dragged Britain into the revolutionary glare of European floodlights. In 1954 half the country, mesmerized, watched them beat Moscow Spartak 4–0 on television one heady, bewildering November night. A month later they beat Honved Budapest 3–2 and the *Daily Mail* front page screamed 'Champions of the World!'

Cullis's teams were direct, no-nonsense and devoid of frills: two wizard wingers and three incisive front runners, all feeding off the half-back line of Wright, Clamp, Slater or Flowers – all internationals, so every week one of them was in the reserves! No wonder in that time the Central League title was won four years on the trot. Last year Wolves dropped miserably out of the Central League – not enough money to run a reserve side.

A generation's chivalrous idol was Billy Wright, gent and goldilocks captain of England and now a TV executive. The bright eyes mist up as he recalls those days now, 'for Chorley has to be the lowest of the low for the old club: I weep for Wolves'.

Stan Cullis, England's centre-half as well, is less emotional. His Black Country accent, nevertheless, is tinged with a little melancholy. 'Contrary to what you want me to say,' he twinkles, 'I certainly don't sit around in my slippers in front of the fire with tears running down my face every time I hear Wolves have lost again. It's just a different club now.'

The old maestro, 70, lives at Colwall in a lively house nestling in the bliss of the plump and friendly Malvern Hills. 'It's like being on holiday every day here,' he says. So don't get him dwelling on the past. 'To be honest, I've thought it better to stay out of the way there this season. There is a sadness, I suppose. My Wolves was not only a football club, you see, it was the very integral part of its community. We considered ourselves far more than footballers: we were carrying a banner for the town and its people. The whole industrial and social parts of life and leisure have changed now.

'We all lived in the town, summer and winter, we walked to work. Where do top players live now? They commute in big cars from country mansions miles away. I'm not blaming them, mind you. I'm just telling you how life has changed.'

John Richards saw such changes during his devoted service to the Wolves, bridging the 60s to 80s. He wore the gold in Europe, Wembley and the doldrums. He is now the town's sport and recreation officer, as honest, charming and articulate as his football always was. 'Of course I go and watch them whenever I can. Sure, it's a little upsetting, not only the way the football has slumped but the stadium. We always say each year "things can't get worse at Molineux". But then they always do.'

Richards insists the players are still trying their darnedest in spite of the club's penury and apathy. He desperately hopes the council might win the probably forthcoming appeal. 'We could build the club up again and give it back to the people and the town,' and he grins that determined grin and you know he is happier recalling some of those days when he had the terraces and whole town on a raw: 'early 70s v. Everton, I'm outside the box, ball comes over, I bring it down, on my left foot, not my best, I pirouette in one movement and let rip, thwack! a perfect volley, bliss, top corner past poor old Gordon West, what a beauty! We won 4–2', and the grin is as wide as a penalty area.

Richards, always loyal, played through the crass era of exhorbitant transfer fees. 'Don't blame me,' says the ever-chirpy and unrepentant John Barnwell, Wolves manager at the time. 'If you deal in the marketplace you pay the market price, whether it's apples or football players.

'So I sold Daley for over £1 million and bought Gray for over £1 million. That was my job. And the place buzzed. When Gray signed we sold 20 private boxes that week at 15 grand.

'I had good years at Wolves and, of course, I'm sad at what's happening, but don't you go around blaming me for it. All I did was balance my end of the books.'

So, Dave Potts is not putting on his trilby and setting off to report on a Cup tie today. The faithful local scribe, whose translated adjectives bounced around the world in the 1950s, had said to himself this autumn when Wolves were beaten in a friendly by non-League Telford: 'Once, I climbed up Everest with the Wolves; now they can't even struggle up the ruddy Wrekin.'

Poor Wolverhampton. Like another poet said the night Stan Cullis got the sack: 'Wolverhampton wandered round in circles like a disallowed goal looking for a friendly linesman.'

6 December, 1986

Frank Keating

Do you understand?

Esperanto is celebrating its centenary this year. Unfortunately my plan to learn the language has come unstuck. I was walking down Portobello Road in the direction of the Esperanto Centre in Holland Park Avenue when I noticed on a junk stall a little blue book called *Introduction to Chinyanja*.

Its authors are Dr Meredith Sanderson, MRCS, FRGS, etcetera, of the East African Medical Service and W. B. Bithrey, FRAL, of the Nyasaland Police and it was printed at the Government Printing Office and published in Zomba, Nyasaland, in 1925.

A brief inspection of the contents made it clear that Esperanto was going to have to wait. It was Chinyanja for me. After a brief discussion with the proprietor of the stall, a dangerous-looking gentleman with a black eye, we settled on a price of 20p and the transaction was completed.

The Preface sets out the work's modest aims. 'This little book,' it says, 'does not pretend to be a complete handbook to Chinyanja either in its grammar or its vocabulary. It has been written for the increasing number of settlers in Nyasaland, both official and non-official, who require only a working knowledge of Chinyanja.'

It starts with a section on pronunciation, giving examples of words which evidently were needed early on when a settler was chatting with the people of the Nyanja. The complete list gives the Chinyanja for the following: A chair, A house, That chair, That house, Bring (singular), Bring (plural), I want, You may go, Get out!, Do you understand?, Work, Cattle, (Some) cold water, (Some) hot water, Go and bring, Come here, A native, An European, Maize, Food, There is not, There are not, It doesn't matter, No, Yes, Sir, Mister.

You get the picture. The European Sir or Mister is sitting in his chair in A house or That house, ordering a native to work, to bring water of various temperatures, to come here, to bring cattle, maize and food, and to Get out!

You might think that there was nothing further that a settler needed to say in Chinyanja but we're still only on the fourth page of the book, which runs to nearly 100 pages. Here are a few handy phrases and sentences that the student of the language would acquire by persevering through the book.

Chipongwe means insolence or cheek. *Chikoti*, whip, lash. Go and bring the hide of that beast. That woman has some good string. I want some more salt. That child is very cheeky. How many wives has the chief? Where is my whip? One is here, but I want that other one.

Here's a selection from Exercise 7. Translate into Chinyanja. Fetch my gun. Don't give any meat to that man, he did not come yesterday. Go and bring some more earth. I don't want mud but earth, do you understand? Go and ask Bwana X to come here. Don't you understand what I say?

Meredith and Sanderson were ahead of their time. Their dialogue often anticipates that of Harold Pinter, Samuel Beckett, Eugene Ionesco and N. F. Simpson. What a charming playlet could be made that contained lines like 'This hat is the one that I wore when we started to fight.' Or like these:

'If I had not arrested him he would have run away into Portuguese Territory. If you do not do as I tell you, I shall discharge you at the end of the month. Where is Juma? He has not come yet. Where has he gone? He has gone to bathe. The people have not eaten their porridge because there is no relish. Give them some beans. The people have not yet paid their tax.'

Page 58 yields the following continuous dialogue. 'Why are

you standing there like a fool? I am waiting for my pay. Come back again when everyone has stopped working. Mr Jones is going to England. Is he really? Yes, he has been in this country for five years now. Will he return? Yes, he will come back after a year. That white fowl lays more eggs than that black one. Are these the same pumpkins that I saw yesterday? No, my wife gathered these this morning.'

It's obviously hard work being a settler, what with constantly having to be asking for your hat or for Juma or your axe or your favourite whip. And then you have to complain that the pot hasn't been washed or that the bananas aren't ripe and so on. For a settler there can't have been an idle moment in the day. Unlike some I could mention. People who sit about doing nothing are numerous, or (as we say in Chinyanja) *Antu amene angokala chabe ngambiri*.

27 April, 1987

Richard Boston

Slogger's return

Slogger-Ogger they used to call him as a student at the Royal Manchester (now Royal Northern) College of Music, a good-natured tribute to the combination of power and quiet patience that promptly took John Ogdon in 1962 to a first prize – along with Vladimir Ashkenazy – in the Moscow International Piano Competition, the most prestigious in the world. His dogged determination also took him much later, through overwork, into a serious mental breakdown, movingly and graphically described by his wife and fellow-pianist, Brenda Lucas, in her book, *Virtuoso*.

Now, having just celebrated his 50th birthday, Ogdon is performing at a series of celebration concerts. His own large-scale piano concerto will be the main work, when on Monday he appears with John Lubbock and the London Philharmonic

Orchestra at the Royal Festival Hall. Though nowadays he takes things much more easily than he did, Slogger-Ogger is still very active.

It was in 1981, when Brenda's book was published, that a great deal of fuss was made over what was described as Ogdon's comeback. The implication was that he had been away from the concert platform for ten years. In fact, his absence – or rather absences, when his illness recurred more than once – bought several small gaps rather than a long one. Since 1981 progress has been steady if unspectacular.

He is now quieter than ever, a gentle giant of a figure, even broader of girth, but still radiating power and concentration. Talk to him on music for a few seconds and he is telling you eagerly about some new work he is planning to perform. Though, as he says, the breakdown led him away from twentieth-century music back to the classical repertory as his base, he still talks in loving admiration of a big range of modern music, not least that of such Manchester contemporaries of his as Harrison Birtwistle and Alexander Goehr.

Ogdon was a leading member along with Birtwistle and Goehr of the New Music Manchester group, all of them at the Royal College, with Peter Maxwell Davies, then studying at Manchester University, as an important associate. Brenda, who first met John when studying at the college, has particularly vivid memories of Birtwistle at the time with his red hair, wearing shorts even through the winter, regularly commandeering the stage in the big hall to play the clarinet raucously: 'Not a nice noise.'

'Who would have thought when we were in Manchester,' she says, 'that Harry Birtwistle was such a genius?' Ogdon himself remembers visiting Birtwistle's home near Accrington, where his father was a farmer. He also remembers a year at the Dartington Summer School, when Birtwistle wrote a two-minute piano piece, *Precis*, which he still likes to play as an encore in recitals.

If Birtwistle's background was unexpected, Ogdon's own had its odd side. Brenda remembers going to visit the family in Wakefield, where Ogdon's father, a grammar-school teacher, would play Wagner records all day in a sanctum at the back of the house. There, with books and papers piled high, he was a Faust-like figure. As a recreation he played xylophone and trombone in Besses of the Barn band.

John, like his elder brother and sister, had piano lessons from childhood. As the youngest and most talented, he cannot remember having ever had to compete for a place at the keyboard. From Manchester Grammar School he went straight to the Royal Manchester College and there, in addition to becoming a piano virtuoso, learnt the craft of composing.

His Piano Concerto of 1968 is his biggest and most ambitious work to date. It was written for the first year of the festival of modern music in Cardiff, which he founded with Alun Hoddinott. In retrospect, remembering the pain and violence involved in his later breakdown, one can detect from the inner expression it contains what was already brewing inside him.

The first movement in particular has violence in it, and the contrasted first and second subjects do a sort of Jekyll-and-Hyde change between exposition and recapitulation. So the violent opening theme returns in the recapitulation as a gently lyrical flute solo, while the quiet second subject is later made to bite hard, symbolic perhaps of changing human character and relationships.

Ogdon as a composer is uncompromisingly tonal, but his idiom is far more abrasive in such a movement than you would expect from one whose favourite composers include Rachmaninov, Scriabin and Vaughan Williams. Not that he dislikes atonal music, but 'we hear tonally – I even interpret the Variations of Webern as being in B minor'.

He began writing the Piano Concerto in Japan in 1966, but broke the back of the main task of composition during three weeks he spent in Ischia, borrowing Sir William Walton's idyllic house. So Brenda and the children would go down to the beach, and John would lock himself in Walton's air-conditioned studio, there to hammer out more of the concerto. He rarely writes at the piano, but likes at once to check what it sounds like at the keyboard.

Knowing Walton well, he repeatedly asked him to write a piano concerto for him, but his regular excuse was 'too many notes'. I suggested that it was time that Walton's early Sinfonia

Concertante for piano and orchestra, dedicated to the Sitwells, a movement apiece, was revived, and who better to do that than Ogdon?

Another suggestion he embraced eagerly, if only it might be arranged, was to play a concerto with his once-rival, now long-time friend, Vladimir Ashkenazy, as conductor. His immediate suggestion was that Scriabin's *Prometheus* would be the ideal work. Some ten years or so ago, he remarked to Ashkenazy that he could not find a score of *Prometheus*, and within a week or so one arrived for him from New York, sent by Ashkenazy.

Ask Ogdon what pianists of the past he admires, and he will quickly go on from listing Paderewski, Busoni and Ignaz Friedman to mentioning Ashkenazy as the one among his contemporaries who has influenced him most, for 'the naturalness with which he approaches so many different styles'.

Ogdon himself ranges wide, and though immediately after his breakdown he had temporary memory problems, he still likes to keep some 35 concertos in his repertory, with ten or so current in any one season.

He and Brenda both enjoy the discipline of the recording studio, never feeling intimidated. Among his most recent records have been compact discs of Beethoven sonatas and Chopin pieces for the Pickwick label. Not yet issued is an enormous recording he has made over several years for a small company, Altarus, of a work of epic length by the Parsee composer, Khaikhosru Sorabji, his Opus Clavicembalisticum, which Ogdon estimates will fill five LPs.

He would be glad if some of his EMI recordings from the 1960s and 1970s were reissued – a pity no one thought of his 50th birthday as an excuse. Meanwhile, his birthday celebrations will be rounded off on 22 February, when at Queen Elizabeth Hall the Park Lane Group presents John Ogdon and Friends. He will appear in partnership with a series of artists.

7 February, 1987

Edward Greenfield

For Mahler's sake

Mahler's Second Symphony can't stop wars, can't make the young older, lower the price of bread or erase solitude: thus Luciano Berio, in his Sinfonia (part of which adds several layers of commentary to Mahler's third movement), voices the hopes of all who listen that it might be endowed with such powers.

To be sure, a great performance of the work can transcend particular circumstances and intermittent technical weaknesses to stimulate and satisfy human cravings for the sublime.

Here, Yuri Temirkanov conducted the Royal Philharmonic Orchestra and Brighton Festival Chorus in an interpretation which, though splendidly exact and often brilliant, only belatedly penetrated far beyond the notes.

It was not for want of trying. Temirkanov rightly insisted on a steady, inexorable tread for the opening funeral march which he only relaxed at the end of the exposition, so that the start of the development section was a real plunge into the abyss.

But his concern for detail became self-conscious. In his hands, the succeeding *andante* sounded extremely laboured: for instance, the initial up beat was nearly a bar long, and the RPO strings had to be really cunning to synchronize on the final cadence in response to Temirkanov's contortions.

For instance, the dream-like refuge from the agonies of the rest of the work, which this movement can conjure, didn't materialize. Moreover, the timpani outburst that shatters this dream, at the start of the *scherzo*, was postponed until the solo singers had made their entry on to the stage and been applauded, destroying thus the dramatic continuity of the symphony.

Matters improved greatly in the forth and fifth movements, notwithstanding Temirkanov's fondness for excessively long pauses whenever the opportunity arose. Here, cued in by the singing of the mezzo soprano Sarah Walker and (later) the soprano Karita Mattila, Mahler's apocalyptic vision began to unfold with true grandeur.

The clarity and vividness of the RPO's execution and the

strength of the Brighton chorus gave an irresistible momentum that made the impact of the music awesome. Even the man seated near me, who was counting £10 notes in his wallet during the *andante*, suddenly lifted his eyes heavenwards. I trust (for Mahler's sake) he gave the notes away afterwards.

18 November, 1986

Meirion Bowen

La Dolce Vita returns

Has Britain been overtaken by Italy as an economic and industrial power? In Rome, the outgoing Prime Minister, Mr Bettino Craxi, believes it has, and in a series of moves, some abrasive, some subtle, and one which verges on self-parody, he is telling his compatriots the good news.

It is not an easy task, since national boasting at the expense of other countries which are meant to be friends and allies is not considered good form. But Mr Craxi, after serving longer as Prime Minister than any of his post-war predecessors, clearly feels a historic duty to put Italy back on the map. What better way to do it than draw a flattering comparison with a country which most middle- and upper-class Italians tend to admire?

France is too near and closely related. The connection with Germany is still awkward after the embarrassing fascist alliance 50 years ago. Britain is remote enough to be neither envied nor feared.

The evidence for the much discussed 'sorpasso' – overtaking Britain – emerges from a revised calculation of Italy's gross national product published recently by the Central Statistical Institute. The Institute used a complicated input–output formula to try to measure the intriguing gap between private spending and reported income.

The difference, of course, is the black economy. The mathematical extrapolation, backed up by sample surveys, concluded that more than 6 million Italians have undeclared, and untaxed, second and third jobs. Estimating the previously

244

uncalculated output of goods and services from small shops, restaurants, and home-based piecework making shoes and clothes, the statistical office decided that an extra 15.4 per cent should be added to Italy's GNP. About 46 per cent of the service sector's revenue was never officially declared.

Although the statistical office did not draw any international comparisons, the Italian treasury has. It calculates that Italy's revised GNP is $579 billion, putting it in front of Britain's $567 billion. Opponents of 'il sorpasso' say that if you divide this by the larger Italian population, Britain is still ahead in income per head by $10,486 against Italy's $10,230.

They also say that the pound has lost 20 per cent of its value compared to the lira over the past 12 months, so the basis of the comparison is faulty. The 'sorpasso' advocates retort that the lira's rise proves their point.

To those who argue that Britain also has a black economy, the Italians counter that the statistical office made no effort to calculate another key factor – their criminal economy. This could tot up to another $15 billion a year, well above Britain's.

One immediate consequence of the finding was the row at last month's meeting of finance ministers in Paris of the Group of Five – the United States, West Germany, Japan, France and Britain. The so-called 'G5' met in secret at the Plaza Hotel in New York 18 months ago to hammer out a deal on exchange rates.

Italy was annoyed by more than the snub of not being invited. Its Central Bank lost billions of lire by not being told in time that the dollar rate was to be deliberately eased down. It was a new twist to the humiliation felt over President Nixon's notorious expletive – 'fuck the lira' – when he was interrupted during the Watergate crisis by news that the Italian currency was on the slide. This time the dollar was being made to slide, but Italy still suffered.

At last summer's Tokyo summit of the Group of Seven major industrial nations (G5 plus Italy and Canada), Mr Craxi extracted a promise that Italy and Canada would be invited to G5 whenever exchange rates and improvements to the international monetary system were to be discussed.

Imagine Mr Craxi's anger when he heard that the G5 had

met in Paris and prepared a communiqué before the Italian Finance Minister, Mr Giovanni Goria, arrived. He asked Mr Goria to come straight home. (The soft-spoken Canadians made no fuss. They understood the Tokyo summit 'concession' in the spirit of polite brush-off which was intended.)

Mr Goria's abrupt return home went down well in Italy. The issue could mean that this summer the G5 meets its death in Venice. The Seven assemble there in June, with Italy taking its turn as host, and the meeting may be forced to concede that the G5 has had its day. Its passing would not be mourned by many bankers, who say that 'G3', the United States, West Germany and Japan, are the only economies which really count.

Building on Italy's new confidence, Mr Craxi has taken a second step, this time slightly ridiculous. He has announced a competition to design a new national emblem. The present emblem, which dates back to 1947, consists of a star inside a cogged wheel surrounded by leaves of oak and laurel.

Mr Craxi's close adviser, Mr Giulio Amato, told reporters the cogged wheel was outdated as a symbol of work. The country needed something as recognizable as the United States' bald eagle or France's fleur-de-lys. 'A symbol must be easily recognizable around the world. If ours didn't say "Republic of Italy" on it, who would recognize it?'

Umberto Eco, a member of the panel which will judge the entries, says that from the point of view of memorability, 'the Coca-Cola symbol is a true work of art'. His panel expects a flood of designs but is insisting that groups of at least five people, including children, must collaborate on each entry.

This is being done for two reasons, 'one noble, the other ignoble. The first is to achieve a socialization of the problem and obtain an imaginative, collective proposal. The second, frankly, is to prevent millions of separate entries.'

More seriously, Mr Craxi is not only concerned about Italy's image abroad, where he wants it to be seen as a modern, productive, efficient country. No more jokes about spaghetti, please. He is concerned that too many Italians do not care about their country's status.

In his resignation speech this week he took issue with what he called the 'provincialism' of people who shrink away from anyone who underlines the importance of Italy's international role. He talked of Italy's success in defeating domestic terrorism and regaining stability while maintaining a broad dialogue and cooperation with neighbouring Arab countries as an example of Italy's peaceful nature. Using the English phrase he described it as a special product with the proud trademark 'Made in Italy'.

He quoted an American study (which he did not identify) as saying Italy has the second highest quality of life in the world. He also claimed, lest anyone think he is obsessed with materialism, that, according to the EEC, Italy was Europe's top spender on culture.

Not all Italians share Mr Craxi's faith in statistics as proof of Italy's status. Guido Rey, the head of the Statistical Institute, himself warned against glib international comparisons. 'On per capita income terms the Arab Emirates and Kuwait ought to join the Group of Five,' he said. He also recalled Italy's high unemployment rate (13.9 per cent compared with Britain's 11.3 per cent) and the growing gap between the Italian north and south. Dr Stefano Silvestri, vice-president of the Institute of International Affairs, says political, diplomatic and military weight must also be taken into account.

What of the other indications of affluence, which reflect different national tastes? Italians like driving (359 cars per 1,000 Italians) more than the British (312 per 1,000). But they watch less television (336 sets per 1,000 in Britain, 243 in Italy) and phone less (521 telephones per 1,000 in Britain, 405 in Italy.)

Simple visual observation also confirms that Italians, men and women, are better dressed and manicured, and apparently better washed. It is standard practice for any new two-bedroomed council flat in Rome and the north to have two bathrooms. 'The same is true in the private market. People wouldn't take flats without them,' says one long-term resident.

There is little doubt, too, that Italy's northern cities feel, look, and probably have become more prosperous than their counterparts in the south-east of England.

What this all adds up to will be a matter for endless dispute. At the least it should bring a belated European recognition that

Italy has made impressive economic progress in the last two decades. It also means that by playing the triumphalist card, Mr Craxi may come out as Prime Minister after the next election.

7 March, 1987   **Jonathan Steele**

A shot in the park

In our stairwell hang old maps showing our parish of St Mary Le Bone as it used to be. The earliest are wisps from the centuries of pastoral prologue, when the gateways west out of London were Charyncros and St Gilles in the Fyeldes, and a traveller would want a Marrowbone comfort stop and perhaps change horses at the inn. Then away he'd go down the Pike, past Tyburn, Bayswatering and the Pest House, off in earnest for Oxford.

The Tyburn River has gone underground, but in a cobbled mews that starts opposite our front door, the same old pub perseveres in quenching thirsts, though the haylofts all round were long since converted into bijou flats. Indeed it looks from the maps as if the pubs are the most enduring of the parish's institutions.

The Pike became Oxford Street, always the great divide between us and the Soho Goths and the Mayfair dandies, and now the front line of tourism. A south wind carries the polyglot clamour of the foreign hordes as they get the scent of 'last crazy reductions'. But they do not penetrate into the lattice of austere terraces beyond.

As Surtees wrote in 1850, Oxford Street was to the north what the Strand was to the south: it brought a man up; he could hardly get across either without knowing it. His hero Soapy Sponge was daunted and went the length of it before taking a cab up the Edgeware Road, thereby skirting our demesne – and today's tourists take Soapy's line, though some

248

will tack across a bit to ponder on Sherlock Holmes in Baker Street, and the waxes of Tussaud's.

At one end of our street is the rag trade (and Fitzrovia, and the Post Office Tower rearing up like Grendel's mother) and at the other end the High Street. Since we moved in 17 years ago, there have been some pretty rococo shopping developments down there, and any time I go away for a few days it adds another coco.

I could, within minutes of receiving your request, buy you a cuirasse or a duelling pistol, a Twenties rosbif trolley made by Drake's for £10,000, a banana tree with a dehydrated natural trunk and polyester silk leaves for £215.50 (cleaning visits by arrangement), a Sanson map c.1700 showing the Canadian frontier with Florida, a micro bipolar coagulator, a working model of a human ear two feet high or, a really banal item, a villa in the Cayman Islands. Of course, if you wanted to rent fancy dress, or have a half-head perm (£35), you'd have to come yourself.

The new shops incline to name themselves with a Carnaby Street whimsicality. The supermarket likes to be a Food Hall, the jeweller to be Nuggets, the sandwich bar Yummies, the outsize clothes shop Largesse, the boutiques Rich Bitch and Petal and Whistles and Bambino. We could buy cakes from Bonne Bouche, meat from Wainwright and Daughter, vegetables from Daisy Buchanan's. The day may soon come when the Midland Bank will call itself Gelt, the Harley Street Clinic become Sawbones, and the National Heart Hospital Ticker. One old pub has already turned into Nicki's, and before I enter The King's Head or The Prince Regent I like to be sure it hasn't become Drinkies.

The nineteenth-century poet Barry Cornwall, who lived three doors along from us, had regular intercourse with his Muse in the crowded street, and the inopportune flow of his verses then obliged him to dart in to buy cheese and sugar, so he could get them down on the wrappings. The search for such ordinary goods would make his method a gamble today, though he might filch a beer mat.

There's much thirst here, probably because we spend so much time talking. We hardly make or grow anything: our bent is diagnostic and discursive. Albeit fictional, Sherlock Holmes in one sense was truly typical: he was a consultant. Our stock-in-trade is experience; we've been there, done that, we're soaked in the stuff.

We won't push our opinions, though just over the way in Broadcasting House they make rather a meal of them, but if you want to sit at our feet you can have them, and we'll invoice you in guineas – discreetly, perhaps just a handwritten line. Nine times out of ten if you press our doorbells you won't get a householder, but someone in a white coat, or it'll go 'Zzzzzz' at you, and open of its own accord into a hallway festooned with artificial plants and country prints.

We have handsome little squares and the Wallace Collection, music in Wigmore Street and a nice little church like a witch's hat in Langham Place. The electors themselves commonly have, like ourselves, vistas of roofs, or of area railings. We live either at the top in the servants' quarters of merchants' townhouses, or in the basements. In between are doctors and dentists, abortionists, relaxers, osteopaths, physios, account-ants, solicitors etc., who go away at five and for the whole weekend.

Macaulay, urging the Reform Bill in 1831, when we had no representation, pointed out that the rental of this dense patch was more than that of the whole of Scotland, and that could well be true today. My neighbour is asking £1.8 millions for the freehold of his drab brick pavilion, squatting between us and the colossal Chinese Embassy. But we are not smart, more like ponderous.

Among innumerable talking shops are councils of architects and builders, Actors' Equity and the Monarchist Society, and the paramount terraces of Wimpole Street and Harley Street, where Arabs may have crossed half the world to find themselves discussing their fertility problems with Jewish doctors. I walked down it the other day and counted the brass shingles of 797 medics, and no doubt Wimpole could muster a similar tally.

Few of us have gardens of our own. The Regent's Park is our garden of delights, our floral fizz and common playground, our Sargasso Sea, broadwalk of bloods where skateboarders mesmerize the pram people, our wildfowl sanctuary and sporting champaign. You will find there football pitches, the American game too, and cricket nets (a lofted Botham drive from Lord's), archery butts and scullers. In the summer the open-air theatre bravely takes on the Bard near Queen Mary's Rose Garden – I wonder now if they're allowed to insure with a Pluvius Policy.

There's still a lot of flirting going on in Regent's Park (as Ronald Frankau used to sing in the war) and a stretch of Nash Terraces, or the classical aplomb of the Holme, is not a bad backdrop to flirting. At the north end the dogs cavort under the complacent eyes of the simian gazebo of London Zoo, but generally the grey squirrel begs at ease, and only seagulls are ominous. My favourite creatures of the lakeland are the dinky little ducks, cheeky chunks of brilliant plumage.

A fine place for casual encounters, too. A week or two back my son, trying to beat his record of keeping a football in the air through 45 kicks, heard a Welsh voice soliciting a game, and turned to find the leader of the Labour Party, out with his dog. At the end of the knock-up the eminent man observed ruefully that he was more at ease with the oval ball, and added that he hoped he had been playing with a Labour supporter. Actually yes, my son replied, 'but you won't find many of those round here'. True, and among the few, I suspect, are often pragmatic accountants who enjoy the challenge of Labour rule.

Home is where one starts from, said the poet. From home I vanish, virtually while still waving goodbye, down the bolt-hole of Oxford Circus tube and don't sniff another breath of fresh air until the aircraft doors open on a foreign runway. Conversely, as the returning plane seems, like the Luftwaffe, to be using the Thames to find London, but is actually already beamed on finals to Heathrow, I can pick out my home patch by the Post Office Tower and the Park.

Two hours later (d.v.) I surface again at the Circus, and there is Portland Place is the last landmark, the equestrian statue of Field Marshal Sir George Stuart White, VC, GCB, OM, GCSI, GCMB, GCIE, GCVO, whom military historian Norman Dixon takes as a prime example of incompetent command for overlooking, at the sieges of Ladysmith and Mafeking, Boer access to the railway.

Sometimes, when travelling, I see Sir George in my mind's eye and all around his plinth the Solidarnósc protestors who have kept up a vigil for years outside the shuttered Polish Embassy. And I imagine my children taking tea, as they have done on winter nights, to this sombre group – having perhaps already given the sugar to the horses of the embarrassed policemen, who thought they were hidden, in the mews behind.

23 August, 1986   **Alex Hamilton**

Index